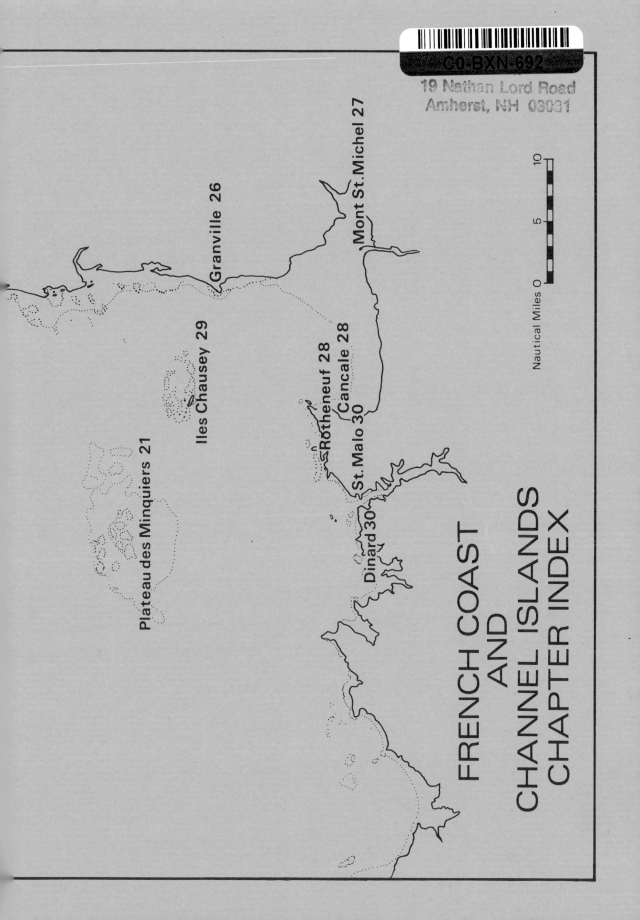

Mont St.Michel 27

Granville 26

Iles Chausey 29

Rotheneuf 28
Cancale 28

St. Malo 30

Plateau des Minquiers 21

Dinard 30

Nautical Miles 0   5   10

FRENCH COAST
AND
CHANNEL ISLANDS
CHAPTER INDEX

Channel Harbours
and Anchorages

K. Adlard Coles

with assistance of Professor A. N. Black
and the Royal Cruising Club

First published 1956
Reprinted   1962
Second edition 1963
Third edition   1968
Reprinted   1972
Fourth edition 1974

Fourth edition published in Great Britain by
NAUTICAL PUBLISHING CO LTD
Lymington, Hampshire SO4 9BA
in association with George G. Harrap and Co Ltd.
London.

ISBN 0 245 52064 3

Filmset and printed by BAS Printers Limited, Wallop,
Hampshire

By the same author:

Heavy Weather Sailing
North Biscay Pilot (with A. N. Black)
Creeks and Harbours of the Solent
North Brittany Pilot (with H. G. Hasler)
Shell Pilot to the South Coast Harbours

Caution
While great care has been taken in the compilation of this book, it is regretted that neither
author nor publisher can accept responsibility for any inaccuracies or mishaps arising
from the work.

Acknowledgements

For contributions and help in the first edition of this book, published in 1956, I gratefully acknowledge my debt to the following: Captain C. Stewart, Extra Master, for Christchurch and other advice and to Mrs Stewart for drawing the charts; to the late Mr A. J. Barber for the sailing directions and transits for Guernsey, Herm and Sark; to Lieut.-Colonel H. A. Stevenson for Jersey and Carteret; to Mr D. P. Richardson for Les Ecrehou, and Mr V. R. Richardson for Mont St Michel; to my own family and amateur crews who accompanied me on many happy voyages of minor exploration.

The charts in this book are largely based on Admiralty charts by permission of the Controller of HM Stationery Office and the Hydrographer of the Navy and reference has been made to the *Channel Pilot* and *Tidal Stream Atlas* by permission of the same authorities. Six of the charts are based on French charts by kind permission of the French Service Hydrographique de la Marine. Photographs, other than my own, are acknowledged individually.

Additional information for the following two editions was gratefully received from Mr D. Russell Anstey (Poole Harbour), Dr J. C. Bulstrode (Guernsey and Herm), Mr J. M. Robson (Sark and Goury), Mr M. Gilkes (Goury), Mr John Marriner (Minquiers) and Lieut-Colonel H. A. Stevenson (N. E. Passage to St Malo), and useful comments were received from Mr Dennis Hall and many other yachtsmen.

For assistance with this fourth edition I wish to acknowledge with thanks the help of the Queen's Harbour Master, Portland, and the Harbour Masters and Authorities at Poole, Weymouth, St Peter Port and St Helier, as also the managers of the various marinas. In addition I am indebted to Mr R. Yeabsley (Christchurch) Mr J. C. H. Tucker and Commander Erroll Bruce RN, Rtd. (Guernsey) Pilot B. Ching (Jersey) Monsieur B. Lefevre (President of the Yacht Club de Cherbourg), and Mr V. R. Richardson for Portbail included in this book for the first time. I am also most grateful to Dr C. Sergel with whom I cruised over the past three years in his *Sequel*, revisiting, checking information and taking new photographs of most of the harbours. I am indebted to Mr Alan H. Irving for bringing the original chart drawings up to date and converting them to LAT datum and metric units as well as for adding a number of new ones.

I wish to thank yachtsmen who have drawn attention to errors or suspected errors. It is all too easy for the eye to miss a mistake time after time: for example, a small error on a chart escaped detection for fifteen years, until a reader drew attention to it. I would therefore, be grateful to receive corrections, constructive criticism or additional information addressed to me at Ailsa Croft, Poles Lane, Lymington.

K.A.C.

Contents

PART III. THE CHANNEL ISLANDS

PART IV. DIELETTE TO ST MALO

General Introduction

When this book was first published the information and photographs were obtained over a period of eight years cruising in the waters described. For the preparation of this fourth edition, I have revisited most of the harbours during the past few years and also received the help of harbour masters and cruising men whose generous contributions I have acknowledged. I have not visited Mont Saint Michel nor the anchorage in the Minquers, and in the absence of fresh information these chapters remain much as before.

Many amendments have been made in this edition, some of the chapters have been rewritten, the anchorage of Chapmans Pool, and the harbours of Portbail and Port du Becquet have been added, nearly all the charts have been altered or redrawn and many new photographs substituted. However, the fundamental differences between this edition and the former ones lie in the metrication of the harbour plans and the alteration to LAT (lowest astronomical tide) datum to conform with the new issue Admiralty charts.

The yachts in which I have cruised had a draft of about 6 ft (1m8). Skippers of shallow-draft yachts can take a more liberal view of shallow harbours, but skippers of deep draft yachts should obviously be cautious, of what is described as 'plenty of water'.

In these days when even very small yachts are fit to cross the English Channel in suitable weather, the Channel Islands and adjacent French coast offer a fascinating cruising ground which, in my opinion, is quite as interesting as the Bay of Biscay and more distant parts. Alderney, Guernsey and Jersey provide pleasant ports of call, although nowadays they are often crowded and there are problems at St Helier, owing to the new roll on–roll off car ferry service and the lack of deep water berths. For 'rock dodgers' there are countless bays and anchorages to explore. The French harbours are equally interesting, and, whether large or small, each has a character of its own.

Some yachtsmen used to be deterred from cruising in these waters on account of the rocks and strong tidal streams. An exaggerated impression of the dangers is given by a casual examination of small scale charts. Here many areas appear as almost impenetrable mazes of rocks and reefs, but given a chart on a larger scale it will immediately be seen that the rocks form groups, between which there is plenty of water; and with the aid of the large scale charts it is found that the approaches to most (but not to all) of the anchorages and harbours are by no means difficult. Furthermore the majority of the rocks which decorate the charts are well covered at half tide, owing to the large range of tide. Before making a passage it is useful to put pencil circles on the chart around rocks which will be inadequately covered at the state of tide when they will be passed. This enables concentration to be given to the dangerous ones rather than wasted on those which will be well covered and harmless except for overfalls in strong streams or bad weather. A liberal factor of safety should be allowed remembering that swell reduces the depth by half its height.

Likewise the streams. Casual references to rates attaining at six or nine knots or more, and setting on rocks, sound alarming to the uninitiated, but the fact is that rates such as these are only attained in certain places, and then only at certain times. Over a considerable area of the Gulf of St Malo the tidal streams are no stronger than in the Solent, although, of course, the range of tide is quite spectacular.

It is true that a steep sea gets up more quickly than in home waters, and overfalls occur in many parts when wind is against tide. For these reasons, when cruising on these coasts for the first time it is wise to choose neap tides, and always, if possible, to avoid the top of springs. I have not attempted to define which harbour approaches may be dangerous because I think the questions are answered by reference to the charts and descriptions. Narrow passages between rocks in strong tidal streams are always risky unless the marks and bearings can be identified with certainty and conditions and state of tide are suitable. For newcomers to cruising obviously difficult harbours such as Goury or Les Ecrehou or for that matter Herm and Sark should not be attempted until experience has been gained in the easier ones. The point is that a single error may possibly bring serious consequences. Auxiliary power is desirable on the occasion of a first visit to enable transits to be followed exactly where necessary without sails impeding vision and to avoid being set on rocks if the wind drops.

To my mind fog or thick weather is the principal hazard of the French coast or among the Channel Islands. It is idle to pretend that it is pleasant to be borne along by the tide on a rock-strewn coast which one cannot see, and in water which may be so deep that it is difficult to anchor. I have found myself in this predicament on several occasions, the worst being when approaching the SE of Jersey from Iles Chausey in thick fog, with my wife and daughter, at a time when I was unfamiliar with this bit of coast, which is the rockiest of all.

To omit mention of these difficulties would be misleading to the reader, but equally it is right to emphasize that in a normal summer there will be weeks of fine weather without fog or gales, when sailing in these waters is a delight to the amateur navigator. The distances between harbours are never great, the tidal streams make good servants, and all that is needed is particular care in navigation and caution in the choice of weather and state of tide suitable for passage-making.

For yachtsmen sailing in these waters I hope this volume will prove useful, and for those entering them for the first time I hope the book will provide an introduction to what I firmly believe is one of the happiest cruising grounds in the world.

Charts, Tides and Navigation

Chart datum and depths. As early as 1965, the Admiralty commenced adjusting datums in accordance with the International Agreement to the level of the lowest astronomical tide (LAT), which can also be defined as the lowest predicted low water. This alteration is also being made in the Admiralty Tide Tables (ATT) Volume I and in other tide tables based upon them. By the time this fourth edition has been published many of the new issue Admiralty charts for the areas covered, will be available.

As explained in the Introduction, the harbour plans of the English coast from Poole to Portland in Part I and for the Channel Islands in Part III of the book have been altered to conform approximately with LAT datum. The theoretical datum on the French coast, in Parts II and IV, is the lowest possible low water. This may be a foot (0m3) or so below LAT datum and varies from place to place, but the datums in ATT and the charts correspond closely enough for most practical purposes. Thus the whole book (except for Christchurch Harbour where the level is impounded by sands at about the level of MLWS) is now referred approximately to LAT datum and the depths are converted from the nearest foot to metres and decimetres to conform with the new issue charts and tide tables.

The low level of datums are of particular significance in calculations of depths in the Channel Islands and on the French coast where the range of the tide is great, because it means that at most states of the tide the cruising man may find considerably more water than shown on the harbour plans. For example, on the St Malo chart the depths at MLWS are 1m3 above datum and at MLWN no less than 4m0 above datum, and these figures can be added to the depths or references in the text as may be appropriate. On the other hand, it is easy to forget that the level may actually fall to LAT datum near the Equinox and nearly as low at other times, so tide tables should always be consulted. Meteorological conditions may also have a considerable influence on the levels which can fall even below LAT predictions.

On the harbour plans in this book the shaded areas show the parts which dry out at chart datum and the dotted line indicates the fathom line (1m8), unless otherwise stated. In some of the harbour plans such as Goury, based on French charts, a rock which never covers may be marked by a symbol like a 'T' with a short transverse, which must not be confused with some form of beacon. Height of land, lighthouses and islets and rocks which never cover are given above MHWS or MHHW. The range of lights given in this book is the lesser of geographical and luminous (or nominal) range. In metric charts the range is now shown at luminous (or nominal) range, which may be considerably longer than before. For definition of terms see *Admiralty List of Lights*.

High Water. Constants are given in relation to high water Dover; for example − oo h 15 m Dover means 15 minutes before *high water Dover*. Where appropriate, constants are also given on the nearest standard port, Cherbourg or St Helier. Tide tables for these and other ports appear in *Reed's Nautical Almanac*, and are, of course, more accurate than working from constants of a distant port. The most accurate method of tide predictions is shown in the *Admiralty Tide Tables* (ATT), Volume I, which is published each year.

Tidal Streams play such an important part in the navigation on the coasts described in this book that frequent reference is made to them and to the more important eddies. Tidal

Stream Charts are given in the *Tidal Stream Atlas* for the Channel Islands and adjacent coast of France and in *Reed's Nautical Almanac*. These are necessarily on small scale where it is impossible to show all the local eddies. The streams generally turn earlier inshore than off-shore and this feature is particularly marked on the neighbouring French coast, where in the vicinity of the Cherbourg Peninsula eddies exist running contrary to the main streams as much as two or three hours early, and in the Channel Isles (especially round Herm) there are fast running reverse eddies in some parts. Times, rates and directions of tidal streams are approximations as they vary between springs and neap and can be materially influenced by winds, barometric pressures and other conditions.

Abbreviations Tidal

ATT	*Admiralty Tide Tables* (Vol. I)
HW	High Water
LW	Low Water
LAT	Lowest Astronomical Tide
MHHW	Mean Higher High Water
MHWS	Mean High Water Springs
MHWN	Mean High Water Neaps
MLWS	Mean Low Water Springs
MLWN	Mean Low Water Neaps

Other Abbreviations

Alt	Alternating		m	Metres or minutes
B	Black		Mag	Magnetic
Bl	Blue		Mo	Morse
Bn	Beacon		Occ	Occulting
Cheq	Chequers		Or	Orange
ev	Every		R	Red
F	Fixed		Ra. Refl.	Radar Reflector
Fl	Flashing		Ro Bn	Radiobeacon
FS	Flagstaff		RW	Red and white
G	Green		S	Stripes
Gp	Group		Tr	Tower
H	Horizontal		V	Vertical
Iso	Isophase		vis	Visible
M	Miles (nautical) or land miles as appropriate		W	White

Bearings. Bearings are expressed accurately in degrees true, and, approximate magnetic bearings, expressed in points, are sometimes used to indicate a general direction.

Sailing Directions. The rocky coasts of France and the Channel Islands change little throughout the years, but alterations may occur in lights, fog signals, buoys and marks, even while this edition has been in preparation and printing. Alterations of this kind are notified in Notices to Mariners and also shown on charts corrected up to date. *Reed's Nautical Almanac* gives the necessary information up to the time when it goes to press. Minor local changes, not necessarily notified anywhere, may take place in leading marks (such as the removal of a chimney or the building of new houses near what had been mentioned as a conspicuous one) and in marinas and facilities. However, provided the probability of changes are recognized, this new edition should be of service for some years to come.

Charts, Tides and Navigation

The alterations in this new edition, including datum and metric conversions, have been so extensive, with numerous amendments on almost every page and chart, that the work involved has proved almost as great as compiling a new book. Great care has been taken over the task, and everything has been double checked individually but in the absence of independent checking, such as is available in a hydrographic office, the reader should recognize that the risk of human error remains and that no responsibility can be accepted for mistakes or omissions.

Radio Beacons. Those most useful in the sea area covered in this book are listed on page 11, but are liable to alteration.

Charts Recommended. Up-to-date charts are, of course, essential for cruising on these coasts. The minimum outfit of Admiralty Charts comprises Chart 2615 Portland to Christchurch; Chart 1106 Cap Flamanville to St Marcouf Islands, for sailing between Barfleur and Diélette; Chart 2669 the Channel Islands and adjacent coast of France which is the key to the whole area; and the following charts for the particular localities to be visited: Chart 60 Alderney and the Casquets; Chart 3400 Guernsey, Herm and Sark; Chart 3367 Jersey and Chart 2700 Port of St Malo and approaches. Navigation is easier and infinitely more interesting with the aid of the very large-scale charts. There are particularly good large-scale Admiralty charts for the whole of the Channel Islands, available from all chart agents, and large scale French charts can be obtained by post from The Service Hydrographique de la Marine at 29283 Brest Cedex, France. This takes a little time involving

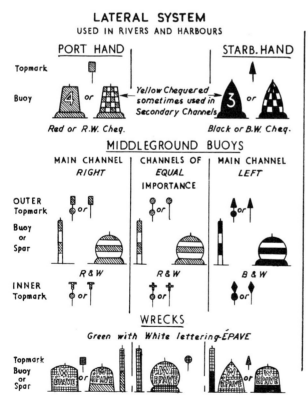

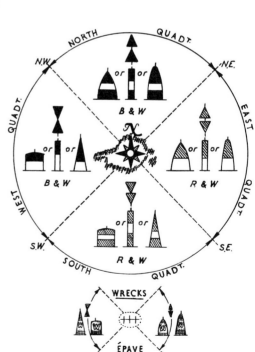

invoicing and payment made through any bank. A list of French charts is available on application. References to French charts has been given in the text and the following are particularly useful: 846 Cherbourg to La Hougue; 845 Vauville to Cap Levi: 5631 Abords de Goury et abords de Omonville (exceedingly useful as it also covers Cap de la Hague); 827 de Port Bail à Diélétte (including Passage de la Déroute and Les Ecrehou on small scale); 824 de Cancale à Bricqueville (which covers the whole of the Baie de St Michel including Cancale, Iles Chausey and Granville); 829 Iles Chausey and 4233 River Rance. Messrs Imray, Laurie, Norie and Wilson of 143 Cannon Street, London, EC4 publish an excellent coloured chart No C33 of the Channel Islands and St Malo and adjacent coasts. They also publish coloured charts of the English Channel.

French Buoyage System. The diagrams reproduced on p. 10 show the characteristics of the buoyage system in use in British and French waters.

French Port Signals

The following signals are used on the signal stations in French harbours for regulating entry or departure:

Entrance prohibited. A cone point up between two balls, vertically, or a red flag. By night. A white light between two red lights, vertically, or a red light.

Entrance and departure prohibited. Two cones, points together, above a ball, vertically, or a red flag above a green flag. *By night.* A white light above a red light and below a green light, or a red light above a green light.

Departure prohibited. Two cones, points together above another cone point down, or a green flag. *By night.* A white light between two green lights, vertically, or a green light.

Customs

It is necessary to notify the Customs of intended departure for the Channel Isles or France. The Customs officers require a list of the crew, and they examine passports if bound for France and satisfy themselves that the currency regulations have been observed. Formal clearance is not usually given unless requested.

For cruising in French waters passports are required. On arrival at the first French port a call should be made with the ship's papers at the Customs. A 'Green Card' (Passport du navire étranger) will then be issued.

On arrival from a British port at Channel Island harbours the regulations are the same as at other British ports, and particulars of the yacht will be asked for at the pier head on entry.

On returning from France to the Channel Isles the 'Q' flag must be worn and Customs cleared at a recognized port of entry (St Helier or Gorey for Jersey, St Peter Port for Guernsey, Herm and Sark). The same procedure must be followed again when arriving at a British port before making any contact with the shore or other vessels.

Radio Beacons

The following radio beacons, which are useful in the sea area described in this book, are listed here from *Reed's Nautical Almanac* and Jersey *Notice to Mariners* 1973 for reference. But, like buoys and lights, they are liable to alteration and the latest Nautical Almanac should always be consulted.

Charts, Tides and Navigation

Marine Radio Beacons

Station	Lat. North	Long. West	Range Miles	Freq. kc/s	Signal	Mins. past each hour
Start Point LH	50° 13½′	3° 38½′	70	298.8	SP (· · · · − − ·)	01, 07, 13, etc.
Casquets LH	49° 43½′	2° 22½′	50	298.8	QS (− − · − · · ·)	02, 08, 14, etc.
Roches Douvres LH	49° 06½′	2° 49′	70	298.8	RD (· − · − · ·)	03, 09, 15, etc.
Cap Frehel	48° 41′	2° 19′	20	305.7	Not yet established	00, 02, 04, etc.
Corbière, Jersey	49° 11′	2° 14½′	20	305.7	CB (− · − · − · · ·)	Continuous
St Helier, Elizabeth Castle	49° 10½′	2° 07½′	10	287.3	EC (· − · − ·)	Continuous
Nab Tower LH *Fog*	50° 40′	0° 57′	20	312·6	NB (− · − · · ·)	00, 06, 12, etc.
Cherbourg (Fort de l'Ouest LH) *Fog*	49° 40½′	1° 39′	20	312·6	RB (− · − · · ·)	01, 07, 13, etc.
Portland Bill LH	50° 31′	2° 27½′	50	291·9	PB (· − − · − · · ·)	00, 06, 12, etc.
St Catherine's Pt	50° 34½′	1° 18′	50	291·9	CP (− · − · · · − − ·)	01, 07, 13, etc.
Pointe de Barfleur	49° 41½′	1° 16′	70	291·9	FG (· · − · − − ·)	05, 11, 17, etc.

Aeronautical Radio Beacons

Station	Lat. North	Long. West	Range Miles	Freq. kc/s	Signal
Hurn	50° 48′	1° 43½′	30	394	HRN (· · · · · · − −)
Cherbourg	49° 38½′	1° 22½′	—	373	MP (− − · − − ·)
Alderney	49° 42½′	2° 12′	50	383	ALD (· − · − · · −)
Guernsey	49° 26′	2° 38½′	25	361	GUR (− − · · · · − · ·)
Jersey East	49° 13′	2° 02′	75	367	JEY (· − − − − · · − −)

PART 1
SOLENT TO PORTLAND

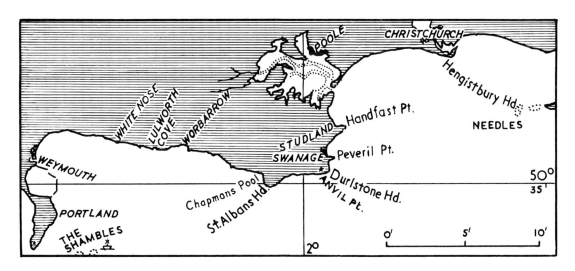

1 Christchurch

Double High Water: In entrance at springs 1st HW highest −1 hr. 55 m. Dover; at neaps 2nd HW highest +1 h. 5 m. Dover. At the Town Quay times are about 25 min. later. Portsmouth HW times give a more accurate result and, if used, the corresponding times are −2 h. 10 m. and +0 h. 50 m.

Heights above datum: MHWS 1m5. MLWS 0m1. MHWN 1m2. MLWN 0m6. The datum is referred to MLWS approximately as the water within the harbour is impounded at this level owing to drying sands on the bar.

Streams: In 'The Run' 4 to 5 knots on ebb, 3 to 4 knots on flood; comparatively weak outside.

Depths at Low Water: 0m4 at Bar (variable); 2m2 or so in 'The Run'; 0m4 to 2m7 between entrance and Town Quay; 0m4 to 1m8 above Town Quay in Rivers Avon and Stour. Apart from the channel and creeks the broad expanse of the harbour nearly dries out. The depths at bar and in harbour are influenced by prevailing meteorological conditions, prolonged N and NE winds tending to reduce the depth.

Yacht Clubs: Christchurch Sailing Club. Mudeford Yacht Club.

Christchurch—at one time Twynham—lies at the junction of the Rivers Avon and Stour and about two miles from their mouth. Three-quarters of a mile below the junction, the easterly flowing rivers open out into a wide shallow expanse of water, sheltered on its southern side by Hengistbury Head and almost closed off from the sea on the east by Mudeford Sandspit. At the northern end of this spit is the harbour's outlet known as 'The Run'.

To owners of small craft the harbour's doleful reputation of a difficult entrance can be somewhat offset by its asset of a double high water and good protection. Any craft with a

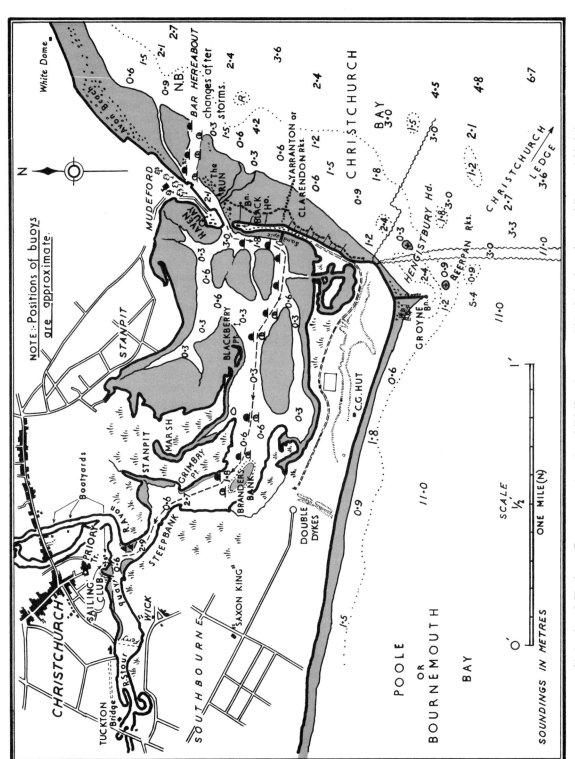

Christchurch Harbour: Datum approximately at MLWS as the water within the harbour does not fall appreciably below this level. (Based on British Admiralty Chart No. 2219 with the permission of the Controller of HM Stationery Office and of the Hydrographer of the Navy.)

draft of 1m4 or less can, with local knowledge, enter the harbour at the top of a spring tide and find deep water berths near the town. For such craft there are winter moorings and slipways at local boat yards.

Buoyage in the harbour and entrance is undertaken privately by the Christchurch Harbour Association (for the convenience of yachtsmen). Buoys may be withdrawn during the winter months, certainly those in the entrance. Further, as the depth and position of the bar is far from stable—it varies from year to year and after storms—great care must be exercised when entering and leaving. Certainly the harbour should not be approached for the first time in foggy or bad weather; although under calm conditions a small boat should be able to 'feel' her way in, particularly if she watches local craft. Advice can be obtained from Elkin's Yachtyard (Tel. Christchurch 4741).

Tides

The most important factor governing entry and use of the harbour is the tides. The double high water, although quite apparent, is in effect a stand of the tide for a period of about 3 or 4 hours. At springs the 1st HW is the higher by about 0m15, whilst at neaps the 2nd HW is higher by the same amount (although under both conditions the actual height of 2nd HW is in theory much the same). However, states of flood (or drought) in the river and meteorological conditions can cause a variation from the predicted height by 0m3 or more.

Flood and Ebb in 'The Run'. Under certain conditions the full rate of the ebb in 'The Run' may be 5 knots or more, although the average is about 3 or 4 knots. Owing to this high rate and the narrowness of the channel it is obvious that auxiliary motor power is required to make the passage into the harbour against the stream. However, on the first ebb, entry under sail only is possible with favourable winds.

The full strength of the ebb—the second ebb—comes an hour or so after 2nd HW, and lasts with diminishing strength until after LW at the bar. (At springs it is not actually slack at LW until half an hour after the tide has begun to rise.)

The flood then commences and comes away more strongly about an hour later (i.e., $1\frac{1}{2}$ hours after LW) when it reaches perhaps 3 or 4 knots, with a strong cross inflow sweeping around close to the end of the Sandspit. This causes minor back eddies and a little turmoil. By 3 hours after LW it has eased considerably and presents little hazard.

At springs the most favourable conditions for entering the harbour are from 3 hours after LW until after the 2nd HW (a period of some 5 hours). At neaps the most suitable period is between the two high waters.

Between the two high waters there is an ebb and flow each with a rate of perhaps 1 to 2 knots.

Navigational Instructions

Off-lying Dangers. To the east there are no dangers except for general shallowness offshore, whilst to the west the groyne on the southern extreme of Hengistbury Head and its adjacent Beerpan Rocks (0m9 MLWS)* should be given a clear berth of about 3 cables, although there is a narrow passage between them.

Christchurch Ledge, which extends from the groyne for $2\frac{1}{2}$ miles, is marked at its SE extremity by the Ledge buoy (R with can topmark). The depths vary from 3m to 8m and rise steeply on the west flank from 14m or more, falling away more gently into an area of

*These have been known to dry out under exceptional conditions.

Christchurch

1.1 Looking SW across harbour to Bournemouth Bay at half-tide. The boat (*bottom left*) has just crossed the bar. The flattened 'c' towards the centre of the harbour is Blackberry Point.

1.2. Looking NNW across the harbour towards Stanpit at half-tide. Note the pleasure-boat landing-stage near the centre of the sandpit in the harbour, whilst on the seaward side the submerged Clarendon (or Yarranton) Rocks are faintly discernible.

1.3. Hengistbury Head from the east, with the low lying Mudeford Sandpit and beach huts. (The Black House is just off the right of the photo.) The groyne shuts behind the Head as the bar is crossed.

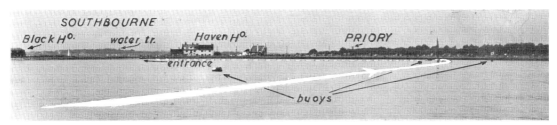

1.4. At the Bar buoy half-tide. Priory bearing about 287°. The bar (about 0m4 MLWS) is approx. 1 cable to the right (east) —it changes often, see text.

1.5. In 'The Run' channel running parallel to right (northern) shore—deep water 2m1 at LW.

1.6. Entering harbour from 'The Run'. Channel bears to port and close to Sandspit shore towards pleasure-boat landing stage.

Christchurch

1.7. Christchurch at the junction of the Rivers Avon and Stour looking NNW. At the bottom right is the Steep bank reach. The Sailing Club with flagstaff is below the centre of the Priory and just to the left of E. F. Elkins Ltd. boatyard.

9m or so in Christchurch Bay. Minor overfalls and general roughness of the sea here can be experienced because of this.

Fallen rocks from the headland and small groynes extend to the low-water mark from Mudeford Sandspit—one particular ledge, an old mouth of the river, known as the Clarendon (or Yarranton or Long) Rocks, is submerged at HW but extends some 2 cables to seaward from the centre of the spit. There is a café on the shore near its root.

The Approach. Hengistbury Head forms a conspicuous landfall from all directions. It is about 30 m high at its western end where it is crowned by a coastguard hut, whilst from its foot Mudeford Sandspit—dunes covered with beach huts—extends NE for about half a mile. At the extremity of this spit is the Black House acting as a sentinel on the seaward (southern) side of the harbour's outlet—the northern side being flanked by a seawall known as Mudeford Haven or Quay, upon which is a small group of charming old houses. Half a mile to NE there is a very conspicuous white dome near the shore.

The Entrance and Run. About 4 cables ENE of Haven Quay is the bar (about 0m4 MLWS) marked in the summer months by pairs of buoys, red-and-white spherical to port, black to starboard. In this area the conspicuous grey square tower of Christchurch Priory, 2 miles inland, may be seen over the top of the low tree plantation bearing about 287° true and open east of the Haven Houses; farther to the east it is hidden. Also the distant higher land of Southbourne with its red square water tower may be seen through the harbour entrance between the Black House and Haven Quay.

However it cannot be too greatly emphasized that *owing to the changing nature of the bar, both in depth and in position, precise sailing directions cannot be given.* The entrance buoys are relaid

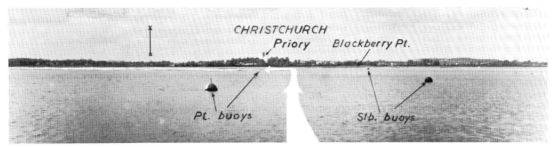

1.8. At the first porthand buoy in the harbour about ¼ mile from landing stage. Priory bearing about 308° over Stanpit Marshes. (The vertical crossed line indicates same position in view 9.)

1.9. Abreast of Blackberry Point. The long reach heading towards the 'Saxon King' (brg. about 274°) has only about 0m3 MLWS.

1.10. At Brander's Bank at the inner end of the long shallow reach. *C. Stewart.*

at Easter, and their position is altered to conform with any alteration in the channel. This rarely occurs in the summer months except perhaps after an exceptional gale. Once over the bar, course is altered to port. The starboard or northern side is then flanked by the seawall, whilst the port side is confined by the submerged shingle and sand extremity of Mudeford Sandspit. This part of the channel is known as 'The Run' and as the quay is approached the fast tidal stream keeps it naturally dredged to some 2m1 or so—the greatest depth being near the quay.

On the quay are a café and public house with a bus service about ½ a mile away. However, craft cannot lie alongside for any length of time, although a landing can always be made at some point.

The Harbour. In contrast to the bar, the channels in the harbour are very stable both in direction and in depth.

From the inner end of the Haven, off which there is a deep pool of 3m0, the channel bears even more to the south and runs close to and parallel to the sandspot shore for about ¼ mile. *No attempt should be made to head up the harbour towards Southbourne from the Haven*—the starboard side of the channel is marked by two small black buoys.

Halfway along the sandspit there is a concrete barge and scaffolding jetty for the use of local pleasure boats; here the channel turns up the harbour. Near the root of the jetty is a public telephone box, the office of the beach attendant and a small café.

The first port-hand buoy (RW spherical) is about ¼ mile from the turn, and when it is reached the Priory should be seen ahead bearing about 308° true (NW mag) over the low-lying Stanpit Marsh.

Shortly before coming up on Blackberry Point the channel bears to port (marked by buoys) and the long shallow reach (0m3 MLWS) heads towards the 'Saxon King', a modern buff-coloured public house with blue tiles, bearing about 274° true. (It is below and to the left of the highest part of the Southbourne skyline.)

On reaching Brander's Bank, where the harbour narrows, the main channel is to starboard and there is a gradual deepening of the water. After passing its inner end do not come too close to Grimbry Point but keep the Priory just touching the edge of Steepbank.

This narrow and deep reach is flanked by tall reeds to starboard and low fields to port. It is known as Steepbank and is usually well lined with craft of every kind as it offers a safe but limited anchorage to deep-drafted boats. The stream is not hard but is appreciable.

It is now only a matter of a few metres before Christchurch Priory comes into full view, but the channel now lies to port of the centre line—it being shallow on the north side. After this head towards the sailing club flagstaff and the centre of the junction of the two rivers, but take care not to go too close to the Stour side of the channel as dinghy moorings cover a shallow patch. (See aerial photograph of Christchurch.)

The Rivers Avon and Stour

Around high water the River Stour can be navigated as far as Tuckton Bridge, a mile or so farther up. The least depth is about 0m5 (LW) between the Town Quay and Wick Ferry, above which the depths are generally deeper—about 1m8. Moorings can be had at Tuckton Bridge, where there is a boat-yard.

The Avon offers a much constricted but pleasant stretch for about half a mile, after which progress is stopped by bridges. As the chart and aerial photograph show, the river separates, forming an island, the sides of which are lined with boats. The right branch leads to Purbrook-Rossiter Ltd, Christchurch Yacht Company, Little Avon Marina and yacht moorings; the depth varies and is shallow at low water. The left branch of the river offers a very pleasant view of the old castle ruins and the Priory and has average depths of 1m with moorings on each bank.

Moorings and Anchorages
Moorings are usually laid privately on the river bed, whilst those off the boat-yards are available on application to the yard concerned. E. F. Elkins Ltd. try to keep two deep-water moorings available to visiting yachts and so also does the Christchurch Sailing Club. Boats can anchor anywhere that is convenient but should keep clear of the centre line of the channel, as many pleasure boats ply up and down the harbour at all states of the tide.

A stranger with a fixed-keel boat wishing to visit the town would do well to bring up in Steepbank and proceed ashore by dinghy.

Facilities
Facilities for yachtsmen are good. There are three yacht yards, shops of all kinds in the town. Early closing day is Wednesday. Good communications by rail or motor bus. Water at Haven Inn, café on Mudeford Spit (also stores) or at yacht yards.

2 Poole Harbour

Double High Water at springs: Entrance, −2 h. 21 m. and +1 h. 14 m. Dover. **Low Water:** +5 h. 4 m. Dover. Poole Entrance.

Heights above datum: MHWS 2m0. MLWS 0m3. MHWN 1m6. MLWN 1m1.

Notes on Tides: Although the above constants are given, the tides in Poole Harbour vary in character between springs and neaps, and for strict accuracy local tide tables should be used from a nautical almanac. The tides are also influenced by the wind and other factors. At *spring tides* the water normally holds up for nearly 3½ hours, falling about 0m6 after the first high water, rising 0m2 or more for the second and then falling for nearly 3 hours. The first high water is thus 0m4 or more higher than the second. At *neaps* the tides are weak and almost unpredictable. Normally the tide rises to first high water, stands easy and finally rises 0m3 or more to second high water, which is therefore higher than the first, instead of lower as at spring tides.

High Water is progressively later the greater the distance from the entrance. For example, compared with the entrance, it is 35 minutes later at Poole Quay, 75 minutes later at Russel Quay, 1 hour 35 minutes later at Wareham Quay. Tides at Bar Buoy are rotary and weaker. Rise at Poole Bridge is 0m2 higher at MHWS than at entrance.

Although the range of the tide is small, the rate is high in the channels, especially in and near the entrance. **Stream Sets** outside near the bar to the east +5 h. Dover and to the west −1 h. Dover. The Channel Flood appears to divide off Anvil Point. The main stream flows towards the Isle of Wight, but inshore it follows the coast, setting NNE past Durlston Head, Peveril Point and Handfast Point towards Poole Bar. On the ebb, part of the water in Poole Bay sweeps along the east side of the Hook Sand, past Handfast Point down to Durlston and Anvil, where it joins the main Channel stream. There are patches of overfalls off this coast, and quite a tide race off Old Harry, off Handfast Point, especially on the ebb tide.

Depth at Low Water. There is normally about 3m7 on the bar at MLWS and as far as Poole Quay. The Main Channel is deep and most of the Channels are navigable by deep-keeled yachts for considerable distances even at low water.

Stakes. The port-hand stakes marking smaller channels are not painted their entire length, but only for 1 metre or so from the top. The tops of these port-hand stakes are painted red and carry a red-can topmark. These red cans are sometimes carried away, but the red paint on the stakes themselves affords some aid to navigation. When only one side of the channel is marked by stakes these are placed on the western side. At the intersection of channels the neutral stake carries a circle top mark and boards carrying names and direction of channels. Yellow stakes indicate oyster beds.

Yacht Clubs. Royal Motor Yacht Club, Parkstone Yacht Club, Poole Yacht Club, Poole Harbour Yacht Club, Lilliput Sailing Club, Redclyffe Sailing Club, East Dorset Sailing Club.

Poole is one of the principal yacht centres on the south coast of England, and being a natural harbour of some 100 miles in circumference it is almost an inland sea. Within its area is the commercial port of Poole itself, several islands, numerous navigable channels and creeks and some anchorages, in lovely surroundings, especially in the southern part near the heath country which lies unspoilt between the harbour and the Purbeck Hills. There is plenty of deep water for large yachts, and for shallow-draft and centreboard yachts the harbour offers innumerable creeks for exploration. The accompanying chart shows the entrance and channels, but as the bottom is uneven it is recommended that the large-scale Admiralty Chart No. 2611 should be used if exploring the upper reaches in a deep-keeled yacht. As a rule, the best water is found on the outer side of bends in the channels. The facilities for yachts and boats are excellent, for on the south coast Poole Harbour ranks second only to the Solent in this respect.

The harbour has the advantage of a long high water, and although the streams run hard it is accessible at any time and in any weather, except in strong onshore winds, when the seas on the bar can be dangerous, especially on the ebb tide.

The Approach

Poole is one of the easiest harbours to find and to enter.

From the east steer for Handfast Point. This is the northerly end of a stretch of chalk cliffs which, viewed from the eastward, look like an island, standing out white against the grey and green hills which rise above them in the background. The chalk cliffs are high to the south and slope to the north, where the chalk pinnacle of rock named Old Harry lies off Handfast Point. On a clear day Durlston Head, 3 miles to the SW, and Anvil Point will also be seen from a considerable distance.

Poole Bar Buoy is situated a mile to the north of Handfast Point, and as soon as it is identified course may be altered towards it, leaving Handfast Point on the port bow, thus avoiding the tide race which lies off Old Harry.

Allowance should be made for the alteration in the direction of the stream which, on the west side of Poole Bay, sets into the Bay on the flood and out of it on the ebb.

Approaching from the westward follow the coast round from Anvil Point, giving a good berth to Peveril Ledges (near Swanage) which are marked by a buoy, and off which there is a race on the ebb, extending $\frac{3}{4}$ mile seaward from Peveril Point. There is a race, although a less violent one, off Ballard Point and, as mentioned, off Handfast Point. In bad weather the seas are steep all along this coast, but in westerly winds some protection is afforded by the land.

Bar and Entrance

There is reckoned to be at least 3m7 of water MLWS on Poole Bar, but the depth varies a little from year to year. The entrance is through the Swash Channel, which lies between shallow water and a training bank on the west side and the Hook sands on the east side. The bar can be very rough in strong onshore winds, but farther up the Swash Channel some protection is afforded either by the training bank or by the Hook Sands, unless the wind is blowing right up the channel.

Poole Bar Buoy (B Con *Qk Fl bell. Ra Refl*) should be left close to starboard, though local yachtsmen often leave it to port as there is plenty of water for a quarter-mile northward of it.

The yacht should then be headed for the prominent Haven Hotel standing on the east side of the entrance at 324° true (say, NNW mag) when the Channel buoy (R and W chequered *Fl R 3 sec*) will be seen on the same bearing. This buoy is near the centre of the channel, but should be left to port and the Hook Sands black buoy (*Fl 3 sec*) to starboard.

The Swashway is marked by small conical black buoys (uneven numbers) on the starboard side and by small red-and-white barrel buoys (even numbers) on the port side, beyond which lies the training bank. This is awash at HW Neaps and covered at HW Springs, but it is marked by 10 red stakes with red can tops and at its southern end by a beacon (*Qk Fl R*).

When the Channel buoy is abeam the entrance will clearly be seen between sand dunes on either side, with the conspicuous white building of the Haven Hotel and new block of flats on the east side. Beyond the entrance Brownsea Island will be seen with its castle. The next fairway buoy, Brownsea Buoy R and W chequered (*Fl R 10 sec*), will be found almost in line with the Castle, just a little to the west of it. Hold on the course to the Haven Hotel, or to

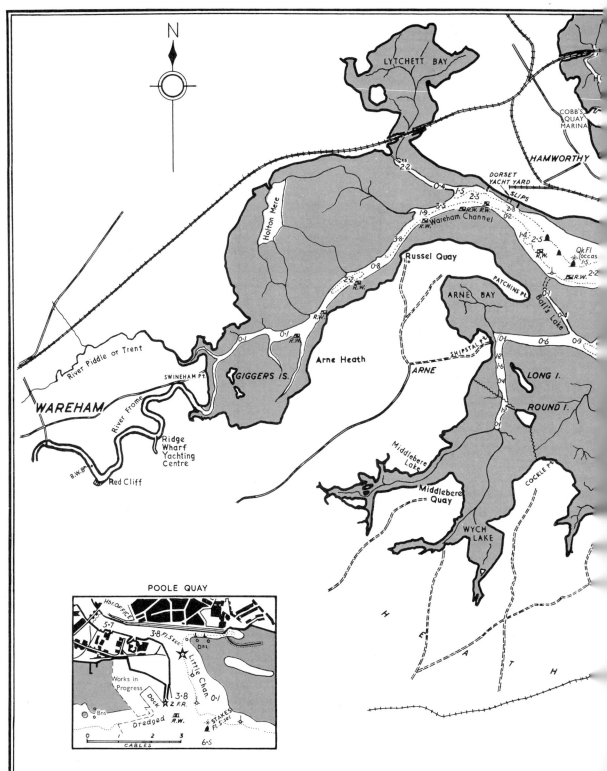

Poole Harbour: (Based on British Admiralty Chart Nos. 2611 and 2175 with the permission of the Controller of Stationery Office and of the Hydrographer of the Navy).

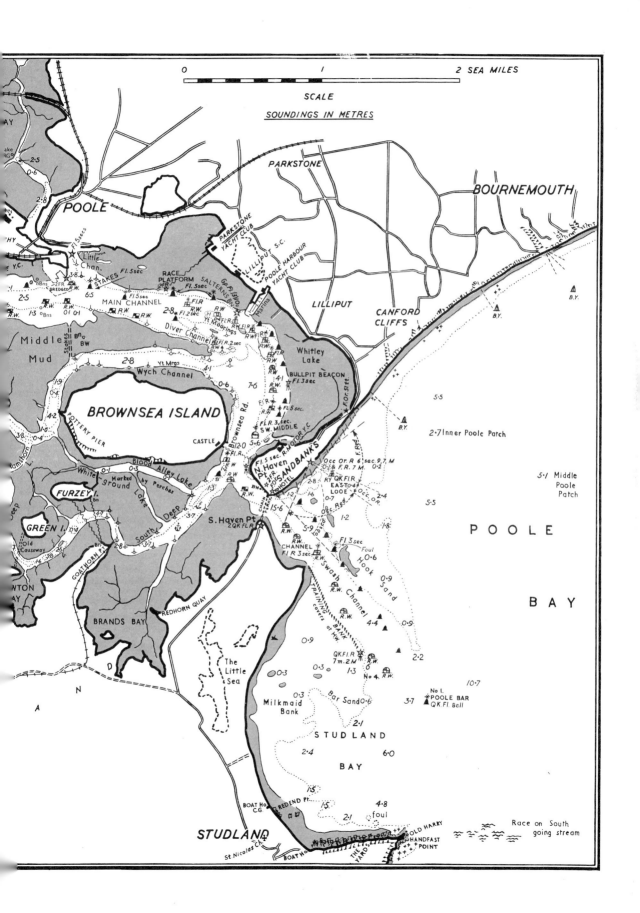

Poole Harbour

2.1. Handfast Point and Old Harry from SW.

2.2. Poole Bar buoy and the Haven Hotel at the entrance to the harbour.

2.3. After passing the Bar buoy two cheq RW buoys and the training bank beacon (shown here) are left to port. The training bank is ¾ mile long and covers at HW but it is marked by ten red stakes with red can topmarks. In the background is the entrance to the harbour to the left of conspicuous white Haven Hotel and flats.

2.4. The east side of the harbour entrance, Haven Hotel on right and the Channel RW light buoy centre with Brownsea Island to its left.

2.5. Brownsea Island, Brownsea Castle and roads to its right with North Haven Beacon in right foreground.

2.6. Bullpit Beacon: starboard hand mark in main·channel.

Poole Harbour

the ferry slipway (*2 FR*) west of it, until Brownsea buoy bears 310° true, when steer for the buoy.

This leads past the sand dunes to port, with the Haven Hotel to starboard, then between the Ferry slips on either side and into the harbour, leaving to starboard a beacon (*Fl 3 sec*) off North Haven Point, which should not be approached too closely. The Ferry has to keep clear of ships, but it is usual where possible to pass under her stern if she is crossing. There is a tidal set through or out of the East Looe (see below) and in the narrows of the entrance the stream is often fierce. For courses from Brownsea buoy to Poole Quay see *Main Channel*.

By Night. Entry into Poole Harbour by night is not difficult. At Anvil Point (*Fl ev 10 sec*) 4 miles to the south there is the powerful lighthouse, visible for 18 miles, and to the NE is the glare of the lights along the long front of Bournemouth.

Poole Bar buoy (*Qk Fl Bell*) is thus easy to locate, and from there course is set between the Channel buoy (*Fl R 3 sec*) port and the Hook Sands buoy (*Fl 3 sec*) starboard, leaving to port the Training Bank beacon (*Qk Fl R*). At night it is best to steer from the Channel buoy towards the 2 *fixed red lights* and the light (*fixed orange*) to SW of the hotel on the east side of the entrance, with North Haven beacon (*Fl 5 sec*) beyond, and not to alter course for Brownsea buoy (*Fl R 10 sec*) until the yacht is approaching the entrance, when she will pass between the two *Qk Fl R* lights to port and 2 *FR* to starboard on the ferry slipways, and then leave to starboard the North Haven beacon. If there is a headwind the tacks up the Swashway should be short, unless there is enough light to distinguish the small unlit channel buoys on either hand and the stakes marking the dangerous training bank on the west side.

East Looe. This short cut from the eastward to join the Swash Channel at the entrance of Poole Harbour lies inshore off Sandbanks, with its entrance nearly ½ mile east of the Haven Hotel. It is much used by local yachts of shoal or moderate draft.

The approach is marked by a RY chequered buoy *Qk Fl R*, but to seaward of this buoy there is something in the nature of a bar, with depths as low as 0m4. The best water will be found by steering for the buoy at approximately 300° true (NW by W). Leave the buoy close to port and alter course to port to make good about 240 degrees (WSW) which gives 1m6 at LAT to enter the Swash Channel between its northern black conical starboard hand buoy (No. 19) to port and the shore near the Haven Hotel to starboard, distant about ½ cable.

The depths over the sands in the vicinity of the bar are liable to occasional changes, so when attempting this short cut a stranger should choose good weather and a rising tide and take frequent soundings. When using the East Looe for the first time it is easier to leave rather than to enter by it. The channel is not difficult but as the rise of tide is only 1m6 neaps, 2m0 springs, there is little margin for error, especially in fresh easterly winds or swell.

The East Looe can also be used at night. Approach in the orange sector of the East Looe shore light *Occ 6 sec, 9M* to the buoy *Qk Fl R*. Then proceed as before at 240 degrees to join the Swash Channel, leaving the South Haven Point ferry lights *2 Qk Fl R* to port and the Haven Hotel lights and Sandbanks *F Or* to starboard.

The Main Channel to Poole Quay

Of the three channels in the northern part of Poole Harbour the Main Channel leading to Poole Quays is the easiest for strangers to follow. It can be summed up by saying 'keep to the right'. When the yacht has entered the harbour, Brownsea buoy will lie ahead and North

Haven beacon to starboard. Alter course to starboard to pass between these two marks, giving a good berth to the beacon. A quarter-mile to NE will be seen the red-and-white spherical Middle Ground buoy (*Fl R 3 sec*) which is locally known as the 'Bell' buoy, but with no bell on it. The Main Channel is immediately east of this buoy and follows a semi-circular course along the mud flats on the east and north sides of the harbour. It is marked by RW barrel buoys on the port side and black conical to starboard, but these buoys should be given a good berth as some of them are in shallow water, especially on the port hand. On the starboard side off North Haven many yachts are moored, some in shallow water, and ½ mile up on the starboard side is Bullpit beacon, (*Fl 3 sec*). Beyond this beacon the Main Channel continues to curve turning gradually through north to NW leaving the Poole Harbour YC Marina and Saltern's beacon (*Gp Fl (3) 10 sec*) to starboard. South of this beacon there is the port hand No. 36 RW cheq light buoy (*Fl R 5 sec*). In this vicinity and SE of it the channel is very narrow. On no account sail direct from the No. 36 light buoy direct to the yachts on moorings seen about west magnetic of it as this would cross shoal water. The main channel bears towards NW here and two more port hand buoys must be passed before rounding Parkstone Shoal to reach them.

The course of the channel from Saltern's Beacon to the Little Channel leading to Poole Quays is best followed on the chart. There are four black conical light buoys (*Fl 5 sec*) and Parkstone YC starting platform (*2 F R vertical*) on the starboard hand and four RW cheq port hand buoys, of which No. 40 is a light buoy (*Fl R 5 sec*). Note on the chart that the main channel is very wide west of the black conical Diver Light Buoy No. 49 (*Fl 2 sec*) which marks the junction with the Diver Channel and does not mark the Main Channel, although there is plenty of water north of it. Yachts not confined to the channels by reason of their draft should give larger, deeper draft vessels as wide a berth as possible.

2.7. Entrance to the Little (or Stakes) Channel to Poole Quays. The direction of the Channel is towards the ship with a black hull at right angles to the entrance, leaving to port the Hamworthy Oil Jetty and to starboard two stakes and a beacon.

Little or Stakes Channel. This leads to Poole Quay at roughly N mag leaving on the port hand No. 42R and W barrel buoy, and the breakwater quay. On the starboard hand there is Stakes buoy at the entrance, two posts and a B conical buoy, which mark the edge of the mud on the east side. At the entrance the tides set athwart the Little Channel, and when approaching the blind corner into the channel between Quays keep to starboard and

Poole Harbour

a sharp look out should be kept for vessels which may be leaving the quays correctly on their starboard side but hidden behind buildings on the quays. The streams run hard and there is a bridge $\frac{1}{4}$ mile up the reach between the quays, so warps and fenders should be ready for berthing at the quay on the north side.

By night. The Main Channel is easy to follow at night as it is well marked by the light-buoys white flashing to starboard, red flashing to port referred to and shown on the chart, but a look-out should be kept for the unlit buoys.

If proceeding from the Main Channel to Poole Quays enter the Little Channel midway between Stakes starboard hand lightbuoy (*Fl 5 sec*) and the two *F R lights vertical* at the southern end of the Hamworthy Oil Jetty, leaving an unlit buoy and the jetty to port. Follow up the line of the quay leaving a beacon (*Fl 5 sec*) to starboard and bear to port. There are lights along the inner quays so that the channel is well illuminated.

2.8. Poole Quays as entered from the Little Channel showing yachts berthed at the North Quay (shown left of the power station) as directed by the Harbour Master.

Parkstone Lake. This shallow creek is $\frac{1}{2}$ mile above Salterns Pier and leads up to Parkstone Yacht Club. It is occupied by permanent moorings, but is useful for dinghies and offers a good landing, if permission is obtained from the Club.

Holes Bay. This is reached from the channel between quays by passing through Poole bridge into the Back Water Channel. The bridge clearance is only 1m8 at very high springs or about 4 metres at LAT. The bridge opens if required for yachts with high masts at specified times (available from Harbour Office) five times on weekdays and eight times on Sundays. Signal to open—three blasts. The stream through the bridge may be strong at springs.

Above the bridge, the first reach, with 2m7 to 4m0 of water, leads NE, leaving the Quays to starboard and the Power Station and piled moorings to port. At the first of two derrick cranes on the starboard side, the channel bends to NNW and is marked by stakes. Keep to the centre near the craft on moorings. At the end of this reach head for a marker stake with a horizontal RG board. Here the channel divides into Creekmore Lake running about NNE, and Upton Lake leading to Cobbs Quay and marina and then continuing NW. For Upton Lake bear sharply to port WSW just before reaching the marker stake. The channel is well marked by stakes but keep to the centre in the best water, about 1m2 MLWS, 1m8 MLWN close to moored craft, and bear to NNW leaving Cobbs Quay and Marina pontoons to port and a trot of moorings to starboard.

Diver or Middle Channel to Poole

This channel lies to the SW of the Main Channel, separated from it by a Middle ground, and in the middle of the three big channels on the north side of Brownsea Island. The minimum depth in the centre is 2m2, but there is only 1m2 where it is entered at its eastern end. It provides a useful short cut to Poole Quays.

After rounding North Haven Point Beacon steer about north true in the direction of Saltern's beacon just W of Poole Harbour YC marina, through Brownsea Roads, leaving the "Bell" RW cheq buoy, No. 20, (*fl R 3 sec*) about a cable to starboard. On this course the yacht will pass the big yacht moorings to port and, when the northern shores of the island open up, steer for Aunt Betty RW cheq light buoy No. 54 (*Fl R 2 sec*) at about 325° true distant three cables. An intersection stake with circular top mark and direction boards for the Wych and Diver Channels will be left close to port, as also a stake with BW triangle top. Leave Aunt Betty buoy to port and alter course to port, steering for the starboard hand black conical No 49 Diver lightbuoy *Fl 2 sec*, bearing about 300°, distant three cables. The channel is marked by stakes on either side (red can tops to port) and the Diver buoy marks the junction with the south side of the main channel.

By night the Diver Channel is not difficult, navigating by the Aunt Betty and Diver buoys, steering nothing south of their line for the first cable and nothing north of their line for the last cable short of the Diver buoy.

Poole Quays. The port of Poole offers yachts complete protection in all weathers, although it can be uncomfortable in S or SE gales and good fenders will be required.

It is a busy commercial harbour for coastal shipping, colliers, pleasure vessels, tugs, etc., so that its capacity is often taxed, especially during the summer months when the port is visited by many yachts. These yachts moor alongside the North or Town Quay but not at its eastern end; the South Quays are generally used by commercial concerns. Owing to the limited space available at the North Quay, yachts often have to lie alongside each other, and should not be berthed until the Harbour Master has given directions. Yachts are usually hailed as they enter, and the Harbour Authorities take considerable trouble to make them welcome, and to berth them in the most convenient place that is available. Warps should, of course, be carried out fore and aft, in addition to breast ropes and springs to quay or other vessel, and yachts berthing temporarily must be ready to move to a more permanent berth. Arrivals and date of departure must be reported to the Harbour Master (Tel. Poole 3845).

There are no Quay Berth charges for the first six hours, for lying alongside the quay, or outside other yachts, but are made after a 6 hours stay. Harbour dues are also raised on all vessels entering Poole.

The Customs Office is near by, with day and night service; clearance for a yacht can be obtained quickly.

Poole Harbour

Water can be obtained by hose from two points on the quay free of charge. A public telephone call box is handy and it is only a short distance from the Quay to the shops. As Poole is a regular yachting centre, facilities are excellent, and in the district there are some ten yacht yards (the largest is able to slip yachts up to 3m3 draft aft), and engineers, designers, brokers, ships' chandlers, sailmakers, etc. Early closing day Wednesday. There are frequent buses to Bournemouth and neighbouring towns, and a main line station.

Marinas

Poole Harbour Yacht Club Marina. Situated in the Main Channel just E of Salterns Beacon adjacent to the Yacht Club at Lilliput, this marina has 217 berths, with dredged depths from 1m0 to 2m5 MLWS, maximum length 25m O.A. and 70 chain moorings outside in the harbour. The marina is open to visiting yachts depending on berth vacancies, usually around 10 pontoon berths and/or chain moorings. Tel: 0202 77321. Temporary membership of the Club available to visiting yachtsmen and excellent restaurant. All facilities, water, fuel, chandlery, etc. and yacht yard adjacent.

Cobb's Quay, Hamworthy. Situated in Holes Bay. Quay, river moorings and finger berths. Depths about 1m2 MLWS, 1m8 MLWN, very soft mud bottom accommodating deeper draft. All facilities, licenced club and restaurant. Car parks, chandlery, water and fuel, and refueller often stationed east of Aunt Betty buoy. The boat yard slips up to 2m4 draft and provides comprehensive services, including laying-up and repairs.

Other Anchorages

The best positions in Poole Harbour are occupied by moorings, but there are places in the deep channels of Poole Harbour where large and medium-sized yachts can anchor, and many anchorages available to shallow-draft yachts. When choosing a berth a stranger should remember it is a big harbour and at high water it is like a large lake, with a considerable fetch for the seas which can render an exposed anchorage uncomfortable. Furthermore, although the range of the tide is small, the stream runs hard and when opposed to a fresh or strong wind makes many anchorages rough, with too much sea for a dinghy. Therefore, in considering an anchorage a yachtsman should select one in the lee of the land in unsettled weather, and in gales should allow for the probable shift of wind when the depression passes. For example, in the Wych Channel there are sheltered positions in a southerly gale on the north side of Brownsea Island, but when the wind veers towards the NW weigh anchor and find shelter on the east side of the island. Do not anchor in the Main and Diver fairways.

The following are a few of the principal anchorages or mooring positions:

1. Brownsea Road, north of Brownsea buoy and E of Brownsea Island, which is sheltered in the winds off the island. With strong winds from north and south this anchorage can be very rough, and the water is deep. The best positions are occupied by permanent moorings owned by members of the Royal Motor Yacht Club at Sandbanks, and they should not be picked up without first applying to the club launchman or at the club for permission. The RMYC welcomes visiting yachtsmen.

2. Off Sandbanks. The fairway must be left clear for ships, and there is little room for anchoring outside the fairway, owing to permanent moorings. Repairs and laying up are undertaken by the Sandbanks Yacht Co. Ltd., to whom application for a mooring may be made.

3. Clear of the fairway between Poole Harbour YC Marina and Parkstone Yacht Club starting platform, or SE of the Marina. All the best positions are occupied by moorings, so care must be taken not to foul the anchor. In strong winds, especially southerly, the anchorage is exposed.

4. Off and SW of Poole Yacht Club. This is west of Hamworthy Oil Jetty and the large area being developed west of it for a ferry terminal, which yachts must keep clear of. The anchorage is good in settled weather or northerly winds, but take soundings as much of it is shallow and even dries out a cable south of the club pier. Here again all the best positions are taken by moorings.

5. Off Lake. This is a good centre a couple of miles up the channel off the Dorset Yacht Yard, but it is choppy there in strong SW or SE winds. Moorings can sometimes be hired from the yacht yard and permission given to land at their pier. There may be room to anchor above or below the moorings. Water and petrol from the yacht yard. Shops $\frac{1}{2}$ mile distant, where there are also frequent buses to Poole taking only a few minutes.

6. See also Wych Channel and South Deep.

Wych Channel

This is a broad channel along the north and west sides of Brownsea Island, which then pursues a wandering course between mud flats to Shipstal Point on the Arne Peninsula, thence in a southerly direction west of Long Island and Round Island. It affords several pleasant anchorages.

The approach to the Wych Channel from the harbour entrance is easy to follow, as it curves round Brownsea Island. There is deep water fairly close to Brownsea Pier, but on the NE of the island is a mud flat, marked by stakes with red can tops, which must be given a wide berth. The entrance to Wych Channel lies between these port hand stakes, and the Intersection Stake with circle top mark bearing directional boards to Wych and Diver Channels. Bear round to port and follow the line of yacht moorings on the north side of Brownsea Island (where the depths in the centre range from 2m8 to 4m0 and more in parts for the first mile). The channel is well marked by piles on either hand, but do not approach these closely as they stand in shallow water.

When west of Brownsea, care is needed in pilotage, as the piles are less frequent and the bottom is uneven, depths varying from 0m4 to 4m0. There is an extensive mud flat off the NW of Brownsea, and the channel turns rather sharply round this, from west almost to south. The next pronounced turn is just over a cable south of the pottery pier situated on the western point of Brownsea. This is a 'V' bend through west to NW. Whiteground Lake and Ramshorn Lake (see *South Deep*), joins the Wych Channel here. There are many shallow patches. The black starboard hand stakes at the entrances of these creeks are port hand when sailing up the Wych Channel. After passing these creeks the channel becomes deeper nearly as far as Ball's Lake, where it shallows again to about 0m5 and turns towards Shipstal Point off which there is another 'V' bend towards the SSE. Just short of this bend the channel is only about 12 metres wide and 0m1 deep, and is marked by a stake on either side. It deepens again in the reach between Shipstal Point and Long Island where a pool with 1m2 to 1m6 LAT can be found by taking soundings. There are moorings here so, if room can be found to anchor, use a trip line in case of fouling one. Shallow draft craft can anchor south of the moorings in about 0m5, which gives 1m6 at neaps. There is also a narrow creek running

Poole Harbour

northwards from Shipstal Point into Arne Bay with 1m8 in parts, but here again there are many moorings.

There is a hard (rough and muddy at low water) at Shipstal Point from which a private road leads to Arne. This affords a delightful walk through woods and heathland to the old village and church, but there are no facilities. Long Island, where there is a bird sanctuary, and Round Island are private property. The channel is staked as far as Round Island pier and a ¼ mile south of this it forks into two drying creeks; the western one winds up past the disused Middlebere Quay and wanders deep into the heathland.

Middle Mud Channel. This channel provides a useful short cut between the Wych Channel and Poole Quays across the Middle Mud. It is nearly awash at LAT but carries about 2m2 HW springs, 1m8 HW neaps. The channel lies straight on a line from a cable E of Brownsea Pottery Pier to the notice board at the end of Hamworthy Oil Jetty. It is well marked on the west side by six stakes with the usual red can tops.

Ball's Lake. The most westerly of the creeks between the Wych and the Main Channel. Like the others it is about awash at LAT and staked on the western side.

Anchorages. The anchorage in the Wych Channel on the north-east and north sides of Brownsea Island provides one of the most sheltered in bad weather, except in strong west and NW winds when Brownsea Road is better. Brownsea Island is owned by the National Trust. Landing from yachts is permitted at the Pottery Pier on the west side, 1st April to

2.9. The anchorage in the pool off Shipstal Point in the Wych Channel. Be sure to use a trip line if bringing up close to local moorings.

30th September, on payment of a small landing fee. There is a sheltered anchorage in easterly winds off the pier clear of the oyster beds marked by yellow stakes. The most westerly anchorage is in the pool between Shipstal Point and Long Island. The best positions near landing places are now occupied by moorings.

34

Wareham Channel

West of Hamworthy Oil Jetty the Main Channel continues to be wide and well marked. Note from the chart the sharp bend at No. 53, B Con starboard light buoy (*Qk Fl occasional*), which is moored nearly 4 cables off the northern shore; it is small and easily overlooked. Depths as far as the Dorset Yacht Yard's Lake Shipyard (off which there are many yacht moorings) are about 2 to 3 metres, but as some of the port hand buoys are in shallow water it is best to keep to the starboard side of the channel.

From the yacht yard to the pier ¼ mile beyond, the best water in the Wareham Channel lies on the north side, and a wide area of mud on the south side dries out at low water. This part of the channel and for some 3 miles is buoyed on the port hand only and it gradually bends round over to Russel Quay on the Arne Peninsula. The depths in the channel off these buoys are as low as 1m0 in parts and the deep water lies on the starboard hand close to a vast area of drying mud flats, which are covered near HW.

The channel follows near the line of the NW side of the Arne peninsula for nearly a mile and the depth of water progressively decreases and dries at LAT where it leaves the Arne Peninsula and turns SW towards Wareham, but it is staked on both sides. It then forks close to the land NW of Giggers Island, the northern arm being the River Piddle or Trent, which is hardly navigable, and the southern one being the River Frome, which runs through Wareham.

In the River Frome there is little water at Wareham itself, but below there are depths up to 1m5, and off Ridge Wharf there are over 2 metres. Local advice can be obtained at the Ridge Yacht Centre. The bottom of the river is uneven and has shallows as well as deeper pools, so that it is really suitable only for centreboard or light draft craft. Care should be taken in navigating at the point where the two rivers join, and again just before entering the river itself, as it is not always very well marked.

By night. There are no lights in the Wareham Channel above No. 53 lightbuoy.

Anchorages. There are moorings and all facilities at Lake, which has already been referred to, and the chart shows many positions further up the channel offering anchorages which are secluded (such as off the demolished Russel Quay), but far from facilities. In the River Frome it is possible to anchor anywhere where sufficient depth is found, clear of passing craft and of salmon holes where anchorage is prohibited.

Rocklea River. This is the largest of the several creeks on the starboard hand of the Wareham Channel above the Dorset Yacht Yard. It carries 0m5 to 1m5 and leads under the low railway bridge to Lytchett Bay. Except at slack water the tide, which runs diagonally under the bridge, is dangerously fast for passage by dinghy.

River Frome. There are about 2 metres alongside the quay at Ridge Wharf Yachting Centre, and also berths at the stagings in the basin for yachts of shallower draft. Buoyed moorings in the river. Yacht yard, fuel and usual facilities.

Wareham. Stores of all kinds and petrol. Early closing Wednesday. Yacht yard where small repairs can be effected. Frequent buses and main line station. Yacht Club: Redclyffe Sailing Club.

South Deep

The entrance to South Deep lies on the west side of the entrance channel south of Brownsea Lightbuoy and almost opposite North Haven beacon. The entrance is marked on the port hand by No. 18 RW barrel buoy, close to the shingle bank known as Stoney Island, and on the starboard side by No. 50A black conical buoy.

When in the entrance of Poole Harbour do not alter course for South Deep too rapidly when the RW buoy comes abeam, as this is situated very close to the spit of shingle which projects somewhat into the channel. It is better to enter midway between the two buoys, and then steer SW until the lines of stakes have been identified. These are the usual black to starboard, red to port, and the port hand stakes have a can at their tops. Frequently yachts are at anchor or on moorings in the centre of the channel near the entrance.

The channel is clearly marked, but the stakes are on the edge of the mud, and should be given a liberal berth and, as may be expected, the best water is found on the outer sides of the bends in the channel. A possible source of confusion to a stranger lies in the red poles placed at the entrances of the two creeks which run into South Deep on the north side. These are placed on the port side of the entrances to the creeks, and will lie on the starboard hand when sailing up South Deep, so must not be confused with the larger red stakes to the south of them which mark the port side of South Deep itself. The paint on the stakes sometimes becomes faded and weatherworn.

On the south side of South Deep there is a wide creek named Redhorn Lake, and $\frac{1}{4}$ mile beyond this South Deep takes a sharp bend to the NW towards Goathorn Point. Care should be taken when rounding this bend, as the best water lies on the port hand.

There are a few private moorings SE of Goathorn Point, but plenty of water remains for anchoring. A cable beyond Goathorn the best water (2 to 7 metres) lies on the starboard hand near the black stakes on the outside of the 90° bend from NW to SW. Two cables cross the bed of the channel NW of Goathorn to Fursey Island. At the second one the depth is only about 1m0 and course should be altered diagonally across to the other side of the channel close to the red port hand stakes. This leaves to starboard a small drying middle ground and the water is deep. The channel then continues south of Green Island (where there are remains of an old causeway) and then northward into the narrow but well staked Ramshorn Lake to join the Wych Channel. The least water is about 0m4 so with the help of the large-scale Admiralty Chart No. 2611 a keel-yacht drawing 1m8 can be navigated through the channel near high water on a rising tide. Certainly the effort would be rewarded, for the surroundings are really beautiful and there are deep pools in which to anchor.

Anchorages. It is possible to anchor almost anywhere in South Deep except in the parts where permanent moorings are laid. In fresh or strong winds the reaches where the wind and tide are opposed should be avoided. The first reach in South Deep is convenient for obtaining facilities at Sandbanks, but the crossing from South Deep can be rough in a dinghy and the streams strong.

Redhorn Lake is suitable for shallow-draft yachts drawing less than 1m2. Larger yachts can anchor off its entrance, and row up in the dinghy to Redhorn Quay. A short walk leads to the main road, thence by bus to Studland (see Chapter 3 for facilities) or to Sandbanks by bus and ferry.

The author's favourite anchorage is near Goathorn Point, although some of the best berths are now occupied by permanent moorings. It is protected even in gales, though if the wind is blowing hard up or down the channel it is uncomfortable at high water especially at Spring tides. To the south of the point the holding ground does not seem quite so good and anchors have been dragged in bad weather. Goathorn Point is private and no facilities are available nearer than Studland. A sheltered and peaceful anchorage in from 2 to 4 metres can be found round the bend in the channel. It lies between Goathorn and the SE corner of Green Island beyond the drying middle ground.

Blood Alley Lake. This creek and its continuation in White Ground Lake lies to the south of Brownsea Island and links South Deep and Wych Channel. It carries a minimum of 0m3 MLWS and is marked by stakes, but there is a drying area west of Furzey Island pier and another one before the creek joins the Wych Channel.

3 Studland Bay

High Water (approx.): −2 h. 30 m. and +1 h. 5 m. Dover.
Heights above datum. Chart 2175, MHWS 2m0. MLWS 0m3. MHWN 1m6. MLWN 1m1.
Stream Sets outside to the west −1¼ h. Dover and to the east +5 h. Dover, but sets approximately NE and SW inshore between Old Harry and Anvil Point.

3.1. The line of chalk cliffs from Handfast Point westward into Studland Bay. The three prominent projections are known as "The Yards" off which there is foul ground.

Studland provides a delightful anchorage in offshore winds from south, through west to NW. The bay (see Chart of Poole) affords plenty of room to anchor, with a sandy bottom and good holding ground. In fresh northerly winds it is uncomfortable, and it is entirely open to easterly winds. However, Poole is near at hand as a port of refuge, if the wind comes in from the wrong quarter.

Studland Bay is easy to enter anywhere between Poole Bay buoy and Old Harry Rocks. The best water between 2½ and 1½ fathoms lies in the southern part, as to the west of the Bar buoy there are the Bar Sand and the Milkmaid Bank, which have depths of under a fathom.

On the chalk cliffs west of Old Harry there are conspicuous projections, known locally as the 'yards'. The remains of old wrecks make a foul bottom between the first and the second 'yard', about 1½ cables offshore, which should be left to port.

At night Poole Bar buoy (*Qk Fl Bell*) is left to starboard, and the bay is so wide that there is little difficulty in entering, provided it is not too dark to see the cliffs against the sky.

The recommended anchorage is about 3 cables off the 'yards', but in practice it is usual to enter the Bay and to take soundings in order to anchor as far inshore as is prudent in relation to the draft of the yacht. A yacht drawing 1m5 will be able to bring up less than ¼ mile offshore, while deeper yachts will anchor progressively farther offshore. There are boathouses and bathing huts on the shore, but little of the village itself can be seen from the sea. Redend

3.2. The pretty anchorage in the SW corner of the bay off the bathing beach.

Point will be noted, and there are rocks off the point extending over a cable seaward. The anchorage is over $\frac{1}{4}$ mile from the shore, where landing is effected on the open beach. A path leads up to the village, where there are small shops, a hotel or two and a post office. There are frequent buses to Swanage and Sandbanks. The surroundings are beautiful, and there are many pleasant walks. The church of St Nicholas dates from Saxon times.

4 Swanage

High Water: − 2 h. 51 m. and + 1 h. 09 m. Dover.
Heights above datum: MHWS 1m9. MLWS 0m3. MHWN 1m6. MLWN 1ml.
Stream sets in the offing to the SW about 1 h. before HW Dover or earlier, and to the NE about 5 h. after HW Dover. The tides are strong outside the Bay, but weak within it.
Yacht Club: Swanage Sailing Club.

Swanage Bay offers a useful anchorage in offshore winds from south to west. As with Studland Bay, it is exposed if the wind backs east of south and in bad weather the anchorage is uncomfortable if the wind goes north of NW. The author has sheltered there in SW gales when, except for a swell, it is safe, but in the event of a shift of wind Poole as a port of refuge is not so handy as it is from Studland Bay.

The Approach
Swanage Bay is deep and clear of dangers, except for the Tanville ledges off the shore by the Grand Hotel, which a yacht rarely approaches as the rocks are in the bight of the Bay, over ½ mile from the anchorage.

Approaching from Poole give Handfast Point a good berth. If there is a strong wind contrary to the ebb stream the race off the point can be rough. Then shape a course towards Swanage pier. The stream runs hard and the only danger for a yacht without an engine is that of becoming becalmed and carried on to Peveril Ledges; so in light weather keep inshore where the tide is weak.

Peveril Ledges extend off Peveril Point due east towards Peveril Ledge buoy (RW cheq *no light*) which is nearly ½ mile off the Point. There is a tide race, especially on the ebb, between the Point and the buoy and for ½ mile to seaward of it. The tide sets straight across the ledges, and the outermost dangerous rock lies under 2 cables off the Point, so that in moderate weather a short cut can be made a cable inside Peveril buoy. The race is a lively one when the wind is over the tide, but in westerly winds there is some shelter from the land.

Approaching from the west, allow for the tide which inshore follows the general direction of the coast. The east and NE inshore stream begins at +4 h Dover and the SW and W stream at −2 h Dover. In light weather give Peveril Ledge a wide berth as the tide sets across it. With a fair tide running NE alter course quickly to enter the Bay once Peveril buoy is abeam, to avoid being set too far north. In a SW gale there are particularly bad seas S and

4.1. Approaching Swanage from northward showing Durlston Head, Peveril Point and Swanage to the right.

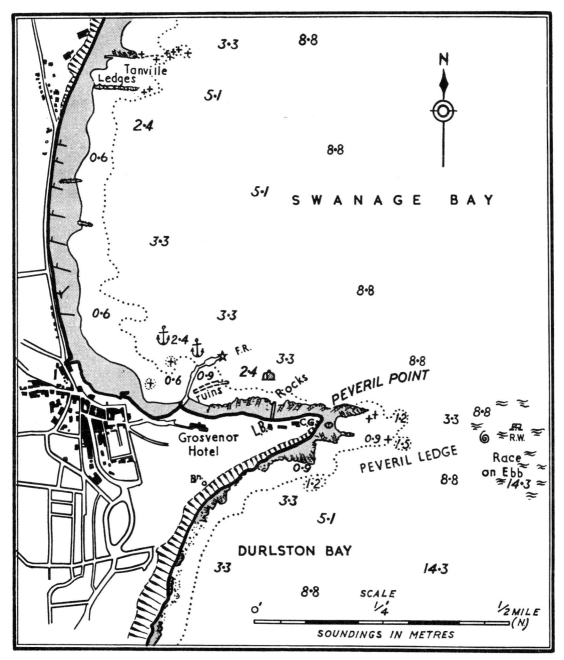

Swanage Bay: (Based on British Admiralty Chart No. 2172 with the permission of the Controller of HM Stationery Office and of the Hydrographer of the Navy.)

Swanage

4.2. Anvil Point and Durlston Head are passed when coming from the westward, and course is altered to leave Peveril Ledge buoy to port.

PEVERIL POINT

SWANAGE PIER

4.3. When the buoy is rounded from the south steer to leave Swanage Pier about a cable to the south. Allow for a possibly strong tidal stream which, if running SW, sets strongly on Peveril Ledges.

4.4. Swanage Bay showing the pier and the anchorage west of it, seaward of the local moorings.

E of Anvil Point when wind and stream are opposed. Some shelter may be gained close in under the cliffs in Durlston Bay, but a yacht has to come out again to avoid Peveril Ledges and may pass a cable W inside the buoy in about 4m5 where the race is fairly narrow in extent.

By night. There is a fixed red light on the pier and stronger shore lights in the town.

Anchorage. The usual anchorage is about a cable NW of Swanage Pier in 2m0 to 3m3 of water. A number of moorings for local boats of modest draft will be seen inshore and yachts anchor outside these, taking soundings to find a suitable depth. The holding ground varies. In some places it is good; in others there is weed on the bottom and it is indifferent. Buoy the anchor unless well clear of inshore moorings, as it was reported that a yacht fouled her anchor here. On the eastern side of the pier there are the ruins of an old pier, a lifeboat house and a few local moorings.

Facilities. Swanage is a small town and seaside resort with hotels and shops of every kind (early closing Thursday) and bus services. Landing from the dinghy is on the shore, where a boatman will keep an eye on it, or to the west nearer the centre of the town. There is an active sailing club which races dinghies and other classes, and on a summer's day the bay is dotted with pedal-boats which are let out on hire. Petrol and water are easily obtained. Although crowded by visitors in the summer the town is a pleasant one and there are good walks along the cliffs either towards Studland or to Durlston and Anvil Head.

5 Chapmans Pool

5.1. Rounding St Albans Head from the eastward by the inner passage.

5.3. View from Hounstout Cliff facing east over the anchorage in Chapmans Pool. Shading of the water indicates the best anchorage. Note the rocks off the small buildings opposite. *C. Sergel*.

44

This little cove lies a mile NNW of St Albans Head, at the foot of the Purbeck hills. It provides a strange anchorage dwarfed by its surroundings and at night, when the few day visitors have left, it seems to be in another world remote from civilization.

The anchorage is only a fair weather one which is sheltered in winds between N to E, but gusts come down in strong winds from the heights above. There are sands, good bathing and lovely coastal walks to the west up the cliff path to the summit of Hounstout (150 metres high and once called 'Adlard's Peak' by his disrespectful crews in memory of a great ascent). From here, where the photograph was taken, one looks down on the gently shelving shore and along the coast southwards to St Albans, which provides another rewarding walk. No facilities are available but visitors arrive in daytime down a rough road to the shore. The nearest village appears to be Worth Maltravers, 2 miles distant.

Approach and Entrance. The approach from the east is easy with the aid of the Admiralty chart 2615. It will be made inside St Albans Race, leaving the head about 50 to 100 metres to starboard. The inshore E running stream starts about $+4$ h Dover and the W running about -2 h Dover. After rounding St Albans and passing through only a few overfalls if the wind is offshore steer WNW for 3 cables and then alter course to N by W for Hounstout Cliff on the west side of the cove, gradually closing with the shore to starboard. This can be followed up at distance of a cable off the shore. As the entrance of the cove is approached there are rocks projecting westward, as shown in the photograph, near some small buildings on the hillside. There are usually lobster pots on the outer fringe of these rocks. Keep seaward of these and enter in the middle of the pool. Approaching from westward keep seaward of Kimmeridge ledges and shoals extending 6 cables SW of Hounstout Cliff, making good a position about $\frac{3}{4}$ mile NW. The stream on the east going tide will be setting strongly towards St Albans Head. Then steer for the middle of the cove and the stream weakens as it is approached.

Anchorage is on sand in the centre of the cove in about 2m5, but with the aid of soundings it is possible to get enough water a little nearer the shore at the NE corner. The holding ground is good and there is little stream inside the cove but it may be unwise to remain at night if there is any prospect of a shift of wind or break in the weather.

6 Lulworth Cove

High Water: −4 h. 38 m. Dover. **Tidal Data:** approximately as Swanage, page 40.
Tidal Streams: See tide chartlets Swanage to Portland, and note stream turns early inshore. Within the cove itself there are no tidal currents of significance.

Lulworth Cove is part of the Lulworth Castle Estate. It is a famous and popular beauty spot and in summer time is visited by thousands of tourists by road, foot and steamer. The Cove and the cliffs around it offer a fascinating study in geology. The cove was formed when the seaward strata of Portland and Purbeck stone were breached by the sea. Behind them the soft layer of Wealdon and Upper Green Sands was worn away by the sea, air and rain; but this erosion was held up farther back by the harder consistency of the chalk of Bindon Hill. To the east, low down on the cliffs, where the Purbeck stone joins the soft and hard cap of Portland stone, is the Fossil Forest.

For the yachtsman it offers a beautiful and unusual anchorage. But it must only be used in fair weather, as it is exposed to all winds with south in them. When it blows hard from one

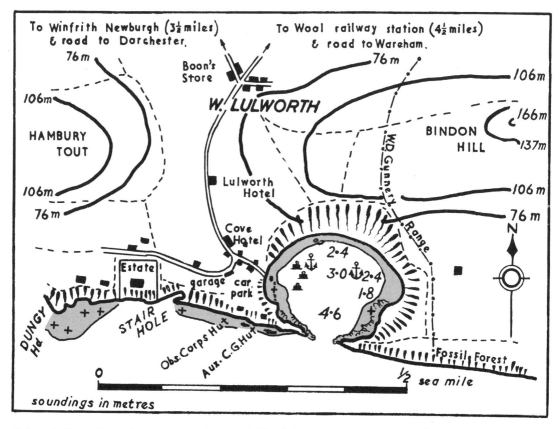

Lulworth Cove: The drying contours are drawn at 0m3 and the dotted contour lines at 1m5.

6.1. White Nose, the prominent headland, 3 miles west of Lulworth Cove.

6.2. Worbarrow Bay, with Worbarrow Tout shown on the right, some 2 miles east of the entrance to Lulworth Cove.

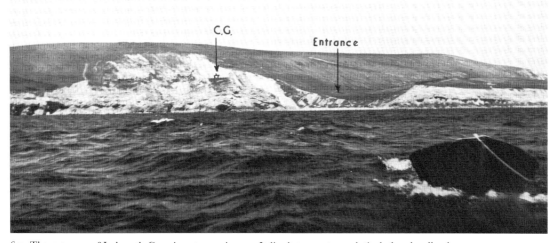

6.3. The entrance of Lulworth Cove is not conspicuous. It lies between two relatively low headlands.

Lulworth Cove

6.4. Taken from the cliffs during a gale, this picture clearly shows the rocks on each side of the entrance. A yacht should enter just east of the midway between the headlands on either side. *R. Coles.*

6.5. View facing eastwards across Lulworth Cove. The yacht is in the middle of the cove, but there is also sufficient depth of water to anchor further to the NE.

of these directions a heavy swell comes in, and in addition the winds funnel down and around the cliffs and through the narrow entrance, causing a yacht at anchor to sheer about in all directions. Because of this and the narrowness of the entrance it is essential that yachts should leave the cove before bad weather arrives.

Approach and Entrance

The entrance of Lulworth Cove is through a gap in the limestone cliffs, which is about 3 miles east of the prominent White Nose headland, and 2 miles west of Worbarrow Tout which is at the east end of Worbarrow Bay—see photographs. The coast to the west of the entrance comprises a series of high turf-topped chalk cliffs, bitten into by the sea. On the cliffs to the west of the entrance are two huts, one belonging to the Observer Corps and the other to the Auxiliary Coastguard Service, and beyond and behind it is a large rounded hill, Hambury Tout, 138m high. When approaching from the east a conspicuous white chalk road will be seen running diagonally down from the Tout. The entrance lies close at the lower end of this road. To the east of the entrance the cliffs are of less height and are fairly steep-to, except for a few rocks lying up to $1\frac{1}{2}$ cables off Dungy Head. Red barrels are sometimes placed on each side of the entrance.

The navigable width of entrance is about half of that which is apparent; its centre being just to the east of the mid-point between the cliffs. There are ledges of rocks running out from the edges of the cliffs on both sides, those to port on entering extend rather farther than those to starboard, leaving a channel is about 70 metres wide, 4m5 deep. Ahead, as the yacht enters, is a 90 metre high chalk cliff where the western end of Bindon Hill has been eroded by the sea. On the port bow there are rocks and a few small mooring buoys and a portable landing stage. To starboard there is clear water.

Anchorage, Facilities and Surroundings

The best anchorage is in the NE corner of the cove. Here the anchor drops into a good holding ground of clay, sand and seaweed in about 3m0. It is found from experience that it is a good plan to put a kedge astern towards the shore to hold the bows of any yacht anchored in the cove towards the entrance, thereby reducing the effect of swell which often enters even in good weather. The anchorage is sometimes crowded and one has to anchor as best one can. There is no anchorage outside the cove owing to telegraph cables.

There is no regular coastguard at Lulworth; auxiliaries (fishermen, local residents and the like) keep a bad weather watch only. No special rescue facilities are available from them. There is a boatman who will give advice and help to visiting yachtsmen.

Fresh water may be obtained from a tap beside the attendant's hut in the car park; or nearer at hand at the café where they will oblige if not too busy. Petrol can be obtained from the garage behind the car park. There is a post office in the village, also several restaurants, cafés and hotels. Near the Cove there are a few small shops and stores, and up the road at West Lulworth is Boon's store, which stocks most provisions required, Church of England and Roman Catholic churches are also at West Lulworth. Buses run frequently to Wool in the summer time. Trains run from Wool to Weymouth and to London. Excursion steamers to and from Weymouth.

Danger Areas

Many footpaths provide some lovely walks along the cliffs and hills west of Lulworth Cove but to the eastward they are limited by the War Department Gunnery Ranges. Red flags and notices at the perimeter give warning of the land danger area.

The sea danger area is divided into parts and the times of firing and areas to be used are notified in a weekly firing programme sent to all yacht clubs within the area. Information is also available on application to the Range Safety Officer, telephone: Bindon Abbey 462721 Ext. 219. When firing is in progress Red flags are flown by day from a flagstaff or at night red flashing lights are exhibited on the summit of Bindon Hill, about 2 cables E by N of the Cove entrance, and at St Albans Head. In addition the sea danger area is patrolled by two Range Safety vessels except in inclement weather.

Yachts are allowed to pass through the sea danger area provided they do not stop, but anchoring or fishing will not be permitted. The range areas and regulations are always liable to alteration.

7 Weymouth

High Water: −4 h. 38 m. Dover. **Heights above datum:** MHWS 2m1. MLWS 0m2. MHWN 1m4. MLWN 0m7.
Yacht Clubs: Royal Dorset Yacht Club, Weymouth Sailing Club.

Weymouth Harbour offers good yachting facilities, although it is primarily commercial in character and has become increasingly busy since the Channel Island ferries have used it as a terminal port instead of Southampton. The town itself is a popular holiday resort, with bathing and boating sands, hotels and all the usual amenities.

St Albans Race, the Approach and Entrance

Approaching Weymouth from Poole and the Solent, the race off St Albans Head provides the principal navigational consideration. The race is not so severe as Portland Race and in moderate weather extends little over $1\frac{1}{2}$ miles. Its position varies according to wind and tide, being rather to the east on the flood stream and to the west on the ebb. Except with strong onshore winds a passage of relatively smooth water is found close inshore, though this is never entirely free from overfalls. Close inshore the tide turns to the west about − 2 h Dover and to the east + 4 h Dover. In moderate weather the inshore passage is a useful one, and the only disadvantage is that it takes a yacht across the gunnery range, referred to in the previous chapter. At $1\frac{1}{4}$ miles south of St Albans the W stream starts $-\frac{1}{4}$ h Dover; E stream $+5\frac{3}{4}$ h Dover. For Portland Race and approach from the westward see the following chapter.

The entrance to Weymouth Harbour is rather inconspicuous. It lies behind a breakwater which runs out from a low green hill called The Nothe. This hill is easily recognized by the fortifications at its base, and its isolated situation. It separates Weymouth Harbour from Newton's Cove, and is the only headland between Portland Harbour and Redcliff Point, the latter being at the northern end of Weymouth Bay.

The mouth of the Harbour faces NE and if it is approached from east a sharp alteration of course to port is required before the harbour is actually entered. Five cables to the eastward

7.1. The south side of the entrance to Weymouth Harbour showing the Nothe and visitors' fore and aft moorings mostly for large yachts.

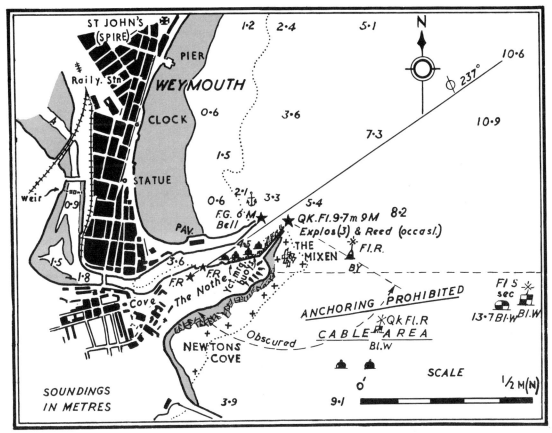

Weymouth

Weymouth Harbour: (Based on British Admiralty Chart No. 2255 with the permission of the Controller of HM Stationery Office and of the Hydrographer of the Navy.)

of the entrance is a blue and white buoy, which has a light (*Fl 5 sec*). This is the seaward of two buoys placed two-thirds of a cable apart. The other buoy is also blue and white, but is much smaller and unlit; between them is a degaussing range. Closer inshore is a conical lightbuoy (*Fl R 5 sec*) with black and yellow stripes. This marks two sewer outfalls and the edge of the deep water.

In approaching Weymouth Harbour leave all these buoys to port and open out the breakwater (south) pier to bring the yacht off the entrance to the harbour. Course is then altered to the SW and the yacht enters between the two piers. Keep clear of motor boats etc. rounding close to the south pier head, which should not be approached closely.

About 3 cables inside the entrance on the southern side of the harbour are two white triangular boards placed one above and behind the other. At night they carry *fixed red lights*, they are the *leading marks*. When in transit they lead up the centre of the channel in 4m5 MLWS at 237°.

On the two piers at the entrance of the harbour are lights and fog signals. The South breakwater pier has a light (*Qk Fl*) at an elevation of 9m7. Its fog signal is either explosion 3 ev. 5 m or a reed. The Northern pier has a fixed green light (occasional) and in thick

51

Weymouth

7.2. The entrance to Weymouth Harbour showing the leading marks and the pier on the NW side.

7.3. Further up the channel showing the leading marks. The Cove where most yachts of average size bring up lies on the south side beyond the yachts in the middle of the picture.

weather a bell. Fog signals are only used in exceptional circumstances when a large ship is expected.

The harbour is long and narrow. It extends some 6 cables from the entrance to end at the Town Bridge. Above this the water is shallow and is seldom used by vessels of any size, for which the bridge has to be swung open. The upper harbour is used almost exclusively by local boat-owners, and by the town's by-laws people are not allowed to live aboard craft moored here.

Moorings and Anchorages

Yachts entering should close the North pier where they will be hailed by the Pier Master or his deputy at any time between 8 a.m. and 10 p.m. He will direct them to a suitable berth, either on one of the four mooring buoys inside the harbour entrance on the south side, or alongside the quay farther up, most probably the Cove which is on the south side just above the lifeboat station where the harbour widens out a little Note that the harbour regulations provide that boats must not impede the passage of vessels entering or leaving the harbour— see Regulating Signals below. At night it is not so easy to find a mooring and there is considerable traffic in the harbour, principally cross-Channel steamers. If arriving in darkness some yachtsmen prefer to anchor outside, or in Portland.

Owners are requested to give the Harbour Master (Tel. Weymouth 5100) notice of arrival. Harbour dues are payable. The Harbour Master is pleased to give local information and assistance to visiting yachtsmen.

Owners must not leave their yachts unattended for longer than an hour or two, and when the crew is going ashore the hatches and doors should be firmly locked. If the boat is to be left for longer periods, then it is best to seek the advice of the Harbour Master in obtaining a boatkeeper.

In Weymouth Bay the most convenient anchorage is 1 cable to the northward of the Northern pier of the main harbour. The bottom here consists of fine sand and weed, and is covered by $1\frac{1}{2}$ fathoms of water at MLWS.

Regulating Signals

A red flag over a green flag by day or two red lights over a green light by night indicate entrance foul, entry or departure forbidden. Two red flags by day or three red lights by night indicate a vessel is leaving the harbour and no vessel is to approach so as to obstruct the entrance when this signal is shown. Two green flags by day or three green lights by night indicate that a vessel is approaching the entrance from seaward and no vessel is to leave the harbour. When no signal is shown on the mast, it denotes the entrance is clear both inwards and outwards, but a look-out must be kept when a vessel is approaching in case the signal is put against her. Within the harbour and harbour limits, boats, whether under oars, sails or power, are to keep clear of the main channel and are not to obstruct or otherwise impede the passage of vessels entering or leaving the harbour.

Facilities

Customs can be cleared at any time. The Weymouth area extends from Lulworth Cove to Lyme Regis and includes Portland. Coastguards keep a regular watch from Weymouth and there is a lifeboat station on the South Quay. The Royal Dorset Yacht Club welcomes visiting yachtsmen.

Weymouth

Any fuel and calor gas can be obtained either ashore or from the fuel boat. Water can be obtained from a tap at the Cove or from hydrants on the quay side on application to the Harbour Master.

The British Railways Slipway (Tel. Weymouth 6263, Ext. 23) will slip or repair yachts of up to 100 tons, but have no facilities for laying up. Their charges are most reasonable. Cozens and Co., Ltd., have facilities for laying up and hull repairs (Tel. Weymouth 4832). W. L. Bussel and Co. have a yacht chandlery on the South Quay and a small boat-yard on the Cove. The firm also supplies calor gas. In Weymouth itself and on the South Quay there are many shops and stores of all types. Early closing day is Wednesday. Also banks, hotels and all the amenities of a fairly large town. There is an A.A. office on the Commercial Pier.

Train services run direct to London and Southampton. Buses run to Portland and the rest of Dorset. Steamers run to the Channel Islands and in summer to Lulworth Cove.

8 Portland Harbour

High Water: −4 h. 8 m. Dover. **Heights above datum:** MHWS 2m1. MLWS 0m2. MHWN 1m4. MLWN 0m7.
Tides: Inside harbour, negligible; in ship channels, up to 2 knots with eddies off and between Heads.
Yacht Clubs: Castle Cove Sailing Club; Royal Naval Sailing Association (Portland).

Portland Harbour is a large area of water enclosed by land to the north and south, by a shingle beach to the west, and by four breakwaters to the east. It is roughly circular in shape, with a diameter of approximately two miles. It offers a deep-water refuge and anchorage of easy access, but for small vessels it is rather too large and exposed; and at night care is needed to avoid the numerous unlit mooring buoys and, in the western half, the various unlit lighters and rafts moored there. The land mass causes strong or gale SW winds to accelerate across the anchorage and moorings in the SW corner of the harbour and may even eddy from NW outside the outer breakwater.

Portland is a Dockyard Port serving as a sea training base and much activity by ships and auxiliaries of many navies will be encountered on weekdays over most of the year. This activity is much reduced at weekends when most of the ships are berthed alongside the piers in the Naval Base at the southern end of the Harbour. Yachts should take care not to obstruct ships moving in the Harbour and in the fairways leading to and from the breakwater entrance channels. There are several underwater ranges outside the Harbour on which ships may be navigating at high speeds on restricted courses.

Torpedoes are fired from a station mid-way along the North Eastern (detached) break-water in an easterly direction into Weymouth Bay. A red flag at the firing point indicates that a torpedo is about to be fired and safety craft patrol the limits of the range. Ships may also fire anti-submarine mortar bombs in an easterly direction from moorings in Newton's Cove. A safety launch is present during firings.

From seaward Portland is one of the most easily recognized landfalls on the south coast. Apart from the fact that it protrudes so far into the Channel, and from any direction is first seen looking like an island, it has a very characteristic shape. The Peninsula is wedge-shaped when viewed either from the air or from the sea. The high and broad end is at the north and the slope is steep to the summit which is 150 metres above sea level.

The powerful light (18 miles) is situated in the lighthouse on the Bill, and is conspicuous in clear weather from a long distance to the east, south and west. In front of the lighthouse within a few feet of the water's edge is a white obelisk 9 metres in height; this is a Trinity House mark.

The light exhibited from the lighthouse is white *Gp Fl 4 ev 20 sec 18M*, elevation of 43 metres. To the NE and NW there are sectors where the group flash is 1 to 2, 2 to 3, or 3 to 4. Over the Shambles there is a narrow sector over which a fixed red light from a window is exhibited at an elevation of 19 metres (range 13 miles). The fog signal is a diaphone, one blast every 30 sec.

The Approach
The dangers in the approach from the west are the notorious Portland Race and the over-

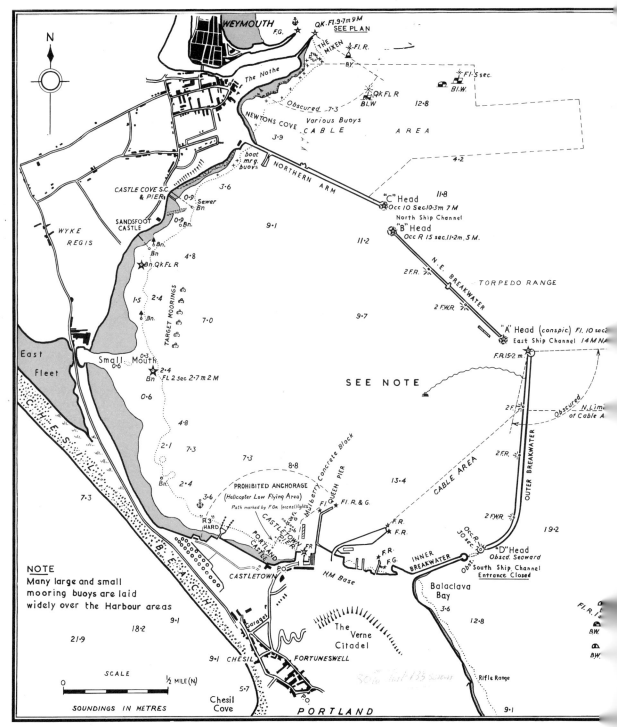

Portland Harbour: (Based on British Admiralty Chart No. 2255 with the permission of the Controller of HM Stationery Office and of the Hydrographer of the Navy.)

8.1. Approaching Portland Bill from eastward by the inner passage.

8.2. Rounding the Bill. Note that there are a few drying rocks on the SW side and usually many lobster pots in the vicinity.

falls over the Shambles Bank. The race extends not more than about 3 miles and it is about 1 mile wide; its position varies, being rather to the SE of the Bill on the flood stream and SSW on the ebb. In bad weather the sea will be rough and disturbed for 5 miles or more, and indeed tide race conditions have been reported as far as 15 miles to seaward when a westerly gale is blowing over a west-setting tide. The Admiralty pocket tidal stream atlas *Approaches to Portland* is essential when navigating in this area, owing to the complexity and strength of the streams.

Accordingly except in fine weather it is best either to keep well south of the race and the whole area between it and the Shambles lighthouse-buoy (*Gp Fl (2) 30 sec 12M*) Horn Morse N (− · *30 sec*) or to use what is called the Inner Passage. This is an area of relatively undisturbed water between the Bill and the main race. In it the streams run strongly but there are only a few overfalls scattered about in small patches. In winds of Force 6 and above, and especially in easterly winds the overfalls are much larger and extend closer inshore the whole way from the Bill to Grove Point.

In navigating the passage the coast should be followed at just over 1 cable's distance, when the race may be 1 to 5 cables farther to seaward. Care must be taken of irregular but strong inshore and offshore sets and the yacht's course shaped accordingly. In approaching the inner passage from the west the land should be closed well northward of the Bill, to allow for the strong southerly set.

Bound *westward*, in order to avoid these overfalls or a foul tide, the passage should be timed

Portland Harbour

to arrive off the Bill between 1 hour before and 2 hours after HW Dover. Bound *eastward* it should be fetched between 4½ hours after HW Dover and 5 hours before HW Dover. There are often lobster pots in the vicinity of the Bill.

The Entrance

The breakwaters are all low but wide. They are constructed of masses of loosely arranged blocks of Portland stone. Around the breakwaters there is deep water except where they join the land. On them are various large and small buildings belonging to naval establishments ashore. At the ends of each breakwater are circular stone buttresses, known as 'Heads'.

Between the four breakwaters there are three channels. The South Ship Channel between the Inner and Outer Breakwaters is permanently closed by the block ship which is exposed at low tide, and by low overhead cables. No craft, however small, should ever try to use this channel.

Between the Outer and North-Eastern Breakwaters is the East Ship Channel, which is 1 cable wide. This is the one most frequently used by yachts, except those sailing between Portland and Weymouth. Apart from tidal eddies of up to 2 knots there are no difficulties in navigating this entrance. As the channel is approached from seaward, to port will be seen the fort on the end of the Outer Breakwater; on the NE end of this is a low iron column from which at night is exhibited a *fixed red light* visible 013°–268°; this light is, however, relatively weak. To starboard on entering is seen 'A' Head and on it a white tower; from this at night is exhibited a white light *Fl ev 10 sec*. Its elevation of 22 metres gives the light a 14-miles range. This light is the highest and strongest one of the harbour itself. In addition, in thick weather there is a horn 10 sec from 'A' Head.

The North Ship Channel lies between the North-Eastern breakwater and the Northern Arm, and has a width of 1 cable, and tidal eddies up to 1½ knots. To port on entering is 'B' Head, which is surmounted by an iron frame-work structure on the tower. From here at night is exhibited a light (*R occ ev 15 sec*) at an elevation of 11 metres. To starboard is 'C' Head on which is erected another iron frame-work structure with a white light (*occ ev 10 sec*) at an elevation of 11 metres.

There are numerous lights marking piers and jetties inside the harbour which are shown on the chartlet.

Anchorages

Although Portland Harbour appears to be well protected by land or massive breakwaters, it is so large that it can be decidedly rough in bad weather. During onshore gales a quite considerable swell rolls in through the entrances and strong winds from the W and SW sweep over the Chesil Beach and seem to strengthen over the harbour.

The two most useful anchorages for yachts are off Castletown, W of the Naval Base at Portland, and off Castle Cove in the NW corner of the harbour. The former is the better in southerly and SW winds (though decidedly rough in gales) and the latter in westerly and northerly winds, besides providing a prettier anchorage within reach of Weymouth. The Fleet is suitable only for craft of light draft, either without masts, or ones that can be lowered.

Castletown. Castletown is situated near the centre of the north side of Portland, just westward of the Naval Base and the Queen Pier. The latter, together with piers and jetties E of it are for the exclusive use of HM ships and boats.

Opposite Castletown is the short Castletown pier with two concrete Phoenix Units to the northward of it. The pier (which is private property) is about 100 yards W of Queen Pier, and between the two is a public landing on the beach.

Yachting activity at Castletown is now centred around the moorings and pontoons of the Portland Naval Sailing Centre, near the Castle less than a quarter mile west of the pier. Here it is sometimes possible (on application) to have the use of a mooring and yachtsmen are allowed to land at the pontoons. There are also many private moorings in the SW corner of the harbour.

Yachts are only permitted to anchor west of R.3 Hard which is $\frac{1}{2}$ mile from Castletown pier beyond the low flying helicopter prohibited area shown on the chart. The hard is Admiralty property and landing may be effected only by prior arrangement with the naval authorities as helicopters operate from it.

Ashore in Castletown are various facilities. Immediately by the pier is a post office, several small shops and public houses, and a few hotels. Water is obtainable at the Royal Breakwater Hotel.

Petrol, paraffin, TVO and diesel fuel can be obtained from Chesil Beach Motors or Aitcheson's Garage in Victoria Square, Portland, which is half a mile from Castletown. Up the hill in Fortuneswell also about half a mile away from the anchorage are a chemist, a cinema, another post office, several banks, and a much wider range of stores. Early closing is on Wednesday for most shops, but for grocers it is Saturday. Customs may be cleared at any time in the harbour.

8.3. The inner passage under gale conditions. The area of (comparatively) smooth water shows dark against the breakers onshore and the overfalls in the tide race beyond. *R. Coles*.

Portland Harbour

Buses run from the Base, from Fortuneswell and from Victoria Square. They go southwards to Easton and Portland Bill; and northwards to Wyke Regis and Weymouth.

The Fleet. This long narrow strip of water inside the Chesil Beach is entered at Small Mouth in the extreme west of the harbour. Chesil Beach forms a natural breakwater, composed of pebbles, linking Portland with the mainland near Abbotsbury, some 8 miles farther north. Only small craft of centreboard type or shoal draft with lowering masts can enter Small Mouth and sail in the Fleet. For such craft the Fleet provides a quiet and beautiful anchorage. Ashore are the shops, garages, post office and bus services of Wyke Regis. Also the boat-yard of W. & J. Tod, Ltd.

Castle Cove. Half a mile to the north of Small Mouth is Castle Cove. The Castle after which the cove is named is Sandsfoot Castle. Henry VIII built this, but it is now in ruins. It stands in a prominent position on the cliff just to the south of the cove. From this cliff a reef of rocks runs out for $1\frac{1}{2}$ cables and at the end of the reef is a beacon. There are many moorings and local craft in the vicinity and in the cove: these belong to members of the Castle Cove Sailing Club. A visiting yacht should anchor to seaward of and clear of the moorings. For a longer stay inquiry should be made of the boatman, as sometimes a mooring may be available.

In the Cove the Castle Cove Sailing Club has built a new jetty alongside the old one. A new drain pipe runs under it and extends 23 metres seaward of it, the end being marked by a small beacon, as it is awash at low water. The jetty and also the water tap ashore can be used by visitors with the permission of the Sailing Club. There is a post office and also shops a quarter mile from the landing and all facilities of Weymouth, which is $\frac{1}{2}$ mile walk by way of a cliff path, or can be reached by bus. The position of the proposed huge National Yacht Racing Centre lies about 600 metres SW of Castle Cove.

Prohibited Anchorages, Regulations, etc.

As Portland is a naval harbour, the regulations governing its use vary from time to time according to Naval requirements. When sailing in the harbour yachts should not approach HM ships or jetties closely. No vessel may exceed 12 knots without a licence from the Queen's Harbour Master and this rules out water ski-ing in the harbour. The following are the principal regulations which affect yachts:

Vessels to keep clear of HM vessels or other vessels in charge of HM Officers
When one of HM vessels or other vessel in charge of HM Officers hoists ZV flags (International Code-Alphabetical) or a red light by night at the foremast head, denoting she is under way for the purpose of passing in or out of the harbour, all other vessels under way within the limits of the Dockyard Port shall keep out of the way of the said vessel.

Rules in respect of larger vessels under way
Sailing vessels and power-driven vessels of less than 65 ft length shall not hamper the safe passage of large power-driven vessels which are entering and leaving the channels between the Breakwaters, or are under way within the limits of the Harbour.

Signal directing vessels and boats to keep out of the way
When any seagoing power-driven vessel, power-driven vessel towing, power-driven dredger or power-driven hopper under way within the limits of the Dockyard Port shall by reason of the crowded nature of the channel or anchorage or from any other cause find it unsafe or impracticable to keep out of the way of other vessels or boats, she shall signify the same by four short blasts of the whistle blown in rapid succession and all other vessels shall keep out of the way of the vessel making this signal, which vessel shall be navigated with due care and at a moderate speed.

PART 2
BARFLEUR TO ANSE DE ST MARTIN

Introduction

This Part covers the French coast on the north side of the Cherbourg Peninsula from Barfleur to Cap de la Hague, which is the nearest stretch of French coast to the Solent, Poole and Weymouth, with Cherbourg as the natural port of entry, being the only one which offers every kind of facility for the yachtsman. Port Lévi to the east is very small, but Barfleur, which is round the Pointe de Barfleur, is an excellent harbour in westerly winds for yachts which can dry out alongside the quays, or which have legs. Barfleur is a pretty village, and well worth a visit. Although beyond the scope of this book, the harbours to the south of Barfleur provide another interesting cruising ground, calling at St Vaast, La Hougue and paying a visit to the St Marcouf Islands.

Eight miles west of Cherbourg breakwater is Omonville, a charming little place with a harbour in which yachts can lie afloat protected from westerly and southerly winds. Still farther west the drying harbour of Port Racine (the smallest in France) in the Anse de St Martin has a good anchorage a cable outside it in settled weather.

The rise and fall of tide on this coast is greater than on the corresponding English side, Although not so considerable as in the Channel Islands and the Gulf of St Malo. A feature in the navigation in these waters which is frequently referred to in the following pages is the early inshore stream, as the tide along the coast turns earlier than the main Channel stream farther seaward. The rate of the streams along the north of the Cherbourg Peninsula is fast, attaining its maximum at the two ends of the Peninsula, in the Race of Barfleur and the Race of Alderney respectively. (See table page 67.)

Approaching this piece of coast the navigation is aided by the powerful lighthouses of Barfleur on the east and Cap de la Hague and Alderney on the west, and by other lighthouses and numerous lightbuoys on nearer approach. Cherbourg is easier of approach by night than by day and Barfleur Harbour has good leading lights. There are also Radio Beacons at Pte de Barfleur, Cherbourg and to the west on the Casquets.

9 Cherbourg

High Water: −3 h 17 m Dover. **Heights above datum:** French Chart No 5628. MHWS 6m4. MLWS 1m1. MHWN 5m0. MLWN 2m6.

Streams in the Offing: 5 miles of Cherbourg Breakwater, the tides conform approximately with the main English Channel streams, but attain a rate up to 4 knots and have a set into the bay between Cap de la Hague and Pointe de Barfleur. **3 miles N of Cherbourg Breakwater,** the westerly stream starts −1¼ h Dover and the easterly +5½ h Dover, both 3 knots, springs.

Inshore Tides: The tides turn earlier inshore, especially to the west and east of Cherbourg. In the west entrance the west stream starts −3½ h Dover attaining 1¼ knots and the east stream +4 h Dover, streams attaining 2 knots at spring tides. In the Grande Rade the tides turn about half-hour earlier with a rate up to 1½ knots. In the Petite Rade there is a counter-current, which sets westward along the south side towards the naval dockyard, and then turns northward and eastward along the western inner breakwater (Digue du Homet) during the SE stream in Grande Rade. (See also page 67.)

Cherbourg is the natural port of entry in France for yachts stationed in the vicinity of the Solent and Poole. It is a large port with an excellent yacht club and all facilities. It is accessible in all weathers, though in northerly gales it can be exceedingly rough in the offing.

The Approach

In clear weather the approach to Cherbourg from England is easy, as it lies almost in the centre of the indentation between Cap de la Hague (photograph Ch. 15, p. 85) to the westward, and the Pointe de Barfleur (photograph Ch. 12, p. 73) to the eastward, and one or other of these headlands will be seen. In bad weather with poor visibility, or in fine but hazy weather, it is not so easy, and yachts quite often make a landfall either east or west of the entrance. The allowance for a 12-hour passage with the effect of the tides cancelling out is not sufficient. The yacht's position should be estimated hourly, to allow for the strong streams near the English coast and the still stronger ones in the approach to Cherbourg, particularly on a spring tide, when it is usual to plan a landfall up stream of the Cherbourg entrances. Radio beacons assist in an accurate landfall. In fog it is possible for the last 20 miles to home on the radio beacon at Fort de l'Ouest lighthouse.

Cherbourg itself will be recognized by the long high breakwaters and the breakwater forts. The high cliff behind Cherbourg, which is shown in photograph 2, is sometimes considered a help in identifying the position of the harbour. In the offing, 3 miles N of the western entrance, is a pillar whistle buoy 'CH 1', red and white stripes, (*occ white*).

To the west of Cherbourg breakwater there are: 3 miles W, the Raz de Bannes beacon tower; 8 miles W, the headland at Omonville (photograph Chapter 13); 9 miles W, Jardeheu Point (a low promontory, with a white-washed building and semaphore station, and conspicuous rocks off the end) and the whistle buoy (*Fl ev 1½ sec*) 1 mile seaward; 12 miles W is Cap de la Hague Lighthouse (photograph Chapter 15), (*Fl 5 sec, 19 M Reed ev 30 sec*). La Plate light tower (*Gp Fl (3) 12 sec, WR*) is a weaker light situated 1¼ miles ENE of La Hague lighthouse.

At the eastern end of Cherbourg Harbour is Ile Pelée with its fort and beacon towers on the rocks extending 4 cables off it; 5 miles east is the low headland of Cap Lévi with lighthouse (photograph next Chapter) (*Fl R ev 5 sec*) and the BW buoy (*Gp Fl 2*) off Cap Lévi Race.

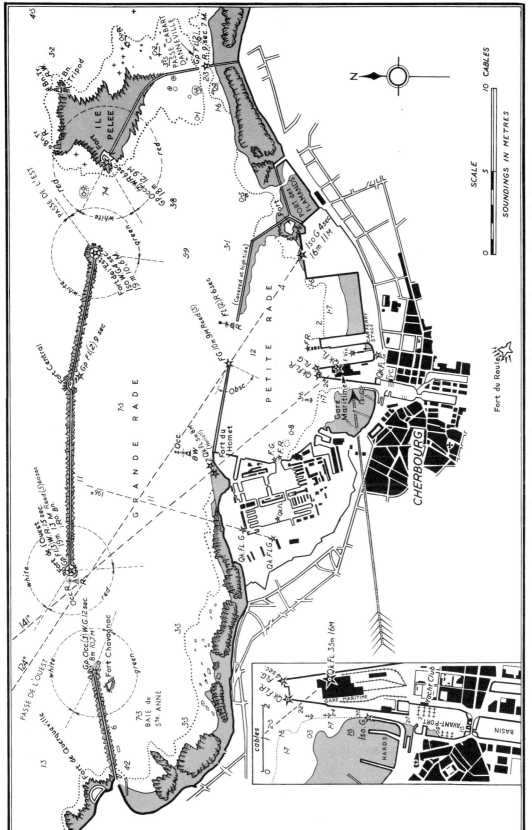

Cherbourg Harbour: (Based on French Chart No. 5628 by permission of the Service Hydrographique de la Marine.)

Cherbourg

There are two buoys (*Qk Fl and Fl*) offshore farther east, and 15 miles east is Pointe de Barfleur lighthouse (*Gp Fl (2) 10 sec 22 miles*), see photograph Chapter 12, *Reed (2) ev min*.

Approaching from east or west keep well to seaward to avoid the numerous outlying dangers, and refer to tide charts, for, as previously stated, there are reverse eddies near the coast at certain states of the tide. Sometimes the division between the eddy and the main stream is clearly marked, with the main English Channel stream one way and the inshore stream (which varies in width) running in the opposite direction. There will be overfalls in whichever stream is running against the wind. With large-scale charts and experience there is plenty of scope for rock-dodging inshore, but it is dangerous for those unfamiliar with the coast, as the tides are very strong. There is a considerable tide race off Cap Lévi, and it is rough off *all* headlands to the east and west in fresh winds and a weather-going tide.

By night. The approach to Cherbourg is usually easier at night. There are the powerful lights of Anvil Point and St Catherines on the English coast, and not long after these have been lost the loom of the French lights at Cap de la Hague (*Fl 5 sec 19 m*) (and probably Alderney to the west, *Gp Fl (4) 15 sec 17 M*) or Barfleur (*Gp Fl (2) ev 10 sec 22 M*) may be seen. The principal light on Cherbourg Breakwater at Fort de l'Ouest (*Gp Fl (3)*) *WR* has a range of 13 miles and the fog signal is *Reed (3) ev min*. The buoy CH 1 is *occulting*, and there are many other lights which are best seen on the chart.

9.1. Fort de L'Ouest and the red buoy left to port when entering the Grande Rade de Cherbourg.

The Entrances

The principal entrance to the Grande Rade (roadstead between outer and inner break-waters) at Cherbourg is the western one, and is wide and deep. It is immediately west of the Fort de L'Ouest *Gp Fl (3) WR* but the fort should not be approached too closely as there is an obstruction on the SW side marked by a buoy *Occ R* (photo 1). On the other side of the western entrance there is another fort at the end of the breakwater (*Gp Occ (1 + 2) WG*) which should not be approached closely. There are also leading lights as shown on the chart, but the entrance is so easy these are not usually followed.

The eastern entrance lies between Fort de l'Est (*Iso WG 4 sec*) and the fort on Ile Pelée

9.2. After entering the Petite Rade steer for the Avant Port which is just to the right of the Gare Maritime shown in this picture. In the background on the left is the high cliff behind the town.

9.3. The entrance to the Avant Port. Keep the inner side of the west jetty just open, to avoid shoal water on the starboard hand off the end of the jetty.

9.4. The Port de Plaisance and Yacht Club (at the foot of the high building) lie on the port hand at the end of the entrance channel to the Avant Port. The berths for visiting yachts are at the first pontoon, but other berths may be available on application.

Cherbourg

(*Gp Occ (2) WR 6 sec*), and has been swept to a depth of 6 metres. There are shoals on the east side of this entrance near Ile Pelée, so a yacht should keep to the west side near Fort de l'Est.

When in the Grande Rade shape a course for the entrance to the Petite Rade, between the inner breakwater (*light FG*) and the red buoy (*Fl R*) to the NW of the eastern breakwater which may be covered at HW.

As the yacht enters the Petite Rade, the Gare Maritime (with prominent cranes and large buildings—see photograph) will be seen to the south. The Transatlantique ocean dock is on the east side, but the entrance to the Avant Port, in which the yacht basin is situated, lies immediately to the west of the Gare Maritime, between its quayside and a shorter jetty on the west side. There is a light (*Qk Fl R*) on the NW of the Gare Maritime Quay, and an *Iso green light* on the end of the west jetty.

The entrance channel to the Avant Port is dredged to 2m2. Avoid getting too far west when approaching the Avant Port as the sands dry out over $\frac{1}{2}$ cable at LAT to the north of the western jetty and for over 2 cables to the NW.

Steer for the end of the west jetty pier, keeping the eastern side of it just open, and then sail up the entrance between the quayside and the jetty. Here the wind often baffles, but the distance is short to the inner basin, where there is plenty of room to tack or manœuvre. Once in the Avant Port there are *lights* along the quays.

Passe Cabart Danneville. This is a boat passage at the eastern end of the Grande Rade. It lies in a gap between the outer and inner eastern breakwaters, and there is a light *Gp Fl (2) R 9 sec 7 M* at the end of the breakwater on its southern side. It can be navigated, with great care, with the aid of the large scale French Chart No. 5628, 9th edition, but the channel leading from the Grande Rade to the pass and to the east of it is not easy as it lies between shoals and close to a rock drying 1m8 on its north side. It is better to treat the channel as drying 1m8 at LAT and wait, if necessary, for sufficient rise of tide before attempting it. A course can then be steered from Grande Rade by keeping the middle of the pass bearing east magnetic, and when through it hold on keeping the middle of the pass on a stern bearing of west magnetic. Do not go north of the west–east course, until $\frac{1}{2}$ mile eastward of the pass in 2 metres LAT clear of the shoals. Tidal streams in the pass are strong and eastward of it. It should not be used in rough easterly weather owing to the seas over uneven bottom.

Avant Port, Basin, Anchorage and Facilities

The hospitable Yacht Club de Cherbourg welcomes visiting yachtsmen and has excellent facilities. It is the centre of all yachting activity at Cherbourg. Just below the club is the Port de Plaisance with marina pontoons to lie alongside, the ones nearest the entrance being reserved for visitors. Charges for use of berths are usually collected at the pontoons, but can be paid at the office in the caravan next to the club. There are also two pontoons at the Quai de Caligny on the opposite (West) side of the harbour but, except at Neaps, these are only suitable for light draft craft, as there is little water at LAT.

During the yachting season, especially after races to Cherbourg, the harbour may appear to be absolutely packed with yachts, and local advice about berthing must be sought. Alternatively, anchor outside or proceed into the inner wet basin and lay alongside the quay. The basin is mainly commercial and sometimes dusty, but it is completely protected from the weather and close to the centre of the town. The dock gate opens about 1 h before to 1 h after high water. Signal to request opening of the swing bridge is one long and two short blasts. Tide gauges indicate depth over the sill and the depth within the basin is usually maintained at about 3 metres when the dock gate is closed.

There is a good anchorage outside the harbour, protected from East through South to West and comfortable even in light northerly winds. It lies west of the Gare Maritime (clear of the fairway to the Avant Port) in 1m7 to 2m3, or more further seaward. With the aid of an outboard engine this is convenient to reach the club, or at Neap tides by taking soundings it is just possible to find room to anchor clear of the fairway only ½ cable north of the jetty. Land then on the sands on the west side of the jetty, which is only a ⅓ mile from the town centre. The anchorage and the marina can be very uncomfortable in severe northerly gales, when shelter is best found in the inner basin.

Facilities are excellent. Fresh water by pipe and hose at pontoons. Customs office across road from the Yacht Club. Bonded stores at Henri Ryst a short distance towards the bridge. Yacht and engine repairers and a sailmaker. Small shops and restaurants on turning left at the swing-bridge, but the principal shopping centre is across the bridge to the west side of the town where there is a casino, the Café du Théâtre and a wide variety of restaurants, some of which are on the west quay. French charts from Nicollet, 40 Rue de Commerce. Air Services include Southampton, Alderney, Guernsey and Jersey. Frequent Thoresen car ferries to Southampton and occasional direct passage by ocean liner. Station and buses to all parts.

Inshore Tidal Streams along the Cherbourg Peninsula

The following table is prepared by reference to information in the Channel Pilot and charts, the approximate times being in relation to HW Dover and the rates at Spring tides average unless otherwise stated.

	East Going Stream			West Going Stream		
	Approx. Direction	*Rate*	*Begins*	*Approx. Direction*	*Rate*	*Begins*
West end of Peninsula between C de la Hague and Raz de Bannes 4 miles W of Cherbourg	ESE	3	+0500	WNW	3	−0530
Off Pte Jardeheu	ESE	5	+0500	WNW	4	−0330
West entrance of Cherbourg Harbour	SE	2	+0400	NW	1¼	−0315
Close Inshore, 1 mile E of Cherbourg	E	1½	+0345	WNW	1½	−6000
1 mile W of Port de Lévi	ENE	1½	+0145	WSW	1½	−0130
Close northward of buoy off C. Lévi	E	4¾	+0500	W	4¾	−0100
In Chenal Hédouin, inshore between the shoals W of Pte de Barfleur	E	2¾	+0330	W	2¾	−0300
Offshore, 3 miles N of Pte de Barfleur	SE	5.3 max	+0530	NW	5 max	−0030
Inshore, ½ mile NE of Pte de Barfleur	ESE	4	+0430	NNW	4	−0130

10 Port du Becquet

Tidal Data: See Cherbourg.

10.1. The white leading towers at Port du Becquet. To the left is La Tounette port hand red beacon tower and below the house on the right lies the entrance to the harbour, just behind the end of the breakwater.

10.2. The harbour is opened up immediately after rounding the breakwater end. The yachts in the centre of the harbour dry out on legs.

This small drying fishing harbour lies 1 mile east of Cherbourg. It is sheltered by land or the breakwater from all winds other than NNE and E, but it is stated that there is a violent surge in the harbour during fresh winds from north as well as NE.

Approach and Entrance. The approach is easy by day or night, even with a small scale chart. There are two conspicuous white 8-sided light towers (*Gp Occ (1 + 2) 12 sec, synchronized*) which come into transit at 187°. Follow their line. On close approach a red beacon tower marking rocks will be left to port and a breakwater to starboard. Ahead will lie a rocky shore but the moment the end of the breakwater is passed the harbour opens up and course is altered 90° to the E into its shelter. If coming from Cherbourg use the Passe Cabart Danneville and steer E until on the leading transit of the light towers.

Berths and facilities. The Author has only sailed a short distance into the entrance owing to a falling tide. The following notes are based on the French *Instructions Nautique Series Vol 11* and the *Foreign Port Information* of the Royal Cruising Club.

The south quay is unsuitable for berthing but vessels can dry out alongside the inner side of the north breakwater, drying 1m4 to 3m0 on sand and mud. The RCC notes state that legs are essential to lie in the middle about half way up the harbour. Some provisions can be had. Water from tap in SW corner of port. Petrol at top of main street. Trains or buses to Cherbourg. From the entrance the harbour looks a pleasant little place off the beaten track and well worth a visit.

11 Port de Lévi

High Water: See Cherbourg. **Streams:** See p. 67.

11.1. Cape Lévi lighthouse and headland from the westward. The harbour is out of the picture to the right.

11.2. The entrance to Port de Lévi, showing the white patches on the ends of the breakwaters and the white leading mark open between them.

Port de Lévi is situated just over half a mile south of Cap Lévi and close to the south of Fort Lévi. The approach from westward past Cherbourg is easy, but care should be taken when approaching Port de Lévi to keep well into the bay to avoid being set into Cap Lévi race. Approaching from the eastward keep a good two miles seawards to pass ouside the buoy off Cap Lévi to avoid the rocks and shoals and the worst of the race, except in light weather, when it may be safe to take a short cut inside at the right state of the tide. In Port de Lévi anchorage the N stream runs from +01 h Dover to −03 h Dover 2 knots springs; the S stream −03 h Dover to +01 h Dover, $2\frac{3}{4}$ knots. Eddies occur inshore between Cherbourg and Cap Lévi, west of Lévi the W stream runs 3 hours only. (See p. 67.)

The harbour, which dries 1m2 at the entrance, is formed by two jetties, having a narrow entrance. As shown on the sketch chart there are rocky ledges outside the jetties and widely fringing the cliffs north and south. The ends of the jetties are painted white and the entrance should be made with the end of the southern jetty bearing approximately east, with the end of the north jetty just open. A white rectangle on the inner wall is then open between the piers. There is a rock alongside the outer side of the south jetty, nearly at its end, to the right

69

Port de Lévi

of the white mark in the photograph. Leave the south jetty about 9 metres to starboard when abreast of it and then steer to leave the north jetty about 9 metres to port. There are rocks at the foot of its SE corner of the latter and on its east side and the southern part of the harbour has a rocky bottom. Elsewhere it is hard sand which dries about 1m8 at the quay and more at the northern end.

The harbour is sometimes occupied by fishing boats as shown in the sketch. There are mooring chains on the bottom, but a yacht equipped with legs could lie with stem to a mooring or buoyed anchor and stern to the quay. A yacht without legs would have to lie and dry out alongside the quay near the light on top of the wall on the east side of the harbour. The co-operation of the fishermen is required, as fishing boats may have to be moved from their regular moorings in order to leave a quayside berth. The harbour can be used in east and southerly winds, but there is a surge with even moderate onshore winds and heavy surf if it blows. It dries from 1m2 to 3m6.

The anchorage outside the harbour in 2m5 to 7m0 is sheltered in easterly winds, but exposed from S through W to NNE. The bottom outside the harbour is rock, except for a comparatively narrow patch of sand off the entrance. The tide attains a rate of $2\frac{3}{4}$ knots at Springs. The nearest harbour of refuge is Cherbourg only 5 miles to the west, but to the eastward the nearest is Barfleur, which involves rounding Lévi and Barfleur Races. A mobile restaurant sometimes parks on the harbour. There is a pleasant walk along the coast road to the fort and Cap. Provisions at Fermanville distant one mile.

Light. There is a fixed light with WRG sectors, visible 9, 6 and 5 miles.

11.3. Give the inner breakwater end a berth of 8 or 10 metres and bring up alongside the quay opposite.

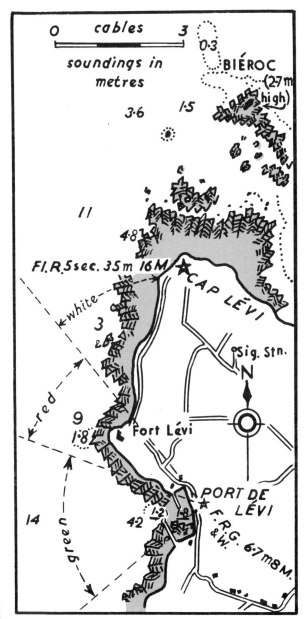

Above: Coast from Cap Lévi to Port de Lévi. (Based on English Channel Pilot Misc. 715 with the permission of the Controller of HM Stationery Office and the Hydrographer of the Navy.)

Below: sketch of the harbour

12 Barfleur

High Water: −2 h 33 m Dover; (+0 h 44 m Cherbourg).
Heights above datum: Chart No. 2073. MHWS 6m4. MLWS 1m0. MHWN 5m1. MLWN 2m3.
Stream sets to the northward between Pointe de Barfleur and the harbour $4\frac{3}{4}$ h before HW Dover and to the south $4\frac{1}{2}$ h after HW Dover, attaining 2 knots.

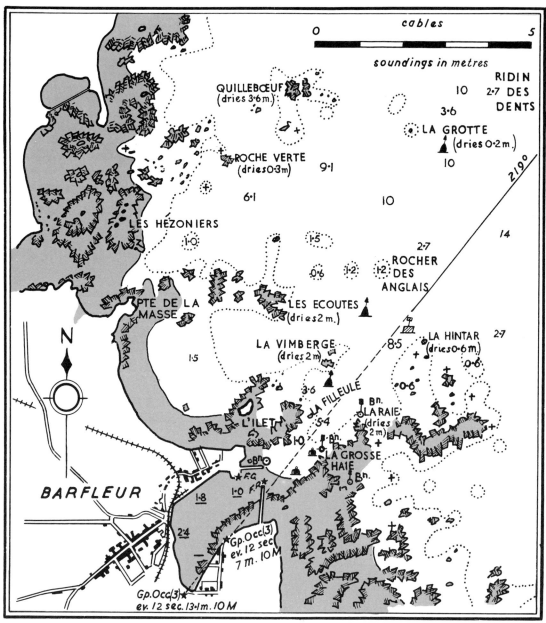

Barfleur: (Based on British Admiralty Chart No. 2073 with the permission of the Controller of HM Stationery Office and of the Hydrographer of the Navy.)

12.1. Pointe de Barfleur lighthouse
and beacon from the eastward.

Barfleur is situated $1\frac{1}{2}$ miles south of the Pointe de Barfleur. The small town is attractive and although the harbour dries out there are excellent berths against the quay, and an anchorage outside which is protected from the prevailing winds. For some reason its convenience and advantages have been overlooked by the majority of yachtsmen. St Vaast, 5 miles to the south, is another good harbour which dries out, and the St Marcouf Islands are also worth a visit, though both are outside the scope of this book.

The Approach and Entrance

Approaching from west or north the race of Barfleur (which extends 3 or 4 miles to the E and NE of the point on the flood stream) should be avoided in rough weather. The tides here require attention. Three miles N of Barfleur Point Lighthouse (*Gp Fl (2) ev 10 sec Reed 2 blasts ev min*) the main streams turn to the NW about $-\frac{1}{2}$ h Dover, and to the SE about $+5\frac{1}{2}$ h Dover, but S of Barfleur Point there is an eddy where the tide runs parallel with the shore north or south, the latter for only about $3\frac{1}{4}$ hours, starting at $+4\frac{1}{2}$ Dover. This eddy is strong in the vicinity of the Pointe de Barfleur and there are overfalls where the eddy meets the main east or west running stream. It is weaker about $\frac{3}{4}$ mile S of the Pointe de Barfleur, attaining a speed of about 2 knots only. When approaching from the eastward keep well south of Barfleur Point to avoid the race. Note that the streams in the Hédouin Channel (the inshore passage W of Pointe de Barfleur) are over two hours earlier than the main streams offshore. (See page 67.)

There are shoals and numerous rocks off the coast between the Pointe de Barfleur and Barfleur Harbour; so yachts should keep a mile to the east of the beacon east of Barfleur Point and $\frac{1}{2}$ mile east of La Grotte, the outer black starboard hand buoy of the channel leading to the entrance, which can be identified by the conspicuous church on its NW side. In moderate offshore winds and in the absence of swell the shoals can be crossed in 2mo least water a cable east of the line from the beacon to La Grotte but nothing to the west.

The leading marks are rather inconspicuous in daylight. They consist of two light structures *within* the harbour, the front one being a square white light tower and the rear a white tower with a black top built over the dark roof of a white dwelling—*see photographs*. These must not be confused with the low hexagonal white light tower at the outer end of the eastern jetty which is very conspicuous. The leading marks should be brought into line at $219°$ true and when in transit will be seen over the top of the eastern breakwater, about a third of its length from its outer end. The channel is sheltered by the land in winds from S through W almost to NW.

73

Barfleur

12.2. The leading lights giving the line of approach must not be confused with the light structure at the end of the breakwater. On near approach leave the transit and head for the entrance.

12.3. Close up view of the leading lights from inside the harbour. The rear one is often difficult to see as only the top peeps over the breakwater.

12.4. Starboard side of entrance showing two beacons and the top of an isolated rock which covers near HW.

12.5. Yachts dried out at LW.

If the leading marks cannot be identified it does not greatly matter as the entrance channel is clearly marked. After passing La Grotte outer buoy it is marked by two more starboard hand black buoys and on the port hand by one red buoy and two RW beacons with can tops. See chart and, although the channel is wide, take no liberties, especially with La Filleule and associated rocks. When about a cable off the eastern breakwater (with sufficient rise of tide) alter course to leave it to port and two BW beacons and the northern breakwater to starboard and enter the harbour. Note the drying rock on the edge of the channel close to the beacon shown in the photograph. At night the approach is clear as the leading lights are synchronized. *Group (3) occulting 12 sec* with a range of about *10 miles*. There is a *fixed green* light at the root of the northern breakwater, and a *fixed red* light at the end of the eastern which is just to the north of the transit of the leading lights. The transit leads close to the unlit La Hintar buoy.

Moorings, Anchorage and Facilities

There is a convenient anchorage in offshore winds outside the harbour NW of La Grosse Haie beacon, close to the leading line (riding light necessary) in 4 to 5 metres LAT clear of La Filleule drying rock, but the holding ground is said to be poor. At neaps with the aid of soundings it is possible to get nearer the entrance with 2 or 3m, where it is better sheltered. It is usual however to enter the harbour and bring up alongside the long NW quay, which dries about 1m8 to 2m4. The best end is near the church but the obliging Harbour Master usually directs to a berth and takes warps. Ladders are provided to the quay. The bottom along the eastern breakwater on the opposite side of the harbour is rough except at the outer end and far from facilities. There is a strong surge in the harbour during fresh onshore winds.

The harbour master lives in the house carrying the rear leading light. Customs Office between church and lifeboat house. Water tap at quay, hose by arrangement with harbour master. Water tap also at public lavatory (not five star) behind the hedge across the road, also laundering troughs and dustbins. Petrol from garages, diesel oil from Garage Mauri, up the road opposite the Hotel Phare in the main street. Hotel Moderne and the PO are in Place de Gaulle a short distance at the back of Hotel Phare. Good restaurants at hotels.

Barfleur is a charming old town extending from the church along the harbour front to the main streeet where there are plenty of small shops for supplies. There is a good bathing beach northward of the town and frequent buses to Cherbourg and elsewhere.

75

13 Omonville

High Water: −3 h 41 m Dover (−0 h 24 m Cherbourg).
Heights above Datum: MHWS 6m3. MLWS 1m0. MHWN 4m9. MLWN 2m4.
Inshore Stream, see page 67. The local inshore eddy runs from about −5 h 30 m to +5 h Dover, setting WNW 3 knots from Le Tunard beacon tower across the rocks south of Basse Bréfort buoy off which the WNW stream begins 2 hours later.

Although Cherbourg is one of the best ports in the whole of France for yachtsmen, many prefer the charm of a small harbour. Omonville la Rogue, which lies less than 8 miles west of Cherbourg, has the advantage of being quiet and unsophisticated, but of course it lacks all the facilities of a large port.

The Approach

Approaching from northward the first landmarks which will be sighted are Cap de la Hague and the tall chimney and buildings on the skyline 3 miles SE of it. The chimney lies to the south of the Anse de St Martin, and stands 2 miles SW of Omonville harbour. The next landmark to identify is the Pointe de Jardeheu, 3½ miles east of Cap de la Hague. It is a low promontory with a white-washed building and semaphore station at the end. Half a mile off the Pointe is the BW whistle buoy, Basse Bréfort (*Fl 1½ sec*) situated in a very strong stream usually setting WNW, with rocks between it and the shore. Take care not to be set too far west as Omonville lies about a mile to the eastward, and on the headland at the entrance sprawl the remains of an old fort, looking more like a wishbone of green-covered walls than

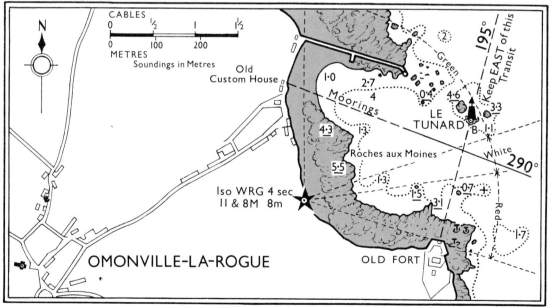

Omonville: Dotted contours indicate the 3 metre lines. (Based on French Chart No. 5631 by permission of the Service Hydrographique de la Marine.)

13.1. The conspicuous high chimney and buildings which stand on the skyline 2½ miles SW of Omonville, and the Basse Bréfort BW lightbuoy 1½ miles NW of Omonville. The stream is very strong running W for over 8½ hours. On the left of the picture is the white semaphore building identifying the low Pointe de Jardeheu.

13.2. The old fort on the hill east of Omonville harbour, Le Tunard black beacon tower and on right the end of the breakwater. Keep the fort open to the eastward of the beacon tower when approaching from a northerly direction.

13.3. The new light structure (Iso WRG) on the SW of the harbour.

the broken pile of masonry one might expect. On nearer approach a black beacon tower (not conspicuous) named Le Tunard will be sighted, and the harbour breakwater over which will be seen the new RW light structure. When approaching keep well to the east of the transit of the beacon tower and the old fort at 195°, to clear the rocky shoals of Les Tataquets, and in particular to allow for the strong cross tide, usually running WNW towards the rocks.

Approaching from the westward keep at least a mile off shore until well east of the transit of the beacon tower and the fort, then steer to leave the tower well to starboard.

From the eastward the approach is much easier, as the coast is less rock-strewn. The beacon tower of Raz de Bannes will be passed three miles west of Cherbourg and soon Le Tunard and the fort will be seen. Allow for the tide, and avoid being set north of Le Tunard.

Omonville

13.4. Composite photograph facing northward over Omonville harbour. When entering from E, the beacon tower is left about 50 metres to starboard, after which the yacht is headed parallel with the breakwater. There are rocks between the beacon and the end of the breakwater and the stream is usually setting hard towards them.

Entrance. The entrance lies between the beacon tower of Le Tunard and the fort. Le Tunard stands on a reef, and there are rocks between the tower and end of the breakwater, and also for about $\frac{1}{4}$ cable E and ESE of the tower, which should, therefore, not be approached too closely. A cable NE of the fort there is a rock which just dries at LAT, and the proper channel is under a cable wide at low water.

When entering from the eastward steer for the former custom house (a tiny building with a high roof and a chimney at each end) at about 290°, or simply leave Le Tunard beacon tower about 60 metres to starboard and make good a course leading south of the breakwater towards the bigger fishing boats or moorings in the harbour. Be prepared for the strong stream usually setting NW off Le Tunard beacon tower and across the rocks between it and the breakwater. When within the harbour keep north of the Roches aux Moines (see chart) which are steep-to and covered near high water.

If coming from the northward leave Le Tunard beacon tower at least $\frac{1}{2}$ cable to the westward before coming on the line for the entrance from the east, when proceed on it.

By night. A light *Iso WRG 4 sec, on a WR light structure elevation 13m, range 11M and 8M,* has been established and added to the accompanying chart. Enter in white sector with the light bearing between 252° and 262°, but alter course to starboard into the harbour when south of Le Tunard Beacon.

Anchorage. The best positions in the harbour are occupied by moorings. Visiting yachts may lie to the big white mooring buoys, if necessary several abreast, as the moorings are very heavy. It is sometimes possible to find room to anchor in good holding ground between the moorings and the rocks south of them, but take care as these are steep-to and often covered. Except near spring tides there is room to anchor nearer to the beach but soundings must be taken. If the harbour is full anchorage can be found to the east of the moorings, but the water is deep, the stream strong and the position less sheltered. Yachts can dry out on sand bottom alongside the breakwater for $\frac{1}{4}$ cable west of the short offshoot or spur, but rocks border the breakwater east of it. There are a few small fishing dories moored south of the jetty on the edge of the shallow water.

The anchorage is sheltered except from winds in any direction from the east, but in a gale from the south it was on one occasion too rough to row a dinghy to the yacht even from the breakwater.

Facilities. Land at steps west of the breakwater offshoot, or in calm weather on the shingle shore. The restaurant facing the harbour was closed in 1972 but possibly a new one may be started there or in the village. Water at tap nearby. Petrol at garage 600 metres up road bearing right. Shops and douanier in village and milk at farm before 8 a.m. or reserved if ordered the night before. Infrequent bus service to Cherbourg. Twelfth–thirteenth century church with attractive gallery.

13.5. The inner harbour. At neaps a vessel can find anchorage as close inshore as soundings permit. The former office of the Douane is the small two chimneyed building to the right of the white house on the extreme left.

14 Anse de St Martin and Racine

High Water: Approx. $-3\frac{3}{4}$ h Dover, $-\frac{1}{2}$ h Cherbourg.
Heights above Datum: Approx. MHWS 6m4. MLWS 1m1. MHWN 5m0. MLWN 2m5.
Stream sets within the Bay SE at $+5$ h Dover and to NNW at -5 h 30 m Dover.

As the chart shows, the Anse de St Martin, half way between Cap de la Hague and Omonville, provides a natural anchorage sheltered from winds between SE through S to W. It has a shelving shore and provides good holding ground. It is however only suitable in settled weather, as in a southerly gale there is the probability of a veer to the NW. As there are no lights in the bay it would be difficult to leave at night in the event of the wind coming onshore. The harbour of Racine though protected from north is small and dries out, but in offshore winds and settled weather the Anse de St Martin affords a pleasant and secluded anchorage with plenty of room.

The Approach
The NW and NE corners of the entrance of the bay are encumbered by rocks but near the centre the three rocks La Parmentière (awash at LAT), and La Francaise and Erte (with less

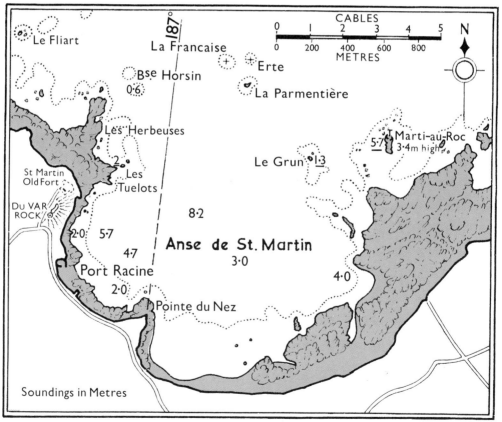

Anse de St Martin and Racine: Dotted contours indicate the 3 metre lines. (Based on French Chart No. 5636 by permission of the Service Hydrographique de la Marine.)

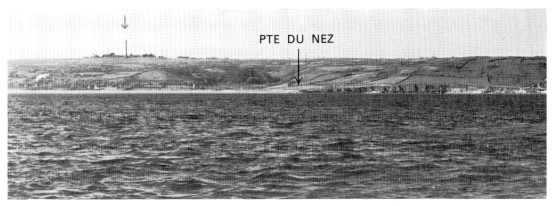

PTE DU NEZ

14.1. The line of approach is with the Pointe du Nez bearing 187°. The Pointe is at the W end of a sandy beach on the south of the bay. The conspicuous chimney will be open to the east of the Pointe but the picture was taken when leaving the anchorage and not exactly on the correct bearing.

14.2. Les Herbeuses from the SE near LW. The rocks appear much the same when approached from seaward and are left about two cables to starboard.

than 1m8 over them) are well covered above half tide, although there might be breakers on them during fresh winds.

The simplest approach to the bay is made with the Pointe du Nez bearing 187°. This is the low promontory on the SW side of the bay with a rock off it which never covers. It is not conspicuous from seaward but its position can be identified as it lies at the W end of a long sandy shore to the east of it. When on the correct line the high chimney referred to in the last chapter will be fine on the port bow. Allow for the very strong streams in the offing, which may at times require an alteration as much as 45° to crab across the tide on the correct bearing on the headland. This leaves La Francaise, Erte and La Parmentière over a cable to port and Basse Horsin with 0m6 over it to starboard. When these have been passed the prominent Les Herbeuses rocks (some of which never dry) will lie about 2 cables to the west. Les Tuélots, drying 2m0, will be left over a cable to starboard and the stream will have

14.3. Port Racine, looking north. It is one of the smallest harbours in France.

weakened to a maximum 2 knots at springs. Alter course to steer into the SW corner of the bay to the west of Pte du Nez and take soundings to bring up in the depth required, probably just to seaward of a number of fishermen's moorings with plastic buoys east of Port Racine. Holding ground good in sand or mud.

Port Racine. The harbour is difficult to find, as it is hidden behind a reef of rocks until the yacht is to the SE of the entrance and in shallow water. The entrance faces south, and the harbour is formed by breakwaters on the south and east, and protected by land to the west and north. There is a reef of rocks extending over 100 metres to the ENE of the east jetty.

The harbour is very small and dries out completely. Yachts can, however, lie alongside the jetties, but should moor as near the outer ends as possible to get the best water, as the bottom is steeply shelving. In practice, however, it would now be difficult to lay alongside the jetties as there are many local craft moored with long ropes aft and by chains forward across the harbour to the east jetty. A deep keeled yacht could only enter with local co-operation. In bad weather a chain is put across the entrance. The harbour provides the best landing place from a dinghy. There is an hotel with bar and restaurant close by. A cheaper restaurant will be found $\frac{1}{2}$ mile on the road uphill to the right on the outskirts of Danneville where provisions can be obtained. Good coastal walks. Occasional bus to Cherbourg.

PART 3
THE CHANNEL ISLANDS

Introduction

Chart Datum: The charted depths and drying heights given in this part of the book have been altered to conform with LAT datums. Tidal data are shown at the head of each chapter.

The principal attraction of the Channel Islands lies in the varied coastlines, the strange rock formations, the sandy bays, the clear water and the constantly changing scene which results from a tremendous rise and fall of the tides. The number and variety of the anchorages under suitable conditions is remarkable. A month could happily be spent with the yacht based on St Peter Port making short cruises exploring the waters round Guernsey, Herm and Sark. Likewise Jersey, although lacking in a good yacht harbour, has many excellent and beautiful anchorages which are available in offshore winds and settled weather. There is no great difficulty in entering the main ports, except in thick weather. Alderney with its deep harbour is only 60 miles from the Solent, and even less from Poole or Weymouth. The Little Russel leading to St Peter Port is rough with a fresh SW wind blowing against a spring tide, but a stranger can avoid this by going round Guernsey and entering from the south. Navigation in the approaches to St Helier is a little more complicated. But if, on the occasion of his first visit, the yachtsman will wait for settled clear weather and a neap tide he need have no anxiety. The Channel Islands form a compact cruising ground with harbours never far apart, and are also convenient for visiting many ports on the neighbouring French coast.

As so much of the enjoyment of sailing in the Channel Islands lies in the coastal cruising and as, at the time of writing, there is no comprehensive pilotage book on the subject, Part III, which follows in this book, has been expanded to include sailing directions in addition to descriptions of the harbours and anchorages themselves. Navigation on the coasts of Herm, Sark and SE Jersey calls for greater experience and caution than elsewhere, and it is due to Channel Island yachtsmen that information is given on the local transits and clearing marks, which are coupled with sketches and the author's photographs to assist in their identification.

The principal requirement when cruising in the Channel Islands is an understanding of the tides. The reader should consult the Admiralty *Pocket Tidal Stream Atlas* for the Channel Islands and Adjacent Coasts of France, and there are many references in the text to emphasize the importance of inshore eddies. Eddies, such as those found on the north coast of Alderney and off Herm, sometimes run contrary to the main stream, and then two opposing currents may be separated by only a narrow band of water. Rock dodgers must be prepared to find inshore eddies which are too local to show on any tidal map, and of course the rates, direction and position vary between springs and neaps, and are also influenced by weather conditions.

In general the direction of tidal streams round the islands constantly progresses in an anti-clockwise direction, being north-easterly at high water (St Helier) (-4 h 47 m Dover), north-westerly at half tide down, south-westerly at low water, swinging round rapidly to south-easterly at the first of the flood, and gradually to easterly about $1\frac{1}{2}$ hours before HW.

Introduction

In the Russels between Guernsey and Sark the NE to N stream begins −2 h 50 m St Helier (+4 h 40 m Dover) and the SW at approximately +3 h 30 m St Helier (−1 h 25 m Dover) both streams attaining over 5 knots springs, 2¼ neaps.

Visiting yachtsmen may find it convenient to work their tides in relation to Dover as the standard port for the whole of the English Channel, but it is more accurate to work on local tide constants. Accordingly constants are given for both Dover and St Helier, and in *ATT* (Vol. 1) or *Reed's Nautical Almanac* will be found the times of HW for St Peter Port and St Helier.

Pilotage in the Channel Islands is based on transits, land marks, beacons and rocks. The compass is necessary to assist in finding these marks, but in narrow waters with perhaps unpredictable (to the stranger) currents it is far easier to keep known marks in line, rather than depend on a compass bearing. Photographs and sketches are reproduced to assist identification of the principal marks, which once recognized will make it easier to find the position of the less conspicuous ones. If a newcomer can kidnap a local yachtsman or pilot as navigator for the first cruise to Herm or Sark so much the better, or failing that, he could do worse than take passage in one of the many excursion boats from St Peter Port in order to familiarize himself with the features of the coast, before piloting his own yacht there.

Finally, for those who are unfamiliar with cruising in restricted waters, with a great rise and fall of tide, the following notes may be of service.

The scene in the Channel Islands at high water is one of islands with a few outlying rocks, towers and tops of beacons standing out of the water; but at low water the rocks will have grown to islets, the beacons may be on top of rocks as big as houses, and vast areas of islets, rocks, ledges and sands will be uncovered. A small isolated rock is known locally as a 'boue', and much can be done to avoid dangerous boues by keeping a watch for them, as was done before the era of aids to navigation. In a smooth sea rocks below the surface can sometimes be seen, and if there is a strong tide they will be revealed by ripples and circles of oily looking water. If it is a little rough there will be overfalls over the rocks, and if a swell is running the waves will break, spurting white columns of spray. It will be seen on the chart that some of the larger rocks which are always above water are steep-to. Such rocks can be treated like beacons as by passing close to them the yacht's position can be fixed.

Overfalls occur in the Little Russel, and are unavoidable on certain passages. But many overfalls such as the Schôle Bank are local, occurring over shoal banks. The navigator should lay his courses to avoid these shoals, but if overfalls are sighted they can be avoided by altering course to go round them, as the patches are usually quite distinct.

Fog and thick weather in the Channel Islands provide the principal hazards, although a flat calm can also be awkward to a yacht without auxiliary power, if the stream is setting on dangers. If a fog comes down when approaching the Channel Islands it is safer to return to sea. It is best to treat a forecast of poor visibility in much the same way as one would treat a forecast of a gale, because gales are preferable to fogs when sailing in restricted waters. Attention is drawn to these risks because if they are recognized they are robbed of half their danger. All that is required in the Channel Isles is an extra degree of caution and vigilance.

15 Casquets, the Swinge and Alderney Race

The SW stream at the Casquets begins westerly about −0 h 30 m HW Dover (+4 h 30 m St Helier) and soon turns SW. The NE stream begins about +5 h 30 m Dover (−2 h St Helier). The streams attain 4½ to 5 knots at springs. It is stated that eddies exist SW from the Casquets during the SW stream and NE during the NE stream. In the channels between the Casquets and Alderney the streams are stronger and there are severe overfalls over banks, shoals or irregularities on the bottom.

15.1. Approaching Alderney Race from NE. *Left to right*: Cap de la Hague, La Plate light tower, Cape de la Hague (Gros du Raz) lighthouse.

Yachtsmen sailing to Guernsey and the Gulf of St Malo will either leave the Casquets well to port, clearing the tide races in the vicinity, or will first visit Cherbourg or Alderney, then taking one of the inshore passages, either through Alderney Race or the Swinge, or more rarely the Ortac Channel. Thus Alderney (see Chapter 16) and the reefs to the west of it may be said to lie in the gateway of the passage to the Channel Isles and Gulf of St Malo. Such being the case they merit special attention.

For navigation in these waters the Admiralty Chart No. 60 of Alderney and the Casquets is particularly recommended. It also contains large-scale local tidal insets.

The Casquets

This prominent group of rocks has been a landmark for shipping throughout the ages, and is situated 7 miles west of Alderney Breakwater. Between the Casquets and the island are several islets, detached rocks and shoals, with wide passages between them. These passages can be navigated but, owing to the strength of the tide, the overfalls and detached dangers, local knowledge is needed, other than for those described below.

The Casquets have accounted for many wrecks, but the hazards have been reduced by navigational aids. The group of rocks is prominent, and the white lighthouse (*Gp Fl (5) 30 sec visible 17 miles*) and buildings can be seen for a considerable distance on a clear day. In fog or thick conditions the whole area is a disagreeable one, but there is a powerful *diaphone* (*2 blasts ev 60 secs*) on the E tower, and as most yachts are equipped with DF the *radio beacon* is invaluable in these waters.

The Casquets group of islets and rocks extends nearly ¾ mile east to west. They may be approached within ¼ mile on the north side as sunken outliers extend less than a cable off the principal rocks which are always above the water. There is little to be gained by approaching closely, as the tide runs very hard, at times setting somewhat towards the rocks, and there are overfalls over the uneven bottom. In particular there are overfalls on the rock drying 2m4, situated ½ cable N of L'Auquière, on 'The Ledge' (covered 2m4), 1 cable NW

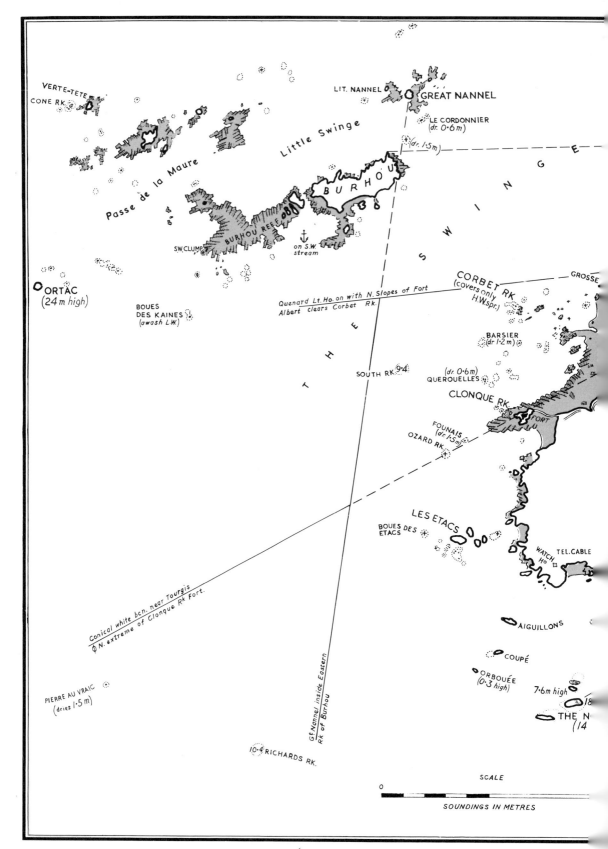

Alderney and the Swinge: (Based on British Admiralty Chart No. 60 with the pe

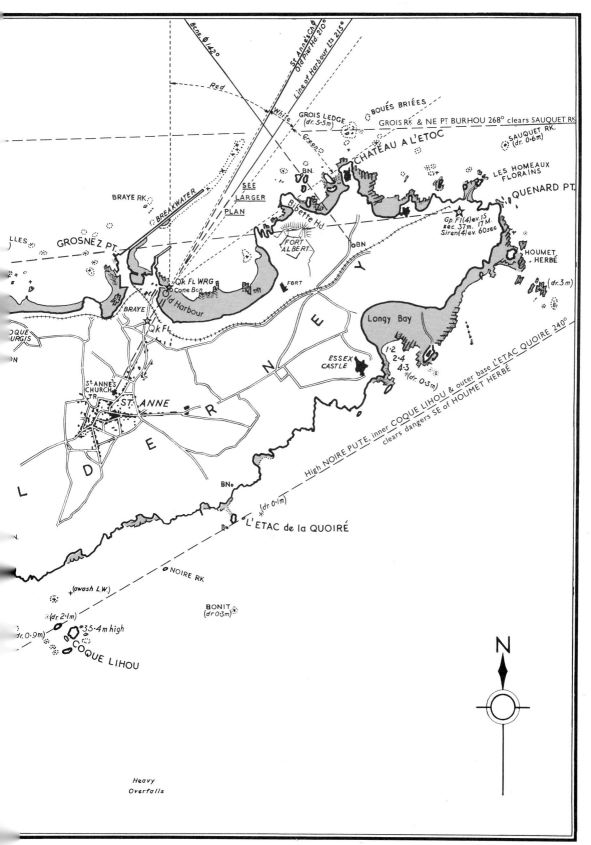

Bcns. Ø 142°

St Anne's Ch. O
Old Pier Hd. 210°
Line of Harbour Lts 215°

Red

White

Green

BOUÉS BRIÉES

GROIS LEDGE
(dr. 5·5m)

GROIS RK & NE PT. BURHOU 268° clears SAUQUET RK

CHATEAU A L'ETOC

SAUQUET RK.
(dr. 0·6m)

BN.

LES HOMEAUX
FLORAINS

BRAYE RK

SEE
LARGER
PLAN

BREAKWATER

Bibette Hd.

QUENARD PT.

GROSNEZ PT.

LLES

FORT
ALBERT

BN

Gp. Fl(4)ev.15
sec. 37m. 17 M.
Siren(4)ev. 60sec

HOUMET
HERBÉ

FORT

(dr. 3m)

Qk Fl WRG
Cone Bcn
Old Harbour

BRAYE

Qk Fl

Longy Bay

OQUE
URGIS

ON

1·2
2·4
4·3
(dr. 0·3m)

ESSEX
CASTLE

A

L'ETAC QUOIRE 240°

High NOIRE PUTE, inner COQUE LIHOU & outer base L'ETAC QUOIRE 240°
clears dangers SE of HOUMET HERBÉ

St ANNE'S
CHURCH
TR.

ST. ANNE

L   D   E   R   N   E   Y

BN

(dr. 0·1m)

L'ETAC de la QUOIRÉ

BN

NOIRE RK

(awash L.W.)

BONIT
(dr 0·3m)

(dr 2·1m)

dr. 0·9m)

35·4m high

COQUE LIHOU

N

Heavy
Overfalls

15.2. The Casquets lighthouse from the northward.

15.3. The Ortac Rock is a nesting place for gannets. It is at the SE end of the Ortac Channel and a useful mark on which to take a bearing.

15.4. The Swinge. The Corbet Rock and associated rocks and the jagged profile of Les Etacs.

of Noire Roque (the rock SW of the group), and over the 'Eight Fathom Ledge' just under a mile west of the lighthouse. It may be said that overfalls may be expected anywhere in the area where banks or shoals exist, even if well covered. For this reason the SW Casquet Bank 2 to 6 miles off, and the Pommier Banks, 2 miles to the NE should be avoided in rough weather or at spring tides.

There are several landing places on the principal Casquet rock which are used for relief of the lighthouse, but landing by the public on the Trinity House property is forbidden, and also risky. The Petit Havre is on the west side, and is simply an inlet between the main islet and the islet south of it. It is narrow, the bottom is rocky, and it is open to the prevailing wind.

Ortac Channel

This channel is rarely used by strangers, but it is a wide one which may be navigated with the aid of the large-scale Admiralty chart. It is entered at the north, to the west of the Verte-

Tête group of rocks. This consists principally of Verte-Tête itself, a two-headed rock 7m9 high, and westward of it the Cone Rock, which is conical and 3m0 high. Westward of Cone Rock is a boue which dries 2m4. The Ortac Rock marks the southern end of the channel, and the yacht will pass westward of this. The rock, which is a nesting place of gannets, is 24 m high and can be seen and identified (see photograph) from a considerable distance. It is most useful for taking bearings.

Simple directions are steer to approach with Ortac bearing 155° true until Verte Tête (7m9 high) and Cone Rock, ½ mile distant, come in line with Great Nannel. Then make good a course of 189° leaving Ortac about ½ mile to eastward. Ortac itself is fairly steep-to on its west and south sides, but there are shoals within 2 cables WNW of it, on which there are overfalls, although they are covered 3m6 even at low water.

The principal consideration in the Ortac Channel is the tide, which attains 7 knots. This causes overfalls, severe when contrary to the wind. NE stream starts +5 h Dover (−2½ h St Helier) and SW at −1 h Dover (+4 h St Helier), but the streams vary in direction, setting at High Water Dover towards the Casquets, and there are eddies, so the tidal charts should be consulted. It should not be attempted without auxiliary power unless there is enough wind to ensure command over tidal eddies. Plan the passage preferably near slack water at neap tides.

The Swinge

The Swinge is the channel on the west side of Alderney, between it and the group of islets and reefs which lie on the other side. This group is about 2 miles long from the Nannels at the NE to Ortac at the SW and the largest islet is Burhou which, if one includes the reef on its SW (which dries at low water), is about 1 mile long.

The Swinge affords the quickest passage between Alderney and Guernsey, and is the one most often used by local vessels and yachts. The streams attain rates up to 8 knots at springs and the bottom is rocky, so there are violent overfalls in bad weather and when wind and tide are opposed. Navigation in the Swinge therefore depends on choosing the right time, and one of the roughest area of tide rips lies about 1 mile ENE of Burhou; less disturbed water may be found nearer Alderney.

When bound southward via the Swinge, a local eddy will be found off Alderney Harbour. Local yachtsmen usually plan to enter the Swinge off Alderney Breakwater at −2 to −1 h Dover (+2½ to 4 h St Helier). See page 92 for times of westerly eddy.

The yacht should be sailed into a position north of the submerged end of Alderney Breakwater (½ mile N of breakwater end) in the line with the beacons—see next chapter. Then steer west towards the southern side of Burhou Island (see photograph).

The stream running to SW should set the yacht to the south. Until the Corbet Rock has been cleared do not allow her to be set south of the line of Alderney (Quenard) Lighthouse (photograph p. 95) on with the northern slopes of Fort Albert at 085° which is the fort on the hill, SE of the breakwater end, on the opposite side of the harbour entrance, and will be seen to the eastward over the breakwater.

The Corbet Rock is the principal consideration in the Swinge, as it lies ½ mile from the shore off Roque Tourgis, and reduces the navigable width of the Swinge to little over ½ mile between Burhou and the Corbet. This rock is covered only at HW springs, and will probably be about 3m3 above water at the state of tide when the yacht passes it, and there is an outlyer ¼ cable west of it which dries 3m0. The Corbet is cleared when Fort Clonque (almost an island joined to Alderney by a causeway—see photograph) is well shut in by the high land of SW Alderney. It is better to hold on the course with the north slope of Fort Albert and the lighthouse astern until Great Nannel (a 14m6 high rock, 3 cables N or Burhou) is just shut inside the extreme eastern side of Burhou at 008°. Then steer on this stern bearing, leaving Les Etacs rocks (see photograph), of which the highest is 36m9, about ½ mile to the eastward.

Keep on this course (or rather to the east of it after passing Les Etacs) until the Noires Putes (a group of four rocks ½ mile S of Alderney, highest 18m9) come abeam, whence steer for Guernsey or as desired, but note the presence of Pierre au Vraic, 1 mile to the west.

Pierre au Vraic is a dangerous isolated rock situated in deep water 1¾ miles W by S of Les Etacs, right in the SW approach of the Swinge, almost on the transit of Coupé and Coque Lihou inner top, best seen on the chart. Pierre au Vraic dries 1m5 at LW springs, and if

15.5. Looking WNW across Clonque Fort and Causeway to the Swinge. The isolated Ortac Rock will be seen on the left and Burhou across the Swinge on the right.

there is a swell running the seas break on it, even if well covered by the tide. It is cleared on its east side by the transit of Great Nannel just shut in by the E side of Burhou, and on its south side by keeping S of the line from the inner (northern) rock of the four Noires Putes to the southern rock (17m7) of the Coque Lihou group, which is unmistakable as its northern neighbour is a rock 35m4 high. On its western side it is avoided by keeping on or west of the conical white beacon just S of Fort Tourgis in line with N extreme of Clonque Rock Fort. Pierre au Vraic has greater nuisance value when approaching the Swinge from the south from Guernsey as if the weather is thick the yacht will be in the vicinity before the transits can be picked up, and allowance for tidal streams must be made as accurately as possible.

In the Swinge the NE stream commences at $+5$h Dover ($-2\frac{1}{2}$ h St Helier) and continues to $-1\frac{1}{2}$ h Dover ($+3\frac{1}{2}$ h St Helier), when the SW stream begins, but north of the Corbet Rock along the north of Alderney, the inshore eddy runs easterly only for three hours approximately $+5$ h Dover ($-2\frac{1}{2}$ h St Helier) to -4 h Dover ($+\frac{1}{2}$ h St Helier). Thus a yacht coming up with a fair tide from Guernsey may meet a foul stream beyond the Corbet Rock, though the eddy is modest compared with the reputed 8 knots springs in the southern part of the Swinge. Other eddies exist which can be used only with local knowledge. A good temporary anchorage on the SW stream is shown on the chart SW of Burhou but a yacht could get closer in under suitable conditions.

Alderney Race

The race of Alderney provides the usual passage for ships and yachts rounding the NW corner of the Cherbourg Peninsula. It is over 7 miles wide and has Quenard Point (Alderney) lighthouse (*Gp Fl (4) 15 sec vis 17 miles, Fog Siren 4 blasts ev 60 sec*) on the NW side and Cap de la Hague lighthouse (*Fl 5 sec vis 19 miles, Fog Reed ev 30 sec*) on the French coast opposite. Strangers may be deterred from using this passage. The rate of $8\frac{1}{2}$ knots attained by the stream in Alderney Race sounds alarming, but it will only be encountered at the peak of an exceptionally big spring tide on the NE side of the race. The yachtsman is not likely to meet with more than 6 knots, and probably less, particularly if he can plan to pass through the northern end of the race near slack water. At neaps the rate does not exceed 4 knots anywhere in the race.

There are overfalls in Alderney Race whenever the stream is running fast over shoals or unevenness on the bottom, such as Blanchard, Inner Race Rock, Race Rock, and Alderney South Banks. The positions of the shoal patches are shown on large scale chart No. 60 and courses should if necessary be planned or altered to avoid them. In very calm weather they will be no more than ripples and oily whirlpools, but if the wind is against the stream, or obliquely against the stream, they will be lively and in strong winds possibly dangerous, though in such circumstances much can be done by easing the yacht through them, letting the tide carry her past.

Although the Alderney streams attain higher rates than in Portland Race, the wave formations are less irregular and are not considered so dangerous. As the tides play such an important part in the navigation of Alderney Race, varying both in speed and direction, they require special consideration, preferably consulting Admiralty Chart No. 60 or Pocket Tidal Stream Atlas.

Tidal Streams. In the centre of the race and its approaches well clear of the land on each side the streams are straightforward. The SW stream starts at $-\frac{3}{4}$ h Dover ($+4$ h St Helier); the NE stream starts $+5\frac{1}{4}$ h Dover ($-2\frac{1}{4}$ h St Helier). Both streams attain $5\frac{1}{2}$ knots at springs. Slack water does not last long, but affords an interval when the tides are weaker and the Race less unruly.

The strongest streams are found on the French side of the Race. Off Gros du Raz light-house the NE stream begins at $+5$ h 10 m Dover and at springs attains $4\frac{3}{4}$ knots 2 or 3 hours later. The SW stream begins at -1 h 35 m Dover and later attains the high spring rate of $6\frac{1}{2}$ knots. A mile W of La Foraine beacon tower the streams begin about at the same time, the NNE stream attaining $8\frac{1}{2}$ knots and the SSW $7\frac{1}{2}$ knots at springs.

Casquets, the Swinge and Alderney Race

If approaching from Cherbourg direction from the east use can be made of the early inshore reverse eddy. Off Anse de St Martin the WNW eddy starts about −5 h Dover and will take a yacht fast along the coast when the offshore stream is foul, but careful chart work is needed to keep north of the outlying rocks. The inshore stream does not bend round towards the rocks off Gros du Raz (which must be given a good offing) to La Foraine beacon until nearly 1½ hours before HW Dover, so there is no point in being too early. If sailing from Cherbourg, Omonville and Anse de St Martin this eddy is useful in good weather, as by this means a yacht can get through the Alderney Race on the east side before the tide attains its maximum. The early eddy which is fair when approaching Alderney Race from the east is of course contrary for a yacht approaching from the south, late on the tide.

On the Alderney side of the race there are notable and most useful eddies. Round the north-east of Alderney the NE stream turns to follow the coast westward towards the Swinge for the last three hours from about −4½ h Dover (+½ h St Helier) and continues W until about +5 h Dover (−2 h St Helier). This stream at springs attains over 3 knots. The division of the main SW stream is near the Sauquet Rock (dries 0m6), on which it sets strongly. One arm of the stream runs west along Alderney while the other sweeps into Alderney Race.

Inshore on the south and east sides of Alderney there is little detailed information but it is stated in the *Channel Pilot* that in an area between the coast within a line from Orbouée to about 1 mile SE of the Noires Putes and thence NE to Brinchetais Ledge off Houmet Herbé Fort the east-going stream begins +3 h 0 m Dover and continues until −2 h 0 m Dover. Maximum rates springs E and NE 2 knots, W and SW 3 knots.

16 Alderney (Braye Harbour)

High Water: −4 h 19 m Dover (+0 h 28 m St Helier).

Heights above Datum: Chart No. 2845. MHWS 6m4. MLWS 0m8. MHWN 5m0. MLWN 2m3.

Well offshore the stream sets SW from −½ h Dover to +5½ h Dover, and NE +5½ h Dover to −½ h Dover. Inshore along the north coast and the west coast as far as the Corbet Rock there is a strong eddy (referred to in the previous chapter) setting westward and towards the Swinge at about 2 to 3 knots for 9 out of 12 hours.

Depths: Deep in the approach and harbour, except off the inner harbour.

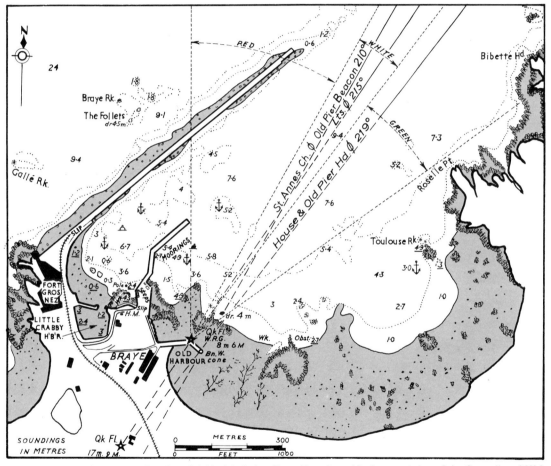

Braye Harbour, Alderney: (Based on British Admiralty Chart No. 2845 with the permission of the Controller of HM Stationery Office and of the Hydrographer of the Navy.)

Alderney Harbour used to be regarded as somewhat difficult of approach and entrance, but in clear weather it is easy enough, except for the strong tidal streams. It is only 60 miles from the Needles, and after Cherbourg it is the most popular harbour in the vicinity of Cherbourg Peninsula. The harbour is deep, the holding ground varies, but it is protected except from

Alderney (Braye Harbour)

N and NE winds. Facilities are good, and the best positions in the harbour are often crowded in holiday months.

The Approach and Entrance

The best approach to Alderney Harbour is from a general direction N to NE, and the island will be seen from a considerable distance in clear weather. When it is sighted fix or estimate the ship's position, and work out the tides over the remaining distance in order to make allowance for them. Close inshore on the N coast of Alderney the stream runs west except between $+5$ h Dover and $-4\frac{1}{2}$ h Dover, so it is usually best to lay a course for the NE part of the island. On nearer approach the lighthouse will be seen, situated about $\frac{1}{4}$ mile west of Quenard Point. There are detached rocks all along this north coast, from the Sauquet rock over $\frac{1}{4}$ mile N of Quenard Pte to Boués Briées $\frac{1}{4}$ mile N of Château à L'Etoc. $1\frac{1}{4}$ miles west of the lighthouse is the harbour breakwater, composed of high masonry, nearly $\frac{1}{2}$ mile long, which will be seen from a considerable distance, and the church at St Annes will be seen in the centre of the island. The stream will probably be setting strongly off the lighthouse along the coast towards the breakwater, which will bring the yacht nicely to the entrance, but take care not to be set too far to the west towards the Swinge and dangers in the direction of the Casquets. See chart, pages 86–87.

If coming from the south either go the long way, giving the Casquets and all dangers a wide berth, and approach Alderney from the north, or approach by the Swinge or Alderney Race as described in the previous chapter.

The entrance to Alderney Harbour lies between the submerged remains of the breakwater (which extend over $\frac{1}{4}$ mile from the end of the breakwater proper) and the rocks off the coast between Château à L'Etoc Fort (prominent on a headland) and Bibette Head. The navigable width of the entrance is only 2 cables, and for a stranger less.

In the immediate approach to the entrance the tidal stream has again to be considered, for the end of the Swinge causes quite a race off the submerged part of the breakwater, and overfalls in westerly winds. As stated the inshore stream varies in width, and towards the end of the easterly inshore stream the westerly eddy has already started within about $\frac{1}{2}$ cable of the breakwater. There will then be a clear demarcation between east and west setting streams, and the sudden change may cause the yacht to sheer as she crosses it. The streams off the submerged breakwater are particularly strong at local high water springs and at 6 hours after, when caution is necessary owing to the strong eddies; they can be dangerous in rough weather.

The remains of the breakwater consist of blocks of masonry; the most dangerous blocks are those within a hundred metres of the breakwater end, covered 0m3 to 0m9 at datum. There are also shoal patches with 1 metre at $1\frac{3}{4}$ cables off and an outer 1m5 patch nearly 3 cables off. They can be imagined as forming an underwater continuation of the masonry for 3 cables, first bulging a little into the entrance then curving slightly outwards to the north. Accordingly, if the inner side of the breakwater is kept slightly open (allowing for an athwartship tide) its submerged continuation will be left to starboard. However, the leading marks will be seen, which consist of a white conical beacon on the old pier head in transit at $210°$ true with St Anne's Church spire—see photograph. These lead close inside east of the submerged masonry. There is also a transit on the east side of the approach which clears the dangerous rocks (dries 4m5) lying to the north of Bibette Head. The transit is the E front of a house in line with the white conical old pier beacon in line at $219°$. There is plenty of water

16.1. Approaching the north side of Alderney, near Quenard Lighthouse.

16.2. Alderney coastline from Château à L'Etoc to Fort Albert, showing the leading beacons, which have opened out as the yacht has altered course towards the harbour.

16.3. The leading marks for the outer approach are the Old Harbour beacon in line with the church at 210°. The principal anchorage lies between the jetty and the breakwater.

16.4. The inside of the breakwater photo-graphed from the Author's *Cohoe I* at anchor during a gale. Within the harbour there was nothing more than an uncomfortable swell. The breakwater has since been repaired.

Alderney (Braye Harbour)

in which to tack between the two transits.

If the yacht is approaching from the W or NW, the end of the submerged breakwater will be cleared by keeping on a transit with the beacon on the prominent above water group of rocks NE of Bibette Head and a beacon on the hill behind at 142° true—see photograph. Course may be altered to starboard to enter the harbour when the transit on the old pier beacon is opened up.

Alternatively, a short cut in good weather across the submerged dangers can be taken at half tide, about 70 metres off the end of the breakwater by keeping the Pepper Pot Tower on the north side of Fort Essex (on the E side of the island see Chart, p. 86) on the southern slope of Fort Albert at 138° true (SE by S mag). The author has not used the transit but the R Channel Islands YC Handbook states that it gives 4m8 at half ebb.

Once inside the breakwater, shelter is found and the harbour widens out. Course may be altered to the anchorage W or E of Braye jetty, which lies between the old harbour pier and the breakwater. There is deep water all along the inside of the breakwater except for some

16.5. The Old Harbour showing the light structure and the beacon. It is a good harbour for yachts and other craft which can dry out.

boulders and blocks of stone immediately below it. The old pier on which the beacon stands and rocks north and west of it dry out.

It may be added that the approach and entrance to Alderney Harbour have the advantage that if there is a headwind, so that the yacht has to beat in, the sea will not be unduly rough, blowing directly offshore.

By night. There are two powerful lights which assist in the approach to Alderney at night. Alderney (Quenard) lighthouse is *Gp Fl (4) ev 15 sec vis 17 miles* and the *Casquets Gp Fl (5) ev 30 sec also vis 17 miles*) is situated 8 miles to the west. Fog Signals: Alderney Lighthouse, *siren (4) ev 60 sec*; Casquets *Diaphone (2) ev 60 sec*.

Alderney Harbour leading lights consist of the front low light on the elbow of the old pier *Qk Fl WRG 6 M* and the rear light on a column 17 m elevation *Qk Fl 9 M*. From seawards they look like fireworks dancing on the land, but there are now many other lights ashore so they do not stand out so clearly. The leading lights come into transit at 215° true (SW mag), but as the entrance is narrow a yacht must not depart far from the transit and should make

16.6. The Inner Harbour, Braye Jetty and the anchorage in the shelter of the breakwater.

short tacks if the wind heads in the approach. The low light has sectors showing red from 180° to 210°; white thence to 218°, green thence to 235°. When the yacht is inside the breakwater, course may be altered to the anchorage north of Braye jetty or as required.

Harbour and Anchorage. While yachts can anchor anywhere under the protection of the breakwater, the usual anchorage is between the breakwater and Braye jetty. The water is deep off the outer arm of this jetty, but SW of this it shallows and dries out in the vicinity of the entrance to the inner harbour.

There is often an uneasy swell in the harbour, especially in NW gales, and small yachts like to go as close to the inner harbour as their draft allows in order to get less of it. For this purpose take soundings when abeam of the point where the pier bends south. There are a few moorings for local craft, and when anchoring be sure to leave plenty of room for vessels to berth alongside Braye jetty. The holding ground varies, consisting of sand or mud or rock and weed in places. A fisherman anchor with plenty of scope of chain (heavy or aided by a weight on the chain) holds best and the anchor should have a trip line. In strong winds or gales it is very gusty close under the lee of breakwater and yachts sheer around considerably and require plenty of swinging room. Those with rope alone or with inadequate ground tackle or on poor holding ground, sometimes drag on others. An anchor light should be exhibited at night. It is proposed to lay moorings for visiting yachts on trots to the N and W of Braye jetty, secure enough to use in almost any weather conditions.

The holding ground on the bank ½ cable NE of Braye jetty in 4m5 or more is said to be better in bad weather than near the breakwater. Some cruising men prefer to anchor on the SE side of Braye jetty. Here private moorings of unspecified holding quality have been laid but there is still room to anchor, if necessary to seaward of them.

The anchorages are well protected in all directions except NE, to which they are exposed, but northerly winds and also SW and westerly gales cause a surge. During W to NW gales the seas sometimes break in a spectacular manner over the breakwater, as is shown by the photograph taken from the author's yacht on one such occasion many years ago. In bad weather from the NE yachts will find the least uncomfortable position in the harbour is to be found in Braye Bay under the lee of the land between Fort Albert and Roselle Point, S or SW of Toulouse Rock in 2m0 to 3m0 or even SSE at neaps, or alongside in the Inner Harbour.

The Inner Harbour (Little Crabby Harbour). This is small and dries out 0m9 to 3m0. It is reserved for local craft, except for refuelling and water or by special permission of the Harbour Master. The narrow entrance should be approached from north and nothing E of 200° true to avoid the rocks drying 3m5 to 4m3 off the NE side of the entrance.

The Old Harbour is situated about 2 cables south of the outer end of Braye Jetty. It is protected by a short pier with rocks on its north side. The harbour dries out 2m4 to 4m6 on sand. Yachts can dry out (by permission) along the south side of the pier and multi-hullers or twin keelers or yachts fitted with legs can dry out on the sand. It is pretty and convenient for going ashore.

Longy Bay. In westerly and northerly winds anchorage may be found in Longy Bay on the NE side of Alderney in 2m0 to 4m0. Allow for the strong stream across the approach and avoid the rock (dries 0m3) in the middle of the entrance. Longy is not a port of entry but is a pleasant anchorage, with a good restaurant ashore. It is a 1¾ mile walk to St Anne's or Braye, but may be useful if late on the tide. If sailing on to Braye a good time to leave is −1 h Dover (+4 h St Helier).

Facilities. In Alderney (Braye) Harbour land from the anchorage at the Braye jetty steps or (with sufficient rise of tide over the rocks) at the dinghy slip SW of the steps. Allow plenty of painter to allow for the large range of tide. Immigration laws are the same as for UK. Report arrival and intended departure to the Harbour Master, who is also the Customs Officer. His office is the square white building near the dinghy slip as also is the Alderney Sailing Club which welcomes visitors and provides showers, teas and Saturday suppers. Mainbrayce Ltd., nearby at the entrance of the inner harbour, are yacht chandlers where with sufficient rise of tide yachts can go alongside the quay for diesel fuel and fresh water by hose. The company is an active concern, undertaking hull, rigging and engine repairs and yacht care, and supplying charts, books and sailing clothes as well as chandlery. The ferry launch provides yacht to shore service (hoist a bucket up the mast to summon). Provisions and their delivery can be arranged and sailing and motor dinghies hired, as also moorings when permission has been granted to lay them.

Water for filling cans is available at the tap outside the men's lavatory near the steps at Braye jetty or at the Sapper slipway. Petrol and oil at warehouse opposite the Diver's Inn just beyond the Old Harbour and groceries at Jean's store. Restaurant at Seaview Hotel or Harbour Lights Hotel $\frac{1}{4}$ mile first turning left to New Town.

The dairy is at the town of St Anne's $\frac{1}{2}$ mile up-hill on the main road. Here there is a doctor and cottage hospital and pubs, hotels, banks, garages, shops, PO together with all the facilities of a small town. Early closing day is Wednesday and during the season hotels (as also at Braye) often require reservation in advance for dinner.

Small cargo vessels run twice weekly to Guernsey, and there are frequent air services to Southampton, Cherbourg, Guernsey, Jersey and thence to Dinard. Alderney is a free and easy little place and there are interesting walks along the coast.

17 Guernsey

High Water at St Peter Port: −4 h 31 m Dover (+0 h 16 m St Helier). **Heights above Datum:** MHWS 9m0. MLWS 1m0. MHWN 6m7. MLWN 3m5.
Tidal Stream to SW in Little Russel begins −1 h 20 m Dover (+3 h 25 m St Helier), and to NE +4 h 40 m Dover (−2 h 33 m St Helier); in the Great Russel 5 minutes later. See Tidal Maps for other streams.
Yacht Clubs: Royal Channel Islands YC and Guernsey YC.

St Peter Port, which is the only large deep water harbour in Guernsey, is popular as it offers good shore facilities for yachtsmen and provides a most convenient port of call, especially for those bound for Brittany. It is also the commercial port which handles the passenger service and cargo produce for the island. The deep water area is very limited especially at spring tides and the harbour is crowded during the season by the ever increasing number of yachts. In order to relieve the problem the old, inner harbour has been dredged and converted into a marina. There is also a marina close south of Fort Doyle at Beaucette Quarry in the NE corner of Guernsey, and the principally commercial harbour of St Sampson where yachts can dry out alongside the quay. Guernsey provides an interesting centre for local cruising as there are numbers of anchorages available in settled weather and offshore winds on the south coast of the island and nearby at Herm and Sark.

The usual approach to St Peter Port is by the Little Russel channel which is not difficult in clear weather, but can be rough if there is a fresh wind against the tide, which is very fast at springs. Alternatively the Great Russel (Chapter 18) is used for approach, although here also streams are strong and there are overfalls.

When coming from England to visit Guernsey for the first time there is much to be said for leaving the island to the east, and approaching St Peter Port from the south. When approaching from the west, the southabout entrance is not only easier but probably quicker, especially if, on approaching the west of the island, it should be between low water and half tide up (local tide Guernsey), as at this time the tide will serve right up to the harbour especially by keeping close to the east coast of Guernsey after passing St Martin's Point. In case of very poor visibility it is quite essential to take the southern route as the west and north west coast from the Hanois light to the Platte Fougère light is a maze of rocks to a distance of two miles from the coast with strong tides running through them, which makes this landfall unwise without special local knowledge.

Approach from the North

The island of Guernsey is about 90 metres high all along the south coast, and slopes down practically to sea level (with a few exceptions) all along the north coast. As a result, seen from the northern approach, the land is frequently not picked up as soon as the higher contours of Sark (114 m) and Herm (70 m).

The Herm group of islands, islets and rocks extends from the Grande Amfroque at the northerly end, to the Lower Heads buoy at the southerly end, a distance of about $5\frac{1}{2}$ miles, and divides the Great Russel from the Little Russel, which latter is the direct entrance to St Peter Port harbour. This whole group will appear as more or less one island when first picked up from the north.

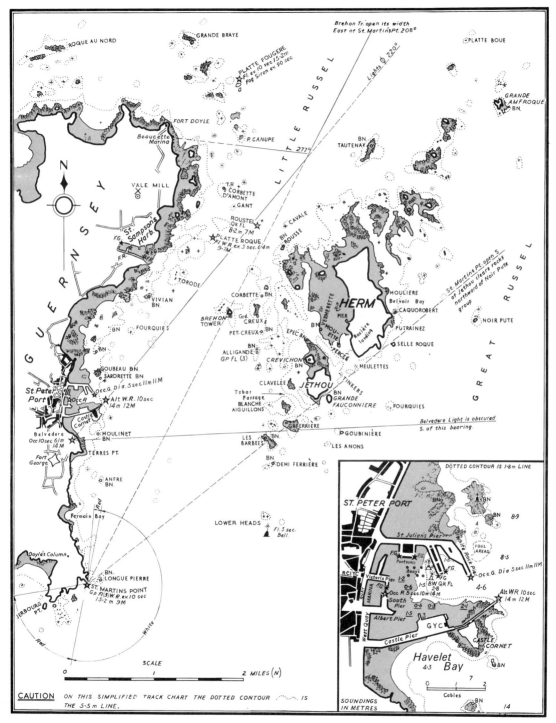

Guernsey, Little Russel and Herm: (Based on British Admiralty Chart No. 3400 with the permission of the Controller of HM Stationery Office and of the Hydrographer of the Navy.)

Guernsey

17.1. The Grande Amfroque is the first port-hand mark approaching the Little Russel and is left well to port. Note the resemblance to the Casquets. *A. J. Barber.*

17.2. Platte Fougère Lighthouse (starboard).

17.3. Tautenay (port).

17.6. Rousse (far to port).

17.5. Roustel (to port). *A. J. Barber.*

17.4. Brehon Tower (far to port).

17.7. Corbette D'Amont (starboard).

17.8. Platte Roque Light Tower (starboard).

17.9. Vivian Beacon (starboard).

17.10. Belvedere House (leading mark).

The Little Russel

On approaching the north of the Little Russel the first starboard-hand mark is Platte Fougère Lighthouse, white with a black waistband, 15m high (*Fl ev 10 sec 12 m. Siren ev 93 sec*). This stands in the sea 1 mile NE of the most north-easterly point of Guernsey. *Note.* Do not let the Platte Fougère bear anything east of due south (mag), or come on with the island of Jethou (which is about the same thing).

The first port-hand mark is the most northerly island of the Herm group called Grande Amfroque, with two stone towers (white, unlighted).

The second port-hand mark is the Tautenay Tower, BWVS (unlighted). The harbour leading lights clear to the west of this about ½ mile and rather more from the Amfroque, but as these are not easily seen in the daytime take as a leading mark Bréhon Tower open its width east of the extremity of St Martin's Point (the SE corner of Guernsey). If you are approaching from due north as from the Casquets you will not be so far east as this and will come on with the leading marks lower down the Russel, but if approaching from the NE, as from the Race of Alderney, this Amfroque may be a close port-hand mark and here is an important point. *Note.* Platte Boue (dries 1m8 LAT), 8 cables NNW of Grande Amfroque, is the most northerly rock of the Herm group and the two Grande Amfroque towers in line lead on to it. It is cleared by ½ mile by the harbour leading lights and by 1 mile with St Martin's Point bearing 208°, and Bréhon Tower open its own width on the port bow. This is very important in approaching with light breeze, as the ebb tide sets very strongly towards the Amfroque.

The next port-hand marks are: Roustel Tower, BW chequered (*Qk Fl 8m vis 7 miles*) and, farther south, Bréhon Tower, 17m1 high, roundish in shape and so fat as to have a silhouette practically square, unlighted, should now be seen between the islands of Guernsey and Herm and just open east of St Martin's Point (SE point of Guernsey). As Roustel is approached it will come in line with Bréhon and will both be port-hand marks. Roustel has plenty of water quite close up, but Bréhon Tower has a half-tide ridge of rocks from W to N of it and about 1½ cables away.

When coming up with Roustel you will see away to port a large conical rock with a black cross on it, the Rouse (unimportant now) but to starboard two black towers, both important because they both have outlying low-tide rocks on their E sides. First the Corbette d'Amont, tower unlighted, black, and farther south the Platte, black tower with red top (*Fl WR ev 3 sec 6m, 7 and 5M*) (light sectors will be mentioned in night approach). *Note.* Gant, awash at low water, nearly half-way from Corbette d'Amont to Roustel and just S of a line joining them.

Before this you will have come on with the leading harbour lights which pass less than a cable from Roustel. The lower one is the South Breakwater Lighthouse (*Alt WR 14m vis 12 M*). The upper one is Belvedere House (white), which is not easily seen in the afternoon when the sun is over the town; but this does not matter as, having passed Roustel, you are all clear to port with the exception of Bréhon Tower with its already mentioned half-tide rocks and after that open water, while for the starboard-hand the Platte tower on with Corbette d'Amont or Platte Fougère will lead well clear of all the small rocks off St Sampson's harbour (the entrance to which is south of the Platte). When Bréhon Tower has come on to the south of Herm all the small rocks to the SE of St Sampson's (the Torode patch) will have been passed, Vivian (BW) tower being to starboard at this point.

At the entrance steer near the North Pier, as the watchman on it will hail you for the yacht's name and probably give instructions through the loud hailer. See St Peter Port Harbour, page 106. When entering keep a sharp look out for mail steamers and other vessels entering or leaving.

By night. Platte Fougère, *Fl ev 10 sec 15m, vis 12 M.* Hanois, *Gp Fl (2) 5 sec, 30m vis 16 M, horn (2) 60 sec.* Sark Lighthouse, *Fl, ev 15 sec, 65m, vis 21 M, horn (2) 30 sec.* Bearings on these lights will give an accurate fix till Hanois and Sark are lost at about 2 miles north of Platte Fougère. When approaching from the NW, keep Sark light visible to clear north of the Grandes Brayes.

Roustel, *Qk Fl, vis 7 M*, should then be brought on with St Martin's Light (white sector) *Gp Fl (3) WR ev 10 sec, 15m, horn (3) 30 sec.* This line will cross from the red to the white of the Platte beacon (starboard-hand mark), *Fl WR ev 3 sec, 6m, vis 7 and 5 M*, at a point about $1\frac{1}{2}$ miles NNE of Roustel, having Platte Fougère just less than a mile on a bearing about 286° true (WNW mag). This mark (Roustel on St Martin's) leads down a line slightly west of the leading lights of St Peter Port Harbour.

Upper Belvedere Light, which is just N of Belvedere House and close to it, *occulting 10 sec white*; Lower Breakwater Light, *alt WR 10 sec 12 miles*, with which it will converge at about 3 cables N of Roustel (port-hand mark) the line of the leading marks at 220° passing less than a cable west of it.

When approaching from the NE the leading lights will naturally be brought on before the Roustel–St Martin's mark. It is important to bring the harbour leading lights on before the Platte Fougère bears more than 245° true in order to be well clear of the Platte boue, off the NW of Grande Amfroque. *Note.* The red sector of the Platte beacon covers all the rocks on the west side of the Little Russel, both north and south of itself *with the exception of* two boues awash at MLWS, one of them 2 cables NE, the other 1 cable due E of the light itself.

Harbour Lights. North Pier (White rock), *G Occ 5 sec.* South Pier (Castle Breakwater), *alt WR 10 sec 12 miles.* Inner Harbour South Pierhead, *R Occ.* Steamer Jetty has small *green lights* on its SW and SE corner. Enter when red inner light comes between North and South pier heads.

West of the Island
(*Admiralty Chart 3400*)
The Hanois Lighthouse, standing on rocks about a mile west of Pleinmont Point at the SW of the island, is cleared on its SE, S, and SW sides by a distance of a $\frac{1}{4}$ mile. To the NNW of it stand the Mauve Rocks (6m7 high) and to the W and NW of these are numerous low patches and $\frac{3}{4}$ mile north of it the Banc des Hanois.

When approaching to round this lighthouse anywhere from the north keep the lighthouse open to the westward of Les Trois Pères (three large black rocks) 1 mile to the NE of it. (These will be seen between Lihou Island and the lighthouse.) This clearing mark coincides with bearing 201° true as marked on the chart and *just* clears W of all the rocks N and NW of Lihou Island, which forms the NW corner of Guernsey, but does not clear the Banc des Hanois, to clear which the lighthouse will have to be bearing 146° true. On this bearing the Mauve Rocks come on with the lighthouse. Give the Mauve Rocks a berth of half a mile till due west of the lighthouse; then all is clear.

Of course all this interesting part can be avoided by just keeping an offing of 4 miles all the way round. It is not advisable to try cutting inside the lighthouse without local knowledge aboard!

17.11. Les Hanois Lighthouse on the SW of Guernsey with Les Mauve rocks to the left of the picture. It is near low water. *A. J. Barber.*

17.12. St Martins lighthouse from the NE. Longue Pierre beacon and rocks lie about $1\frac{1}{2}$ cables east (mag) of the lighthouse and are out of this picture.

Approach from the Southward

The south coast of the island is about 6 miles long running east and west and about 90 metres high all the way along, extending from Pleinmont Point at the SW to St Martin's Point at the SE. The whole of this coast between Les Hanois and St Martin's is clear of rocks at $\frac{1}{2}$ mile from the cliffs.

Just to the south of Pleinmont Point and $1\frac{1}{2}$ miles from the Hanois stands the Gull Rock, or Tas de Pois d'Aval, 21m0 high and $\frac{3}{4}$ cable from the cliff. The Hanois light on with the south tangent of this rock clears south of all rocks along the south coast, except Molière 3 cables to E of it. *Note.* When east of this rock the Hanois light is visible between it and the land and when on with the north tangent of Gull Rock clears of all rocks except those within $1\frac{1}{4}$ miles of it. This is a very close mark for the Kaines and Lieuses. The importance of this Gull Rock will be seen when discussing the night approach.

St Martin's Lighthouse is a small square white house on a rocky point at the bottom of the cliff. Longue Pierre Rock, with a post on it (P) is $1\frac{1}{2}$ cables East of this lighthouse. This is the

17.13. Longue Pierre $1\frac{1}{2}$ cables E of St Martin's Point.

17.14. Goubeau N of St Peter Port.

17.15. Sardrette SE of Goubeau.

port-hand mark of entry to the Little Russel and when kept on with Bréhon Tower leads clear to the east of all the rocks to the S of St Martin's and Jerbourg Points. A straight line from Longue Pierre beacon to the harbour breakwater lighthouse (2 miles) which passes through Anfré (black post 'A') clears east of everything up this coast to the harbour with the exception of half-tide rocks a cable or less just to the SE and south of Castle Cornet. To clear these keep 2 cables from Castle Cornet by having Goubeau (small black tower ¼ mile N of the harbour), a good sail's-breadth open of the Castle breakwater. Get this mark on when abreast of Terres Point and the Bathing Pool.

The starboard-hand mark of entry is the Lower Heads buoy (*Fl ev 5 sec Bell*), 2¼ miles E by north of St Martin's Point. This buoy is 2 cables SE of the Têtes d'Aval or Lower Heads Rocks (awash at MLWS). *Note*. The flood sets very strongly to the NE over these rocks. There can be nasty overfalls here in strong tide against wind.

From the Lower Heads the Ferrières run about due north up to Jethou, well marked by the Demi Ferrière Post ('M') which has 1 cable to its west side a boue called Musé (dries 1m5). Les Barbées Post (black post with barrel on a big rock), and Blanche Aiguillon, unmarked (close up to Jethou).

From a cable or two westward of this line all is clear up to the harbour.

By night. There are no lights on the south coast of Guernsey, except on the west Les Hanois (*Gp Fl (2) 5 sec 30m 16 M. Horn (2) 60 sec*) and to the east St Martin's (*Gp Fl (3) WR 10 sec 15M Nautophone (3) ev ½ min*). The latter has red sectors covering the landward side north and south of itself and a white sector extending from about SSW round to about north north-east.

Approaching from the westward a stranger will prefer to keep well away from the coast by cross bearings on these lights. It may be noted, however, that by keeping just in the red sector of St Martin's light, all dangers west of Lieuses rocks (nearly half-way along the coast) are avoided and by keeping Hanois Light open of (unobscured by) Pleinmont Pt, the Lieuses and all dangers east of them will be avoided, and the yacht will enter the white sector of St Martin's Light about 2 miles to the south, and may then alter course towards the light. As mentioned before the Hanois Light will be occluded by the Gull Rock when the yacht crosses the transit and will reappear again between the rock and the land.

When finally approaching St Martin's Point in the white sector the lighthouse must be given a berth of 1½ cables to the eastward to clear Longue Pierre rock. Open White Rock (North Pier) lighthouse east of Castle Cornet to clear Longue Pierre and all dangers up to and including Anfré. North of this the eastern edge of the northerly red sector of St Martin's Light covers all rocks up the coast to the harbour.

Approaching from the SE direction, if the NE tide is running, or about to run, especially at Springs, keep right on to St Martin's Light until the Lower Heads buoy bears about NE.

St Peter Port Harbour

A red square flag by day or red light by night at the signal station on the north pier-end prohibits entry of vessels. In the absence of these signals, yachts should enter on the starboard hand to report and receive berthing instructions from the signal station. Sometimes they are directed alongside a quay temporarily for Customs clearance if from foreign countries, but usually they are directed to moorings in the Pool, or, with sufficient rise of tide, to the marina in the old harbour. Anchoring is not allowed other than with the permission of the Harbour Master.

17.16. Entering St Peter Port. Yachts report at the signal station when entering and then proceed as may be directed to temporary moorings on the north side of the harbour or to the marina in the Old Harbour in the middle of the picture below the church spire. *J. Tucker*.

It will be noted from the chart that most of the area available in the Pool for yacht moorings dries out at LAT, but this is a pessimistic datum as at ordinary low water there is 1m0 more at MLWS and at Neaps no less than 3m5 above datum. The yachts and craft to be seen in the SW part of the harbour are all on private moorings.

The visitor's moorings in the Pool consist of six large yellow buoys on the north side of the Harbour to which yachts moor fore and aft and a pontoon to lie alongside. These are for use prior to entry into the marina. The pontoon and the inner buoys dry out at LAT and the outer ones lie in 0m9 least water. Fuel (but not petrol on Sundays) and fresh water is available with sufficient rise of tide at Castle Emplacement on the south side of the harbour, where there is a marine engineer and yacht repairs can be arranged. There is a pontoon for tenders at the foot of steps on N side of the entrance to the marina.

In the Old Harbour Marina there are pontoons providing alongside berths some of which are reserved for visiting yachts. A barrier of 1m9 (height 4m2 above LAT chart datum) has been built across the entrance to maintain 1m8 depth within. The entrance is closed for approximately 3 hours either side of low water. The depth over the barrier is clearly shown by the tide gauges on each side. Water is available on the pontoons and there are rubbish bins, toilet and washing facilities nearby.

The only outside anchorage for yachts at St Peter Port lies in Havelet Bay immediately south of the harbour. It is entered from east between the beacons on Oyster rocks on the north and Moulinet on the south. There are private yacht moorings at the north of the bay and plenty of room to anchor in the centre in from 2m1 to 1m1 LAT. The anchorage is a fair weather one, sheltered from WSW through W to N, but even so swell sometimes creeps in towards high water.

Customs regulations at St Peter Port are much the same as for British Ports. Facilities are

Guernsey

17.17. The entrance to the marina as seen from the temporary moorings while waiting for sufficient rise of tide.

17.18. Entering the marina. Light structure and tide gauge in metres on sides of entrance. Visitor's pontoons are on the south side within the marina, but berthing attendants give directions.

excellent. There are many hotels and restaurants and very good shops of all kinds, including yacht chandlers. David Bowker at Pier Steps is a Class A Chart Agent and also stocks French Charts, nautical books, instruments, etc. The Royal Channel Islands Yacht Club is hospitable and faces the Victoria Pier on the N side of the marina, and the clubhouse of the Guernsey YC lies just east of the model yacht pond on Castle Pier. MF and VHF radio is available at the Signal Station, and local weather forecasts can be obtained from Guernsey 64033. Communications by steamer to Weymouth or St Helier. Hydrofoil to St Helier and St Malo. Local services to Alderney, Herm and Sark. From Guernsey Airport there are frequent and extensive air connections.

Marina at Beaucette Quarry

The Channel Islands Yacht Marina was created by blasting a channel from the sea to a quarry about 2 cables south of Fort Doyle at the NE tip of Guernsey. The marina is deep and very well sheltered. The approach presents no particular problems in normal weather

17.19. Local craft lying on pontoons on the north side of the marina. Castle Cornet in background. *J. Tucker.*

17.20. Entering the narrow entrance of the Channel Islands Yacht Marina at Beaucette south of Fort Doyle. The picture shows the leading marks for the approach which are painted red and very conspicuous except when viewed against the sun.

with a free wind or under power and is said to be less rough than the Little Russel, but obviously it should not be attempted for the first time in strong winds between N and E, and in NE winds of no more than force 5 the entrance may be difficult as the swell sets across the narrow entrance onto the south head.

The approach from the Little Russel is made from a point approximately half-way between Platte Fougère lighthouse and the Roustel light tower. The line between them should not be crossed until the leading marks have been identified. The rock faces of the marina entrance are conspicuous from seaward as they are painted white on both sides over a large area. The front leading mark is a wide vertical red line superimposed on white on the North Head of the entrance, and the rear mark is a pole erected on the roof of the Facility Building which carries horizontal cross pieces painted red with a vertical white stripe but is difficult to see when the sun is behind it. The pole has a wind sock, and immediately to the left of the Facility Building two large greenhouses are visible. Care should be taken not to confuse the two diamond shaped submarine cable marks beside Fort Doyle with the marina marks.

Guernsey

Bring the marina leading marks in line at 277° and keep closely to their transit. This leaves to the northward: Petite Canupe dries 3m3, (marked by a beacon), Grune Pierre dries 2m1 and two black conical buoys. To the southward: Grune La Fosse, Pierre and two red can buoys. The buoys are positioned as a guide only and should not be relied upon. The approach channel, until close to the entrance, is deep except where it passes close to the rocks shown on the accompanying chart, so keep strictly to the leading marks. The tidal streams run fast across the approach, but soon weaken towards the land and there is no current within a cable of the entrance.

When 70 metres from the entrance the leading line may be left as a slight southerly deviation will be necessary to clear the North Head, NNE of which there is a rock to be marked by a beacon. Immediately after passing through the entrance channel (18 metres wide) a fairly sharp turn to the southward should be made to clear the green breakwater buoy to starboard.

The sill at the entrance dries 2m1 LAT. There is about 2m7 at half tide and at least 1m5 at MLWN. Tide gauges marked in metres are placed inside and outside the entrance channel. While awaiting rise of tide craft can moor to the red buoy being placed about 100 metres off the marina entrance, a little north of the leading line. No entry at night except by arrangement, when the leading lights will be illuminated.

Within the marina, berths are provided for yachts moored bows to buoys and sterns to pontoons, where water is laid on. Customs clearance and comprehensive facilities including fuelling point, chandlery and grocers shop, good licenced restaurant, telephones, car park etc. Bus or hire cars to St Peter Port. A small number of berths are available for visitors but it is best to reserve in advance. Telephone 45000/47071, or VHF Radio Marina Channel (157.85 mHz).

St Sampson's Harbour

The harbour dries out and yachts lie alongside the quay. There is about 3m0 in the entrance at half tide. Large scale Admiralty chart No. 262b should be used.

The approach is about ½ mile SW of the Platte beacon, between the SW Platte rocks on the north side and the Torode rocks on the south. Off the south side of the entrance is a post on Grunette rocks. Approach with the Harbourmaster's office (clock tower) in line with the south pierhead (not outer breakwater). This leads up to the pierheads. Be prepared for a strong tide setting athwart the course.

By Night the approach is on the transit of the leading lights (*FG* and *FR*) at 295° but close to the transit there are the Torode and Grunette rocks. Do not confuse the leading lights with the lights R and W on the outer piers ends.

Other Anchorages

Anchorages on the N and W of Guernsey require local knowledge, owing to the dangers in the approaches and the strong streams. However, the Admiralty publish particularly good large scale charts covering Guernsey, Herm and Sark No. 262c, 262b and 262a. No. 262c covers SW of Guernsey, and 262b the N, S and E. Note that the datum of new issue Admiralty charts will be reduced to LAT as altered in Part III of this book.

On the S coast of Guernsey there are beautiful anchorages which, in northerly winds and settled weather, are far preferable to the crowded St Peter Port, except that they provide only beach landings except on the rough slipway at Saints Bay. These are easy of access, even on the small-scale chart No. 3400, as although there are rocks in the bays, they are few

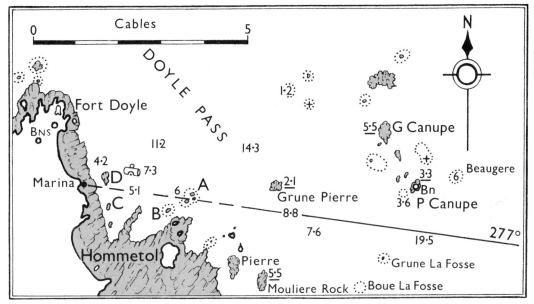

Marina at Beaucette Quarry: (Based on British Admiralty Chart No. 262b with the permission of the Controller of HM Stationery Office and of the Hydrographer of the Navy.) Soundings taken LAT 1973 by J. Tucker: A, shoal NE of Hommetol over which there is 3m0, with several heads. B, rock awash N of Hommetol. C, rock which dries 1m0, normally marked by a small conical black buoy, which lies about 20 m to south of leading line. D, rock which dries 3m7 off north head at entrance, normally marked by a stick beacon. Mooring buoy in approximately correct position.

in number and clearly marked. The first bay is marked on the chart as Petit Port, ½ mile W of St Martin's Point. Guernseymen regard the eastern corner of the bay as the Petit Port, which has some 200 precipitous steps at the landing. The western end of Moulin Huet Bay (the bay proper) offers a relatively easy ascent with few steps. Both bays need care when landing in a dinghy, as there is often an awkward swell, even in offshore winds. There is landing on sand except at high water.

Saints Bay is W of Moulin Huet Bay, but is included on the Admiralty chart under the general heading of Petit Port. It provides a summer fishing-boat anchorage with summer moorings and a rough slipway on its western side. The bay is open to the SE.

Icart Bay lies W of Icart Point and the bays just mentioned. It consists, from E to W, of La Bette Bay, Jaonnet Bay and Petit Bot Bay. The first two have extremely precipitous clambers up cliff paths and are not recommended. Petit Bot, which is stony above half tide, has a tea-room, road and a bus service. The bay is guarded by a group of rocks shown on the Admiralty charts and should be approached with caution at low water. Clearance must be obtained at St Peter Port before landing at these anchorages if coming from 'foreign', and all are subject to swell, occasionally even in offshore winds.

18 Herm, Jethou and the Great Russel

High Water and Tidal Data: See Guernsey.

Herm, originally Crown Property, now belongs to the States of Guernsey and is at present leased to a tenant. The public is allowed to land on payment of a landing fee. As the island has a rocky coast, with wide sandy bays (including the famous shell beach), it attracts many visitors, and there is a stream of speed boats between it and St Peter Port during the holiday months, principally between 11 a.m. and 6 p.m. The island is well worth seeing and has a good anchorage. There is an hotel, a tavern, and a café.

Jethou, with its two satellite islets (attached to it below half-tide mark), Crevichon to the NW and Grande Fauconnière to the SW, is still Crown property. The tenant of Jethou has opened the island to the public.

The Passe Percée

The Passe Percée, called and pronounced colloquially 'The Pershee', is the passage from the Little Russel to the Great Russel between Herm and Jethou and is navigable at all states of the tide.

The stream through this passage runs SE for nine hours from about local low water up to high water and to half tide down, and NW for three hours from half tide down to low water; that is, the SE stream begins $+2$ h Dover (-5 h 30 m St Helier) and the weaker NW stream at -1 h 05 m Dover ($+3$ h 30 m St Helier).

The easiest entry to the Percée is to the northward of Bréhon Tower, half a mile to the NE of which stands Corbette Beacon, black post with a white circular top. In order to clear the sunken rocks to the N of Bréhon Tower keep this beacon well down to the Herm Pier, and then passing quite close to the S of the beacon keep it on with the Vale Mill (the tallest tower on NE Guernsey), which must be allowed to come twice its own width open to the S of Corbette. This mark will lead between two black posts in the Percée, the northerly one Vermerette (V), the southerly one Epec (E) and also, past them, to the S of the Rocher Percée, or Gate Rock (2m1 high) which is the southerly point of all the rocks on the north side of the passage west of Herm. The southerly spur of this rock, which is covered above half-tide, is absolutely sheer to 8m2 deep on its S side and has one part of it flattened rather like an old-fashioned milestone with a hole some inches in diameter through the top.

Legend has it that in prehistoric times this was a gatepost, as there are still in existence some ancient field gates in Guernsey consisting of two stone posts with holes in the tops for a spar to pass through. As, even today, the LWS outline of Herm includes this Gate Rock and also an area of beach and rocks on its west side nearly as large as the island itself the opinion is held by some that it was a boat mooring in ancient times when the sea level was lower—or perhaps the islands higher. There is some considerable evidence along the coasts of Guernsey in favour of this theory, as for instance the peat beds on the north coast which suggest the presence of forest at a time not so very far back geologically.

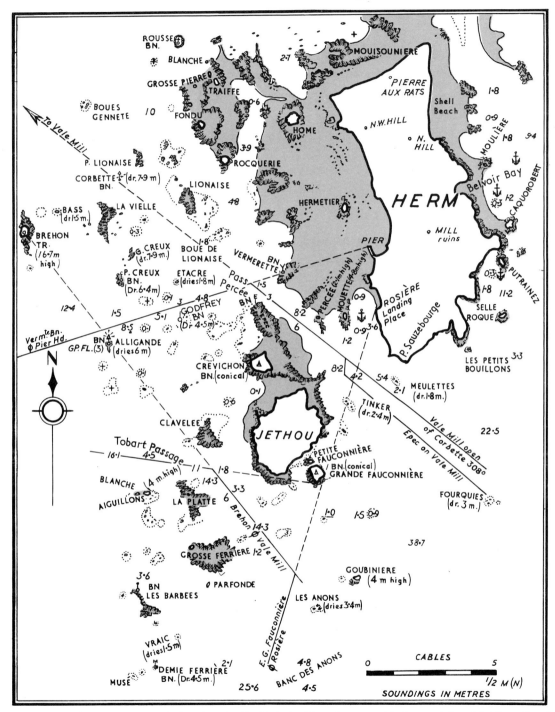

Herm, Jethou and Great Russel: (Based on British Admiralty Chart No. 3400 with the permission of the Controller of HM Stationery Office and of the Hydrographer of the Navy.)

Herm, Jethou and the Great Russel

18.1. Vale Mill, on Guernsey, the principal landmark.

18.2. Corbette Beacon with Vale Tower open twice its own width S of beacon leads through the Passe Percée.

18.3. Vermerette beacon on N of Passe Percée.

18.4. Epec Beacon on S of Passe Percée.

After leaving the Gate Rock to port a second big rock, Mouette, 4m9 high, will be seen to the eastward. Between this and the Rosière landing steps is the anchorage, and Herm Harbour is ¼ mile north. Both are described later.

Continuing on the transit through the Percée, there are no outstanding rocks between Rosière and the Point of Herm (Pointe Sauzebourge); but half a cable to the S of this are the Meulettes (dry 1m8), and 2 cables to the SW of these are the Tinkers (dry 2m4) (near the NE of Jethou). To pass between them keep the Epec beacon on with the Vale Mill. When St Martin's Point comes open of the Grande Fauconnière (see photo. No. 11) you are well clear to the SE of both of these.

Alternative Approach to Passe Percée

Going back now to the Little Russel, the approach to the Percée which is more often used lies between some large rocks to the SE of Bréhon Tower; these are (from N to S) Grand Creux (dries 7m9), unmarked, Petit Creux (dries 6m4) black post 'C'), Alligande (dries 6m0), black post 'A'), on which there is now a light *Gp Fl (3) ev 5 sec*.

Pass between these posts nearer to Alligande and immediately pick up Vermerette beacon and keep it on with the white end of Herm pier. For the next three cables the passage is narrow at low tide and marks must be kept dead on, leaving the Godfrey Beacon (top mark GB) ½ cable to the southward. This beacon lies midway between Alligande and Epec. If Alligande rock is exposed not more than 2m1 there will be at least 2m4 of water over everything in the triangle formed by this leading mark and the previously mentioned one of Vale Mill and Corbette, and a line drawn through the W side of Petit Creux and E side of Grand Creux.

Bear to starboard N of the Epec beacon when Vale Mill becomes twice its width open S of the Corbette beacon, and proceed through Passe Percée as before, or to Rosière anchorage.

18.5. Petit Creux beacon, N side of alternative approach.

18.6. Alligande beacon, S side of alternative approach.

18.7. Corbette Post at Little Russel entrance of Passe Percée, looking SE between Herm and Jethou. *A. J. Barber.*

18.8. The Percées, looking east. *A. J. Barber.*

18.9. The southerly spur of Rocher Percée (The Gate Rock). Photograph taken from author's *Cohoe I.*

18.10. Jethou with Crevichon from Passe Percée, showing the house built by Sir Compton Mackenzie. Photograph taken from near Epec beacon facing SE near low water.

Rosière Anchorage and Herm Harbour

The anchorage off the Rosière steps is virtually a landlocked pool below half tide. The holding ground is indifferent and it is open to the SE and at local high water there is a SE going tide which is quite strong at Springs, rendering the anchorage uncomfortable even in a light breeze from this quarter, until the sands to the northward dry out. If remaining in the anchorage at night remember that it would be tricky to navigate the unlit Percée in darkness, if this should be necessitated by a change of weather.

Herm Harbour, 3 cables N of Rosière landing is not ideal for yachts, as it is very small and dries out so that it can only be used by yachts above half tide when there is about 1 metre depth. It is then crowded by motor boats, but it is often used by Guernsey yachtsmen for an evening sail to the harbour and dinner ashore. When the Vermerette Rock is just awash there is about 1m0 of water at the pierhead. There are leading marks with white drums, the upper and more easterly being situated at the south end of a long field. The drums are very

18.11. The anchorage off the Rosière Steps. On the left of the picture is the Grande Fauconnière, in centre is Jethou and to the right the Mouette rocks. The anchorage is between these rocks and the steps, or north of them. The Passe Percée lies between the Mouettes and Jethou.

18.12. Herm Harbour near high water. It dries out at low tide, as also the sands $\frac{1}{2}$ mile seaward. During the holiday season the harbour is usually crowded until late evening.

close together, so that the slightest deviation from their transit makes a considerable difference to the yachts' position. When approaching on these leading marks with the Vermerette Rock awash or covered the higher, and more easterly, drum should be kept one diameter to the north of the lower drum, in order to avoid being set south on a flat-topped rock on the sandbank which has to be crossed to reach the harbour. The rock is only just south of the transit of the two drums in line. By keeping the drums just open this rock is avoided, but in the outer approach, if the yacht is northward of the exact line of the drums, the Etacre may be crossed. If the Vermerette is awash it will not matter, as there will then be plenty of water over the Etacre which dries only 1m8. Thus the drum leading marks are useful for clearing Vermerette with sufficient rise of tide, but they should not be used for entering the Passe Percée near low water, because they are almost striking marks for the Etacre and rocks SW of it, which would be dangerous at that state of the tide.

Lights will be placed on these drum beacons if application is made at the White House Hotel or the Mermaid Tavern. Guernsey yachtsmen often return after having had dinner in Herm, with the aid of these lights and the light on Alligande beacon, but strangers are not recommended to make this passage at night.

East Coast of Herm

The east coast of Herm is fairly clean up to Belvoir Bay (a mile from the Point of Herm), the only rocks being very large and all more or less attached to the coast with the exception of La Selle, or Saddle Rock, an islet which has a clear passage inside it. Having passed the Meulettes, keep St Martin's Point just open of the Grande Fauconnière until Belvoir Bay opens up to the northward of Caquorobert, a big square rock close to the shore.

In fine weather Belvoir is a good spot to spend a night round about Neap tides. Here all is clear sand though shallow. Anchor opposite the middle of the south side of the small steep bay on a line between Caquorobert and Moulière. Moulière is the rocky islet on the north side of the bay and is joined to the land at LWS. This anchorage will give about 3m0 on a really neap tide, but of course dries out on big springs. One cable E of Moulière will give about 2m1 even at LAT but will be in the tide.

If the wind is NW, there is another good anchorage just S of Putrainez, which is the big slug-shaped rock sticking out from the land between the Saddle and Caquorobert. The south side of this is clean quite close to with about the same water as the other anchorage.

To the north of Belvoir Bay the numerous rocks and strong currents make it inadvisable to explore without local knowledge on board. This also applies to the west coast of Herm.

As a point of interest Caquorobert is said to mean Robert's helmet, and to have been so named by the monks of Mont St Michel to whom this island was given by Robert, Duke of Normandy, father of William the Conqueror.

The Tobart (or Tobar) Passage

The Tobart Passage is between the south of Jethou and the Ferrières. Coming from the Little Russel enter about $1\frac{1}{2}$ cables N of the Blanche Aiguillon (Rocks 1m2 and 4m0 high), the NW corner of the Ferrières. At this point you are S of the leading marks, but steer with the south tip of Grande Fauconnière* just open of the south tip of Jethou. This leads south of the south-westerly boue of Clavelée (just to the west of the south end of Jethou). (If Clavelée is awash or covered there is plenty of water over its south-westerly boue.) When Vale Mill comes into line with Bréhon Tower keep the marks dead on until Herm opens up to the E of Grande Fauconnière.

Notes. (1) Goubinière, large loaf-shaped rock, 4m0 high, 4 cables SE of Grande Fauconnière, with a ledge its own width projecting from its westerly side.

(2) If at low water Spring tides, keep the marks on until the Rosière landing is open E of Grand Fauconnière.

(3) There is a boue awash at LWS one-third along a line from the south corner of Grande Fauconnière to Goubinière.

(4) The leading marks of the passage are almost the striking marks for the rocks Les Anons (dry 3m4 SW of Goubinière), the marks for which are the Vale Mill on the south edge of Bréhon Tower. Cross striking mark Goubinière on Noire Pute.

The Great Russel

Entry from either N or S presents no difficulty in good visibility, as this Russel is practically devoid of covered rocks except along its NW side, that is to say the Humps. By keeping St

*Note. Local sailing instructions give the tip of the white beacon on Grande Fauconnière over the shoulder of Jethou, 100° mag.

Herm, Jethou and the Great Russel

Martin's Point open to the S of Jethou all those rocks to the N of Noire Pute group are cleared.

Noire Pute (2m1 high) is a large black rock having boues around its northerly sides up to a cable's distance. Its position is just under a mile due E of Caquorobert. Two miles SW of it is Goubinière, 4m0 high, quite clean, except its western side where the boues extend out again its own width. Between these two large rocks is the most important patch of rocks in this Russel:

The Fourquies, which dry 3m0, is a large patch over which the ebb tide runs like a mill race. Marks: Goubinière on with St Martin's lighthouse, and Epec beacon (in the Percée) on with Vale Mill. *Note.* The Vale Mill on with either south of Herm or N tangent of Jethou clears it to the NE or SW respectively by at least $1\frac{1}{2}$ cables.

The east side of the Great Russel is quite clear, being bounded by the Bec du Nez, the north point of Sark, and the island of Brecqhou, with its outstanding islet, Givaud, 13m4 high, which is clean up to 2 cables away.

The biggest overfalls in the Great Russel lie between Brecqhou and the Lower Heads buoy. There are four or five patches, the more easterly ones being the worst. The overfalls to the east of Sark right out to the Blanchard buoy can at times be as bad if not worse. These are not places to be with a lot of wind on either strong flood or ebb.

19 Sark

Heights above Datum: St Peter Port. MHWS 9m0. MLWS 1m0. MHWN 6m7. MLWN 3m5. On the east of Sark at Creux Harbour the rise is stated to be 0m6 higher MHWS, 0m3 MHWN.

Situated about 8 miles east of St Peter Port this island is a part of the Bailiwick of Guernsey and thereby is to a certain extent under Guernsey law. Nevertheless it has its own administrative body, the Court of Chief Pleas, and also a Seigneur, some of whose feudal rights have not been altered since the time of William the Conqueror.

It is considered by many the most beautiful of the Channel Islands, and though small (about 3 by $1\frac{1}{2}$ miles) its coastal scenery certainly has a dramatic quality not found elsewhere in these islands, and the visitor's pleasure is undisturbed by motor traffic, cars not being allowed on the island.

Perhaps its most startling feature is La Coupée, a place where the whole width of the island narrows to a knife-edged ridge of cliff, in places only a few feet wide, which has been built up and widened to carry the precariously perched, and only, road joining the two portions of the island—Sark and Little Sark. Standing on this one-cart-wide causeway at a height of about 75 m one can see sheer down to the sea on both sides at the same time. Even at sea level the width of the island here is only $\frac{1}{2}$ cable. From this point there is a pathway down on the west side to Grande Grève Bay, but the east side is practically sheer and scalable only by expert climbers.

Another spot which has to be seen to be believed is the Creux Harbour, which gives one the slightly unreal impression of a film set. It is a tiny rock-bound cove in the middle of the east coast protected by a pier and sheltered outside by grass-covered islands, the Burons. As the cliffs surrounding the harbour are nearly sheer, a tunnel has been bored through the solid rock leading to the bottom of a valley which runs up to the middle of the island. Just to the north of this old harbour the new jetty, in Maseline Bay, has been built which is joined to the same valley by another tunnel.

To complete the bizarre, on the west coast the island of Brecqhou is separated from Sark by the Gouliot Pass, which is only 70 metres wide, a clear cut gash between the islands, yet so high are the cliffs that a small coastal steamer could easily pass underneath the telephone wire which is stretched across it.

The water round Sark is deep and most of the above-water rocks quite sheer, but many are covered at high water and the tides are very strong and the range great, which produces the bad overfalls in some places. Even in fine weather these must be avoided at spring tides. The position of the principal races is marked on the chart.

The East Coast

Coastal Stream along the land on NE coast runs SE for $8\frac{1}{2}$ hours commencing $+6$ h Dover (-1 h 30 m St Helier). Off Bec du Nez at extreme north of island NE stream begins about HW Dover ($+5$ h St Helier) and the SW stream at about $+6$ h Dover (-1 h St Helier). On the SE coast the SW stream (very weak) starts at -2 h 10 m Dover ($+2$ h 35 m St Helier) and the NE stream begins $+2$ h 45 m Dover (-4 h 30 m St Helier). Farther seaward there is an eddy or slack water off NE of Sark during NE stream in Great Russel.

Sark

On the east coast there are three precipitous and grass-capped islets with navigable passages between them and the island. The two northerly ones, Petite Moie 17 m high and Grande Moie 27 m high, are close together and immediately visible on rounding the north of Sark. The third isle, the Burons 20 m, exactly opposite the Creux Harbour, will be hidden by Pointe Robert, on which the lighthouse stands, until the Pécheresse is passed.

The north point of Sark named Bec Du Nez may be passed on the N and NW sides at a distance of 1 cable. Three cables to the E of it is Pécheresse (dries 8m2 at HW springs),

19.1. The Noire Pierre near low water. The Burons just open of Pointe Robert with this rock in the gap clears dangers NE of Sark. The rock may be passed on either side.

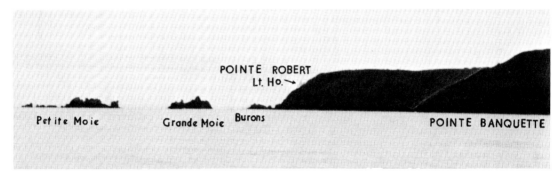

18.2. The Burons just clear of the land.

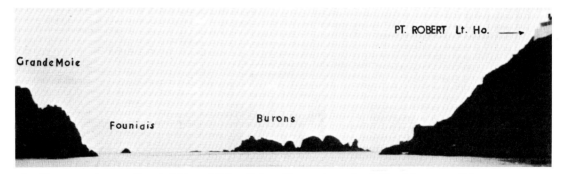

18.3. The passage between Grande Moie and Pointe Robert. Keep rather to land side of the centre of the passage.

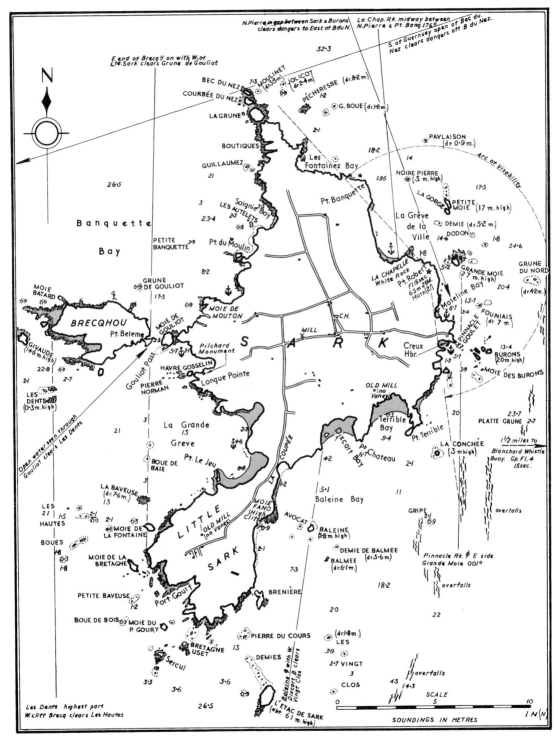

N

N.Pierre in gap between Sark & Burons   La.Chap.Rk.midway between   clears dangers to East of Bdu N.   N.Pierre & Pt.Banq.17·0
S. of Guernsey open of Bec du
Nez clears dangers off B du Nez

32·3

E.end of Brecqᵁ on with W.of
Lte.Sark clears Grune de Gouliot

BEC DU NEZ   MOULINET 7·3   JOLICOT
COURBÉE DU NEZ   (41·5m.)   (dr.2·4m.)
                PÉCHERESSE (dr.8·2m.)
LA GRUNE   ·2
                            G. BOUE (dr.1·8m.)

BOUTIQUES   Les   2·1
GUILLAUMEZ   Fontaines Bay   PAVLAISON
21   18·2   14   (dr 0·9 m.)   Arc of Visibility
3   Saignie   Pt. Banquette   NOIRE PIERRE
LES AUTELETS   1·95   (3 m. high)   17·3
23·4   2·7   LA GORGE   PETITE
Banquette   Pt. du Moulin   La Greve   MOIE (17 m. high)
PETITE   3·9   de la   DEMIE (dr.5·2 m.)
Bay   BANQUETTE   8·2   Ville   14·6   DODON   1·8   24·6
GRUNE   0·3 DE GOULIOT   LA CHAPELLE   5·2   GRANDE MOIE   GRUNE
17·3   MOIE DE   White Rock   (2·7 m.)   DU NORD
MOIE   GRUNE DE   MOUTON   Pt. Robert   20·4   20·4
BATARD   Fl.5sec.   MASELINE   (dr.4·2m.)
                6·5·21M   13·7   Bay
MOIE DE   CH.   Horn(21)   2·4   FOUNIAIS
BRECQHOU   GOULIOT   MILL   6·7   PINNACLE   (dr. 7 m.)
Pt. Beleme   Creux   GOULET   13·4
GIVAUDE   Pilchard   S A R K   Hbr.   1·2   BURONS
(4·6 m.high)   5·7 2·1 Monument   (20m.high)
22·8   2·7   HAVRE GOSSELIN   3·9   MOIE DES BURONS
2·1   PIERRE   Longue Pointe   OLD MILL
LES   NORMAN   (no Vanes)   PLATTE GRUNE 2·7
DENTS   3   La Grande   20   23·7
(0·3m.high)   13   Terrible
   Greve   Bay   1½ miles to
   BOUE DE   5·4   LA CONCHÉE   Blanchard Whistle
   BAIE   Pt. Le Jeu   Pt. Terrible   (3 m high)   Buoy. Gp.Fl.4
   3   LA BAVEUSE   15sec.
LES   (dr.7·6 m.)   4·2   6·7 Chateau   2·4   overfalls
21   13   MOIE   5·1   GRIPE
HAUTES   FANO   Baleine Bay   11   2·9
2·1   (High   Cliff)   AVOCAT   overfalls
BOUES   MOIE DE   Chateau   BALEINE   Pinnacle Rk. $ E side
   LA FONTAINE   L I T T L E   2·1   (5·8 m.high)   Grande Moie 001°
   (no Vanes)   DEMIE DE BALMEE
MOIE DE LA   S A R K   7·3   (dr.3·6m.)   overfalls
BRETAGNE   BALMEE
PETITE BAVEUSE   (dr.6·1m.)   18·2
   BRENIÈRE   20   22
BOUE DE BOIS   MOIE DU   PIERRE DU COURS   (dr.1·8m.)   overfalls
   P. GOURY   LES   14·3
BRETAGNE   13   3·9   SCALE
USET   DEMIES   2·7 VINGT   5
Sercul   3·6   3   0   10
   CLOS   4·3
3·3   3·6   3·6   SOUNDINGS IN METRES   1 N(N)
   26·5   L.ÉTAC DE SARK

Les Dents highest part
W.cliff Brecq. clears Les Hautes

19.4. *Right to left*: Base of Pointe Robert right, the jetty at La Maseline and the Burons.

19.5. Founiais Rock, the photograph was taken from SE when sailing seaward in the passage between the rock and the Burons.

which has several boues around it. Moulinet (dries 3m3) and Jolicot (dries 2m4) lie NW between it and Bec du Nez and Grande Boue (dries 1m8) is 1½ cables E of it. To clear to the N of all these keep the South of Guernsey open of the Bec du Nez.

To the SE of Pécheresse are the Petite Moie and Grande Moie already mentioned. Three cables NW of Petite Moie is Noire Pierre, 3m0 high, a black pillar-shaped rock. Keep Guernsey open until the whole of the Burons have just opened clear of the land. At this point the Noise Pierre will come into the gap. Keep this mark, on leaving Pavlaison (dries 0m9) a cable to port, and pass either inside or outside Noire Pierre, which is quite clean, as also is the land opposite to it (Point Banquette).

After passing Noire Pierre keep the E side of the Burons in the middle of the Grande Moie passage in order to pass inside Demie (dries 5m1), a rock just S of Petite Moie.

The passage between Grande Moie and Pointe Robert, the Lighthouse, is 140 metres wide but looks much narrower, owing to the height of the cliffs. It has a depth of 6 m MLWS, but there is a group of boues (awash at MLWS) which stretch out from the Grande Moie rather less than a third the width of the passage. The rest of it is quite clean.

At this point the jetty of Maseline will be seen dead ahead. Yachts can go alongside inside it, but this is inconvenient, as it is used by the Guernsey ferry, and it is better to anchor clear of the fairway.

Just NE of the jetty is Founiais (dries 7m0 and has a satellite ½ cable to E, 0m3, and one to W, 0m9). To clear inside this (if covered) keep Point Banquette (opposite Noire Pierre) on with, or hidden by, Pointe Robert (lighthouse).

The Goulet (the passage between Burons and the Harbour) has only 0m3 best water at LAT. Tidal streams attain great rates in both directions, especially to the southward at low water. On the land side is a big pointed rock, the Pierre du Goulet (marked on the chart as Pinnacle du Goulet), which is only covered by very high tides and is joined by other rocks to the land except at high tide. A few metres to the SE of this are Les Quarts (dries 2m4). When these are awash there is 2m7 of water in the Goulet, where the navigable water is over 50 metres wide. A local Sark law permits only passage northward through the Goulet.

When at Founiais, and if in doubt as to whether there is enough water through the Goulet, either anchor in Maseline Bay or turn out close round the south side of Founiais and pass right round the east side of Burons, giving it one cable berth all round, especially on its

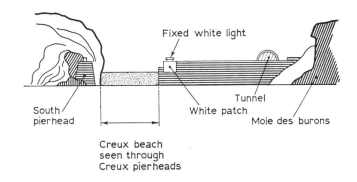

Fixed white light

South pierhead

White patch

Tunnel

Moie des burons

Creux beach seen through Creux pierheads

north side. When the Pinnacle du Goulet comes off the land the South boue of Burons is clear.

Alternatively after passing well through (a cable) the passage between Pte Robert and Grande Moie head roughly E (allowing for the tidal stream) until La Gorge (the prominent rock at the S end of Petite Moie) shows well outside Grande Moie and bears 330°. Then steer 150° to maintain this bearing until L'Etac comes on to La Conchée. Keep on this transit at 215° until Creux beach shows between the pierheads then keep on this (compensating for the tidal stream) in order to leave the boues south of the Burons to starboard.

As the Creux Harbour dries out entirely at LWS the fishing boats have their moorings outside in a cove called Les Laches.

In fine weather it is quite comfortable to lie alongside the quay inside above half tide springs; there is 2m7 at half tide and at neap tides it is said that a yacht with 1m5 draft can lie afloat between the steps and the crane but the berths are usually in use by excursion boats. When there is any sea running outside this may be quite impossible, as the surge in the harbour can be as much as 2 metres.

Half a mile to the south of the harbour is La Conchée, a square rock, 3m0 high, which has

PINNACLE
ROCK

19.6. The Goulet from south. Creux Harbour on left, the Pinnacle Rock centre and to the right the eastern extremity of the Burons.

19.7. The author's *Cohoe I* anchored in Havre Gosselin on the west side of Sark.

some boues around it up to 50 metres. It is $1\frac{1}{2}$ cables from Pointe Terrible and the passage between is clear, but give the east side of the land a berth of a cable here.

The whole of the SE coast from Point Terrible to La Brenière (the islet close inshore on the SE corner of Little Sark) is quite clean inshore and is called Baleine Bay. It includes in its north end the two small bays, Dixcart and Terrible. Anchorage anywhere in this bay is safe with fine westerly weather. The only rocks in the bay are Baleine, 5m8 high with a narrow reef N and E, and a small boue awash MLWS $\frac{1}{2}$ cable due S of it. Close on its western side is its small satellite Avocat (dries 3m9) and a small boue $\frac{1}{2}$ cable SW which is covered even at MLWS.

Outside Baleine are Balmée (dries 6m1), and Demie de Balmée (dries 3m6), a cable apart, the mark for both of which is the west side of the Burons on with Point Terrible. Baleine anywhere on the Coupée and just south of it puts you on these.

To the south of La Brenière the only rocks outside the Etac of Sark are a patch of shingle, sand and boues known as Vingt Clos (curiously enough there are only six of them marked). The northern boue dries 1m8 and the southern is awash at LAT. To pass between these and L'Etac of Sark (which is quite clean on its E side) keep Baleine on the W point of Dixcart Bay. To clear round outside keep the E side of Grande Moie just open of Sark. To clear the Vingt Clos on the south side keep the south of Guernsey open S of L'Etac.

It should be noted when navigating in the east side of Sark that the principal overfalls lie between Pointe Robert and the Blanchard whistle buoy just over 2 miles to the SE, and there are extensive overfalls east and south of La Conchée rock. The Blanchard rock is nearly $\frac{1}{2}$ mile WNW of the buoy, and at LAT there is only 1m2 over it and weed extends to the surface.

The West Coast

The coastal stream in the Gouliot Pass is north-going as in Great Russel from $+4$ h 40 m Dover (-2 h 50 m St Helier) to -1 h 25 m Dover ($+3\frac{1}{2}$ h St Helier) when the south stream begins. When the north-going stream meets an eddy from Bec du Nez inshore in Banquette Bay, it results in a combined set to the NW to join the NE Great Russel stream. Off SW Sark including La Grande Grève the streams are rotary: NE -5 h to -4 h Dover (HW to $+1$ St Helier); then through N and W to SW at $+1\frac{1}{4}$ h to $+2\frac{1}{4}$ h Dover (-6 h to -5 h St Helier); then through S and E back to NE.

The whole of Banquette Bay, which extends from the Bec du Nez down to the island of Brecqhou, is entirely devoid of rocks except within about a cable of the shore with the exception of Grune de Gouliot (with 0m9 of water at LAT), which is $1\frac{1}{2}$ cables from Brecqhou and 3 cables NW of the Gouliot Pass. Marks: E end of Brecqhou on with W side of Little Sark clears well to the E of it.

The island of Brecqhou has on its West side Givaud, 14m6 high and on its South West side Les Dents, 0m3 high. This group of rocks on the South side of Brecqhou has its highest peak at its most southerly end and is quite clean on the South side.

The Gouliot Pass

This has 3m3 of water at LAT, and a reputed speed of 10 knots at flood on Springs. It is entirely clean on both sides with the exception of a spur which sticks out from the SW corner of the Moie de Gouliot, over which there is 0m3 of water at LAT. To clear this see the Bec du Nez (N point of Sark) in the centre of the pass.

19.8. The Gouliot Pass, approaching from southward.

Sark

Havre Gosselin, to the SE of the Moie de Gouliot, is deep and good anchorage in fine weather with clean bottom. Water is clean right up to the cliffs on the north side. The south side of the harbour is guarded by a row of rocks, the westerly end of which is Pierre Norman, which covers at HW Springs. If covered keep the Pilchard Monument (a high tower on the cliff above Havre Gosselin) to the north of the southern spur of the harbour to clear north of Pierre Norman.

On the west side of Little Sark a large patch of boues, Les Hautes Boues (two dry up to 2m1), extends for half a mile. North of these is good anchorage in Grand Grève Bay, the southern point of which Pointe le Jeu, on with the south of La Coupée clears to north of all these boues with the exception of two which dry 0m3 at LAT, and are 3½ cables W by N of Pointe le Jeu. The exact marks for these two are not easy to describe, but the west point of the Moie de la Fontaine and the east end of Moie de la Bretagne (two islets close to the west of Little Sark) puts you about on both of them.

The SW side of Little Sark from Les Hautes Boues to L'Etac should not be explored without local knowledge on board. The highest point of Les Dents on with west cliff of Brecqhou clears to the west of Les Hautes Boues.

Harbours and Anchorages

Sark possesses no harbours sheltered from all winds. Creux harbour on the east side is tiny and yachts must not lie alongside the quay for long. At half tide there is 3m6 at the foot of the stone steps (about 1m5 LW neaps). 2m7 abreast of the crane, 1m8 at the bollard and 0m9 at the iron ladder in the NE corner. A small yacht can thus remain afloat at neaps off the steps, but she will be in the way of the numerous passenger motor boats arriving from Guernsey in the morning and afternoon. The new jetty at Maseline Bay has deeper water, but is also in use by excursion boats. There are anchorages in deep water off Creux* and also to the north of the new jetty which are good in offshore winds in settled weather, so it is preferable to anchor rather than enter the small harbours, as these harbours are equally unsafe with onshore winds or swell.

There are telephone booths at both harbours, the box at Maseline being most used, and tunnels lead to the road up a hill to the scattered villate. In the island there are four licensed hotels, two banks, a telephone service via Guernsey, post office. Many small shops. Petrol, paraffin and diesel oil are obtainable. There is a daily commercial boat service a.m. and p.m., except Sundays, when commercial traffic is prohibited.

On the east side of Sark there are many other anchorages in settled offshore winds. North of Pointe Robert is La Grève de la Ville, where a yacht can anchor 1 cable N or NW of La Chapelle Rock, out of the tide and on good holding ground in sand. When the afternoon sun is casting shadow over the high cliff the anchorage looks somewhat forbidding, but it is sheltered from the prevailing wind between south and west.

In Baleine Bay there are several anchorages, and the deep one is south of Pointe Chateau, in 18 metres on a sandy bottom, or east or west in Terrible Bay or Dixcart Bay, though these anchorages are only protected from west to north. Sark is under 3 miles long and in severe westerly gales the wind comes round the ends of the island as well as gusting down from the heights. Anchorage close in under the lee of the shore in La Grève de la Ville with very good ground tackle may be safe, but landing by dinghy is adventurous and the yacht rolls day and

*There is a notice on the seaward side of the south end of Creux harbour pier reading 'anchorage prohibited west of this notice'.

night in a spectacular fashion, especially when the wind veers towards NW. However, in these conditions the visitor can count on having the whole anchorage to himself.

On the west side of Sark there are several anchorages in easterly winds in Banquette Bay to the north and La Grande Grève to the south. Havre Gosselin, which is the author's usual anchorage, is also good in easterly weather, though it is small and as the yacht swings to her anchor she sometimes appears uncomfortably close to the cliffs. There is a landing here.

By night. The lights on Sark are Pointe Robert lighthouse (*Fl 15 sec 65m 21M Fog Horn (2) 30 sec*) on the east side, and the Blanchard Whistle buoy (*Gp Fl (4) 15 sec*) just over 2 miles SE of it. Fixed white lights of low power (about a mile) are now exhibited from the ends of Creux and Maseline jetties.

On the west side the nearest lights are the Lower Heads buoy (*Fl 5 sec*) south of Herm and St Martin's Point (*Gp Fl (3) white sector*) on the SE of Guernsey. Accordingly, when anchoring off Sark, and intending to stay the night, the position of any light which can be seen should be noted in case of change of weather that may necessitate leaving during darkness.

20 Jersey

High Water, St Helier: −4 h 47 m Dover. **Heights above Datum:** MHWS 11m0. MLWS 1m3.
MHWN 8m1. MLWN 4m1.
Depths: All harbours except St Helier dry out.
Yacht Clubs: Royal Channel Islands Yacht Club (at St Aubin), St Helier Yacht Club, Gorey Yacht Club
and St Catherine's SC.

Although all harbours in Jersey are tidal, with the exception of St Helier (and even there deep-water accommodation is very limited) and St Catherine's, the island has a beautiful sea coast which offers many sheltered anchorages under suitable conditions. Among the anchorages, St Aubin's Bay on the south side and Gorey and St Catherine's on the east may be noted, and will be referred to later. Visiting yachts, especially those fitted with legs, will find much interesting navigation and be assured of a pleasant stay in Jersey. The unusual range of spring tides, sometimes over 12 metres, which run in certain places at 4 knots and over, need attention, and the Admiralty Pocket tide charts should be studied. The principle is to use the tides to advantage and to avoid unnecessary battle against them.

All visiting yachts coming from foreign ports, must clear Customs and Immigration authorities either at St Helier or Gorey, and yachtsmen are not allowed to land anywhere in the island until this formality has been completed.

Approaches to Jersey

Admiralty Charts Nos. 810, 3367 and 62a

(**Note,** 1973. Chart 62a is withdrawn and will be reissued on LAT datum).

Because of the rotary nature of the tide, the approaches to Jersey can be considered separately under the following headings:
1. From the North: (A) for St Helier, (B) for Gorey.
2. From the North-West: (A) for St Helier, (B) for Gorey.
3. From the South-West.
4. From the South and South-East: (A) for St Helier, (B) for Gorey.
5. From St Helier to Gorey and the Violet Channel.
6. From the East.

1. Approach from the North

This approach probably by way of the Race of Alderney at or before High Water Dover (+4 h 47 m St Helier) has only two formidable reefs to avoid. These are the Paternosters or Pierres de Lecq and the Dirouilles, both reefs several miles to the north of Jersey.

(A) **If bound for St Helier** steer for Banc Desormes black conical buoy (*Qk Fl*), just over 4 miles WNW of the Paternosters. At a speed of 5 knots, this course from Alderney should g ve a fair tide and an extra knot until +5 h Dover (−2½ h St Helier) when the tide sets hard to the east. Assuming that the vessel has arrived at the buoy some 4 miles NNW of Grosnez Point (NW corner of Jersey) (*Gp Fl (2) WR sectors 15 sec*) a course should be shaped southward to pass at least 1 mile west of Corbière. Lighthouse (*Iso WR ev 10 sec*) (*Diaphone ev min*

20.1. La Corbiere Lighthouse. *Tourisme Committee, States of Jersey.*

Radio Beacon), allowing for some easterly set of tide. In heavy weather it is well to keep west of the Rigdon bank to avoid rougher seas.

When about 1 mile due west of Corbière Lighthouse, the course may be altered to round Corbière, keeping the same distance off to avoid the detached reefs. In calm weather if the Lighthouse balcony does not appear to be above the high land the distance should be sufficient, but all vessels should guard against a NE set which may take them too close to the outlying reef. Until HW St Helier (−4 h 47 m Dover) the flood tide runs easterly along the south coast at a rate of between 1 and 3 knots, according to the range of tide. To approach St Helier after local HW will mean stemming the tide as it ebbs westward, and this adverse factor may require the use of the engine or the advantage of a fresh and fair wind. There are rough seas off La Corbière in strong winds.

It is advisable to reach certain positions on the passage to Jersey at certain states of the tide. An example of this, described briefly, is the punctual arrival in the Race of Alderney at HW Dover (+4½ h St Helier) or even an hour earlier, the arrival at a position west of Grosnez not more than five hours later and the arrival off Corbière Lighthouse six hours after HW Dover (−1½ h St Helier) when a fair tide will be continued up to St Helier for the next hour, and the maximum strength of the stream, which causes overfalls off Corbière and especially off Noirmont Point, will be avoided.

To maintain an average speed of 6 knots over the ground, it may be found necessary in light or contrary winds to increase sailing speed by the use of the auxiliary engine before reaching Jersey waters. Without this speed, it would be wise to be prepared for a much longer time, say another five hours, on the journey, or to put into Guernsey, or even make for Gorey. Before describing these alternatives let us continue the approach to St Helier Harbour from Corbière.

Keep a good ½ mile south of Corbière and sail 097° between Pt. Le Fret and Passage Rock conical black bell buoy, *Fl W (10 sec)*, *Ra refl.*, in position 9 cables SW of Le Fret, marking entrance to the Western Passage. Alternatively, it is merely necessary to steer to pass about 2 cables south of Pointe le Fret and Noirmont Point (black tower with white band) *(Lt Gp Fl (3) ev 10 sec) 4 M*. There is a race off Noirmont Point and a black Buoy (Les Fours) *(Qk Fl)* 3 cables south of it. Leaving this buoy to starboard the next leading marks should be picked up. These are the Dog's Nest (a rock with a RW beacon, 4 cables SE of the Breakwater end—see photograph No. 3) in line with the red daymark on the tall, white light-structure of

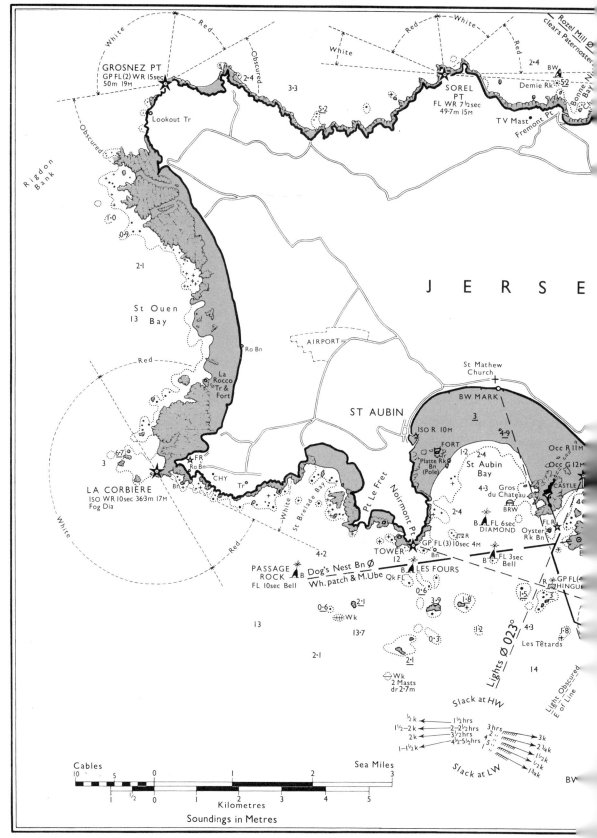

Jersey: (Based on British Admiralty Chart No. 3367 with the permission of the Controller of HM Stationery Office an

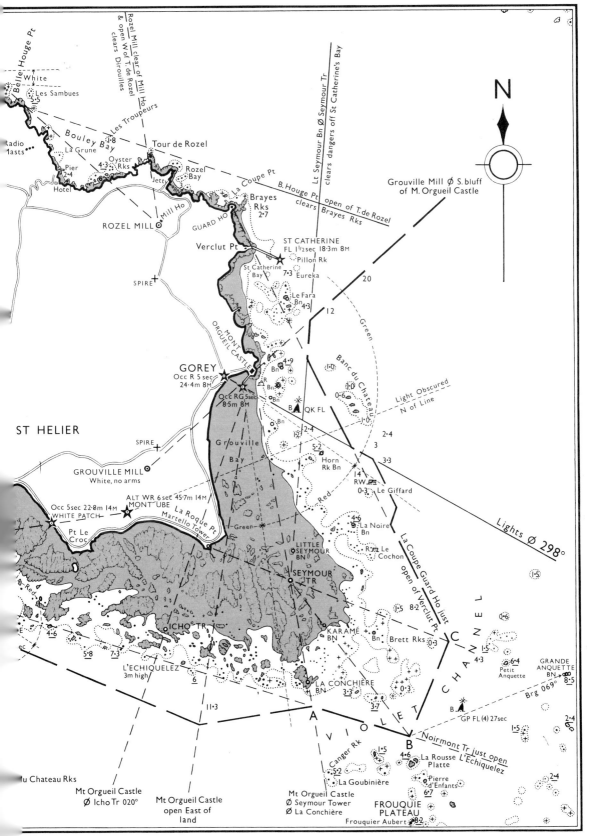

N

Belle Hougue Pt
White
Les Sambues
5·5
Radio Masts
Bouley Bay
La Grune
Les Troupeurs
Pier 2·4
Oyster Rks
4·3
Hotel
Jetty
1·8
Tour de Rozel
Rozel Bay
3
La Coupe Pt
Rozel Mill clear of Mill Ho & open W of T. de Rozel clears Dirouilles
Rozel Mill clear of Mill Ho
B. Hougue Pt open of T. de Rozel clears Brayes Rks
Lt Seymour Bn Ø Seymour Tr clears dangers off St Catherine's Bay
Grouville Mill Ø S. bluff of M. Orgueil Castle
Brayes Rks 2·7
ROZEL MILL
GUARD HO
MILL HO
Verclut Pt
ST CATHERINE FL 1½sec 18·3m 8M
SPIRE
St Catherine Bay
Pillon Rk
7·3 Eureka
Le Fara 4·3
20
12
Green
MONT ORGUEIL CASTLE
GOREY Occ R 5 sec 24·4m 8M
Occ RG 5sec 8·5m 8M
Bn 4·9
Bn
Bn
Bn
Banc du Château
10
10
0·6
B QK FL
Light Obscured N of Line
0·6
2·4
2·4
2·4
3
ST HELIER
SPIRE
Grouville Bay
5·2
Horn Rk Bn
2·4
3·3
GROUVILLE MILL White, no arms
14
RW
0·3 Le Giffard
Lights Ø 298°
ALT WR 6sec 45·7m 14M
Occ 5sec 22·8m 14M
WHITE PATCH
MONT UBE
La Roque Pt
Martello Tower
Green
Red
4·6
La Noire Bn
R Le Cochon
Pt Le Croc
La Coupe Guard Ho just open of Verclut Pt
VIOLET CHANNEL
Red
LITTLE SEYMOUR BN
SEYMOUR TR
1·5
8·2
1·5
1·5
ICHO TR
KARAMÉ BN
Bn
Brett Rks 0·3
C
4·3
0·6
4·6
GRANDE ANQUETTE BN
5·8
7·3
L'ECHIQUELEZ 3m high
6
LA CONCHIÈRE BN
0·3
Petit Anquette
6·4
8·5
Brg 069°
11·3
3·3
3·7
B
GP FL (4) 27sec
Noirmont Tr just open
A
2·4
1·5
Canger Rk
1·5
4·6
La Rousse L'Echiquelez
Noirmont Tr just open
5·2
La Goubinière
Pierre d'Enfants
6·7
2·4
u Château Rks
4·6
7·3
E
Mt Orgueil Castle Ø Icho Tr 020°
Mt Orgueil Castle open East of land
Mt Orgueil Castle Ø Seymour Tower Ø La Conchière
FROUQUIE PLATEAU
Frouquier Aubert 8·2

rapher of the Navy.) When navigating it is preferable to use the Admiralty Chart itself, this being on much larger scale.

20.2. Noirmont Point Tower Lighthouse and Les Fours buoy.

20.3. Dog's Nest surmounted by white pillar and globe beacon, just over ½ mile SSW of the entrance to St Helier, is an important landmark.

the Greve d'Azette Lt. (*occ W ev 5 sec*) in line with Mont Ube Lt. (*Alt W 5 sec R 1 sec*) at 082° (E mag).

If under sail and tacking on a flood tide there is about 1 cable of sea room on either side of the leading marks at Noirmont and up to the Oyster Rocks (dry 4m3) on which there is a RW beacon, 2 cables SW of the Breakwater end (which is marked with black and white vertical stripes). The turn into the inner roads occurs after the beacon on the Oyster Rock comes abeam, on approaching the Light (*Fl R*) structure on the Platte Rock—see St Helier Harbour, page 138 and harbour plan page 141.

(B) **If bound for Gorey**, a course should be set to pass between the Paternosters and the Dirouilles. The marks to clear the Dirouilles on the west side are Rozel Mill just clear of the Mill house and open W of the Tour de Rozel, 171° (S mag). If these cannot be distinguished it would be wise to steer for Sorel Point Lt. Ho. (*Fl WR ev 7½ sec 15 m*), and when about 1 mile offshore to alter course ESE towards the Tour de Rozel. The latter is a conical white-washed rock (see photo No. 4) on the coast just over 1 mile from the NE corner of Jersey. Between Sorel Point and the Tour de Rozel lies the bluff promontory of Belle Hougue, which should be passed at least a half-mile offshore to avoid the Sambues Rocks (dry 5m5). There is little else to bother about on this north coast as long as a vessel keeps ½ to 1 mile offshore. The TV mast in position bearing 117° from Sorel Point at distance 13 cables is a useful additional aid. At night it has three vertical tiers of *Red lights*, of which the topmost lights eclipse for *1 sec* after a *Flash of 1 sec* at elevation 232 m. There are other smaller masts with single red lights at night above Belle Houge Point and Vicard Point to the east. This part of the passage on a sunny day presents most beautiful scenery. The deep water has a dark blue colour and the white surf breaking at the foot of brown rocky cliffs gives a gentle contrast of colours. Beyond this are green and brown fields with patches of heather and purplish granite rock.

20.4. Tour de Rozel, with white-washed conical rock. It lies between Rozel and Bouley Bay.

At the NE corner of the island are the Brayes Rocks NE of La Coupe, which should be passed ½ mile to the north on a line Belle Hougue open N of Tour de Rozel until Mont Orgueil Castle (see photo No. 17) opens to the east of the white house on the land end of St Catherine's Breakwater, when the course is altered to pass 1 cable off the end of the Breakwater (*Fl 1½ sec 8 M*). A strong tide causing broken water can be expected over the Pillon rock (covered 1m0 LAT) and the Eureka rock (covered 3m4 LAT), but there should be no danger except at Low Water Springs.

On rounding the breakwater, Seymour Tower comes into view 4 miles to the south. This square tower (sketch 10), though apparently 1 mile off La Rocque shore, dries like most of the surrounding rocks. Three cables to the north of Seymour Tower is a rock named Little Seymour which is marked with a beacon. These two Seymours in line 184° lead to the south along the east coast until the Black Conical (April to September) buoy (*Qk Fl*) 4 cables SE of Equerrière Rock (beacon topmark E) has been passed and the leading marks into the Port of Gorey can be picked up—see Gorey (page 141).

2. **Approach from the North-West**

(A) **For St Helier.** If sailing from St Peter Port, Guernsey, commence the passage an hour before LW by the shore. With an average speed of 5 knots set a course to pass 2 miles W of Corbière Lighthouse, but see tide maps for set of stream. When in position 1 mile W of Corbière proceed to St Helier in the same way as described in 1 (A).

20.5. La Coupe Point. Viewed from NW. Brayes Rocks can be seen off the point, and St Catherine's Breakwater with white light tower is on the left. The sentry box, pillar and globe barely show in the picture, but they are situated at the summit of La Coupe, ¾ inch to the right of the inner end of the pier.

Jersey

(B) **For Gorey.** Shape a course for Grosnez Point, Jersey, allowing for tidal streams as shown in the tide maps. On the flood tide the passage along the north coast of Jersey can be speedy and pleasant. If set near to the Paternosters, keep the Tour de Rozel shut in with Belle Hougue. If identification of these marks is in any way doubtful it will be best to make for Grosnez Point, giving the Paternosters a wider berth. Keep ½ to 1 mile offshore till the Tour de Rozel is passed, then proceed as described in 1 (B).

3. **Approach from the South-West**

Set a course to pass 2 miles S of Corbière Lighthouse at about half flood and from this position sail on to the St Helier leading marks—Dog's Nest in line with the white patches on the Grève d'Azette sea wall 082° (E mag), passing between Noirmont Point Light Tower and the Les Fours black buoy and from there as described in the latter part of 1 (A), and see St Helier for entrances.

4. **Approach from the South and South-East**

(A) **For St Helier.** The visitor is advised to shape a course to pass not more than ½ mile W of Demie de Pas Tower RWVS (Photograph 6) (*Mo (D − ··) WR 12 sec 10 M. Horn (3) 60 sec*) and to avoid the reefs lying southward of St Aubin's Bay. Demis de Pas is 1½ miles SSE of St Helier harbour. Four cables to the west of St Helier harbour is the historical Elizabeth Castle, from which a breakwater runs SSE to shelter the harbour entrance. On the end of the breakwater are painted BWVS—see photograph No. 7. This breakwater kept end on will lead between Demie de Pas and Les Tetards and east of the Hinguettes Rocks (marked by a red buoy (*Gp Fl (4) R ev 15 sec*) on the north side), but at low water when half a mile off the breakwater the correct leading marks should be picked up. They are the BWVS patch painted on the sea wall, in line with or between the two heads of the Gros du Chateau rock (which lies a cable west of Elizabeth Castle) 341° (N by W mag) and are shown in Photograph 7. The latter marks give a course parallel to and 1½ cables west of the approach keeping the breakwater end on. They avoid the reef running west from the Dog's Nest, which is a danger at LW.

Course should be altered as soon as the leading marks on the northern part of Albert Pier come into line—see St Helier Harbour, page 138.

(B) **If bound for Gorey.** Coming up to Jersey from the south, by day, a course can be set for Icho Tower (round, top half painted white, see sketch), which will be sighted somewhere below the high ground of the east of Jersey.

Icho Tower is built on a rock 2¼ miles east of Demie de Pas and 1½ miles to the westward of Seymour Tower, a square white tower built on a rock about 1 mile seaward from the SE corner of Jersey. Two miles to the northward from Icho Tower and on a hill is another round white tower, Grouville Mill, elevation 60 metres, which makes a useful landmark on the east side of the island.

In thick weather or at night, a passage to Gorey should not be attempted, and course should be altered to pick up the Demie de Pas Tower and to make for St Helier.

Icho Tower in line with Grouville Mill 353° (is a useful leading mark up to within, say, 2 miles of Icho, when the course can be altered NE toward the Conchière Rock (1m8 bent iron pole Bn) whence follow instructions for the Violet Channel (page 136).

This detour towards the Icho Tower is to make sure that the course is well to the west of the Frouquier Plateau, which on the SW side is marked by a black buoy. The highest rock of this plateau, the Frouquie Aubert, dries 8m2, and is just over 2 miles SSE of the Conchière. Another rock 11 cables southward of Conchière, on the west end of the Frouquie Plateau, the Goubinière, dries 6m4 and has no beacon. To pass west of this rock when approaching this end of Jersey and the Canger rock, 1 cable north of it, Mont Orgueil (Gorey) Castle must be kept completely open west of Seymour Tower and the Conchière, 351° (N mag). The Canger Rock (dries 5m2) lies 1 mile southward of Conchière and forms with the Conchière a 'gateway' into the Violet passage.

With experience, in good weather, the yachtsman can shape his course from the Minquiers or Chausey more to the east than Icho tower; but the east safety limit up to the Violet channel is the transit, Mont Orgueil castle full open west of Seymour and Conchière.

20.6. Demie de Pas Lighthouse. White granite tower, 11m high with vertical red stripes.

20.7. Elizabeth Castle and breakwater and Platte Beacon which are left to port when entering the inner roads. When approaching from S or SW keep the end (BWVS) on with Elizabeth Castle to lead between Demie de Pas and Les Tetards and east of the Hinguettes. This transit must be left before approaching the rocky patch W and SW of Dog's Nest, except after half flood. Gros du Chateau Rock is seen left of the ensign hoist. This is the outer leading mark which, on with the BWVS mark on the distant sea wall bearing 341° clears the Dog's Nest rocks at LW.

5. St Helier to Gorey, and Violet Channel

At all states of the tide, with weather and visibility permitting, a passage is possible between St Helier and Gorey by day, but only through the Violet Channel, and then provided that the vessel can make good her course possibly against a very strong tide, unless the passage is made through the Violet Channel at or $\frac{1}{2}$ hour before High Water. At times other than High Water there would be little sea room under sail to tack against an adverse wind, and as the direction of the tide changes hour by hour and also to some extent according to the exact locality, the stranger in these waters should work out the tides beforehand, and be constantly on the watch for set, so that course may be altered as required.

Good large scale charts are, of course, essential on this rock-strewn coast. The most useful are 3367 which covers the whole of Jersey and 62a, when reissued on LAT datum, which covers the East Coast of Jersey on a very large scale.

While there should be no difficulty in following sailing directions in clear weather and preferably at neap tides, it is recognized that the navigation on the south-east of Jersey is considered by strangers to be exceptionally difficult, and a visiting yachtsman may well be

Jersey

advised to have a pilot or local yachtsman aboard to point out the marks on the first occasion when he makes the passage.

The best time to set out from St Helier to Gorey is on the last half of the flood, say − 2 h 30 m St Helier or + 5 h Dover to arrive at the Violet Channel just before High Water.

After leaving St Helier Harbour leading marks (see St Helier Harbour) set course (as shown in 4 A) keeping Gros de Château rocks in transit with the BWVS mark on the sea wall until Demie de Pas bears east. (At half flood the short cut across the rocks south of Dog's Nest can be taken by keeping Elizabeth Castle Breakwater (Photo 7) end on (BWVS)). Then make good, allowing for tide, about 112°, to pass about 2 cables south of Demie de Pas, and hold this course, keeping Noirmont Point (Photograph 2) open to the south of Demie de Pas, until Mont Orgueil Castle (Photograph 17) opens east of the land.

Then steer to a position approximately 2 cables south of La Conchière shown by the transits: Noirmont Point open south of L'Echiquelez (a rock 2m7 high ½ mile SSE of Icho Tower) and Mont Orgueil, Seymour Tower and Conchière rock in line at 351° (N mag), which is marked position 'A'. (At half flood with local knowledge the yacht could come on the L'Echiquelez open of Noirmont transit earlier, but as it leads close to rocks which dry as much as 6m0 at low water, it is best for strangers to keep at least 2 cables southward until within ¼ mile of La Conchière and position 'A'). Around HW the set to the north must be counteracted.

20.8. Brett Beacon.

20.9. Grande Anquette Refuge Beacon.

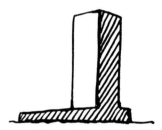

20.10. Seymour Tower 15m8 high.

20.11. Conchiere Rock.

20.12. Icho Tower as seen from seaward.

The Violet Channel

NE Stream begins approximately + 4 h 30 m Dover (− 3 h St Helier) and the SW Stream at − 2 h Dover (+ 3 h St Helier).

From 'A' the transit Noirmont Light Tower just open of L'Echiquelez Rock should be held. Do not allow the stream (which may be very strong and require considerable helm compensation) to set you south of this transit, or north of the transit of Icho Tower open south of Conchière. This course may be held until Seymour Tower (see sketch) becomes open north

136

of Karamé Rock, and Grand Anquette (see sketch) beacon bears 069° (E by N mag). Make this position 'B'.

From 'B' make good 024° (NE by N mag) leaving the black conical Violet buoy (*Gp Fl (4) 27 sec*) about 3 cables to eastward, until La Rocque Tower (near La Rocque Point pier) is in line with Seymour Tower 290° (NW by W) and La Coupe Guardhouse (seen over the land end of St Catherine's Breakwater) is a little open Verclut Point 333°. Call this position 'C'.

Steer on this transit leaving to port Le Cochon red can buoy, *Ra Rfl*, La Noire and the Horn beacons (each beacon having the initial letter at its top). Open the transit a little to avoid Le Giffard till Gorey leading marks are picked up. Le Giffard Rock, awash at LAT, is marked by a RW cheq can buoy, *Ra Refl*, on its NE side.

The reverse passage through the Violet Channel requires the use of the same marks, and is best made to arrive at the Violet Channel at low water or half an hour before to get the benefit of a fair tide. At this state of the tide La Rousse Platte (1·6 miles SE of La Conchière) will be uncovered and may be steered for from position 'C' at 204°, as far as position 'B'. Do not confuse La Rousse (dries 4m6) with Pierre d'Enfants (dries 6m7) to the SE of it.

Note. Some cruising men may prefer to pilot through the Violet Channel simply by chart, if not intending to take the Short Cut east of La Conchière. If so, make a position about 2 cables south of Demi de Pas as before. Proceed by chart leaving L'Echiquelez and Conchière about 5 cables to the northward. Then bring the Violet buoy bearing E mag, and steer to make good this bearing. At the buoy alter course 90° to port and make good N mag, keeping the buoy on a stern bearing of S mag, until the transit of La Coupe open of Verclut Point is reached, whence follow it as before.

This method offers the simplicity of steering for the buoy on a cardinal point so that the set of the stream will immediately be noted and counteracted, besides keeping the vessel in the middle of the channel away from rocks. But it must be recognized that the position of a buoy may on occasion alter. *Author.*

The Short Cut. Near HW only (St Helier) an alternative passage about 1 mile inshore of the Violet Channel can be taken by yachts and ships of light draft. This may be used with local knowledge and passes 4 cables off the Conchière Rock and 1 cable west of the Brett Rock beacon (see sketch). From St Helier the 6 miles to the Conchière might be sailed in the hour before HW St Helier, so that even at HW neap tides, sufficient water and a fair tide can be assured. On the north-going passage there are some overfalls near Brett Rock, which need cause no alarm at the right state of the tide.

The passage from St Helier up to position 'A' is the same as for the Violet Channel, but on arrival at 'A' steer eastward to bring Icho tower close south of the Conchière until St Catherine's Breakwater Lighthouse (5 miles northward) and Karamé Rock 0m9 high K Bn (6 cables SSE of Seymour Tower) are in line. Do not allow the tide to set the vessel north of a line Icho Tower/Conchière until the marks are clearly identified.

From this position steer 028° for about 1 mile to pass 1 cable west of Brett Rock (dries 3m4) beacon. Continue on this course until La Coupe Guardhouse open Verclut Point at 333° is reached about 2 cables east of Cochon buoy (red can, temporary). Then leaving the Cochon and Noire (dries 4m6) and Horn Rock (dries 5m2) to port, course may be shaped for Gorey Harbour.

The reverse passage Gorey to St Helier by the short cut can be made before High Water (St Helier), but an adverse tide of 2½ knots should be expected at Springs until past the Conchière, when a fair tide is found.

Jersey

6. From the East

The two likely approaches from the east are:

(A) from the direction of Carteret and

(B) from the southern half of the Déroute de Terre, as from Granville to Gorey via the passage between the Boeuf Tower and Senequet Light.

(A) **From direction of Carteret.** There are many reefs with little water over them between the Ecrehou and the Normandy coast, so that this passage should not be attempted at Low Water. The French chart No. 826 Du Sénéquet aux Roches de Port Bail, and No. 827 De Port Bail á Diélette, will show all the water between Jersey and the French coast.

South of Les Ecrehou the Ecrevière Bank must be cleared to the south on the mark St Martin's Church spire (Jersey) over the high point Verclut, above the butt end of the St Catherine's breakwater, 250° (W by S mag). A black bell buoy (*Fl 5 sec*) with *Ra Refl* is established to the SE of the Ecrevière bank, which simplifies navigation, and by night, Sorel Point Lt. shows red over the Ecrevière bank and white up to ½ mile to the south of it. *Note.* In the afternoon sunlight the clearing marks on Jersey for the Ecrevière Bank are not easy to distinguish—looking west. The rough guide would then be keep well south, say 2 miles S of the Ecrehou rocks.

Strong tides run SE on the flood and NW on the ebb. About 1 mile to the east of Gorey (Mont Orgueil) Castle lie the Bancs du Château, on the Middle bank of which the least depth is 0m1. At MLWS a detour to the north should be made to close Grouville Mill (white, on hill) with Gorey Castle 230°. Continue on this transit until 6 cables off the Castle when La Coupe mound lies just open of Verclut Point at 333° (about NNW mag), when bear to port to bring this transit astern and continue on this course until Equerrière Rock beacon bears W, when course be altered to the S, leaving to starboard the black conical seasonal buoy (*Qk Fl*), until Gorey leading marks are picked up.

(B) **From the Déroute de Terre** (and along the shallow French coast north of Pointe du Roc) to Basse Jourdan, ½ mile E of Le Boeuf Tower and marked by a whistle buoy *Fl R*. From Basse Jourdan make good a course of 290° passing some 2 miles north of the Boeufs and Grande Anquette (9m1 high white refuge Bn) and thence on to the Gorey leading marks, which lead S of the Banc du Château.

From Gorey to Granville this course reversed is probably the most practicable to avoid the many changes of direction required to travel through the Violet Channel. It can also be negotiated at night in fair weather, if necessary. Given clear visibility, of about 12 miles the Boeuf Tower and rocks may be left to the east, passing between it and the Grande Arconie Rock (dries 3m0), on a stern transit of St Catherine's breakwater end lighthouse on with La Coupe Mound at 315°. Least water is 1m8 over Basse Occidentale des Boeufs (2 miles W of Boeuf Tower) which can be avoided by a ¼ mile detour to W around it.

Harbours and Anchorages

St Helier. The leading marks through the inner roads from south of Oyster Rock beacon to the entrance of St Helier Harbour consist of a white patch (front) on the outer angle of Albert Pier (the long west breakwater) and a white and red patch (rear) at the esplanade end of the breakwater at 023° (NE by N mag). (Photograph No. 13). By night *Occ G* (front) and *Occ R* (rear) lights, (192 metres) apart. For local radio beacons see page 12.

When the harbour entrance opens up abeam course may be altered to enter—see photograph No. 14. *By night* inner leading lights 2 *FG*.

20.13. Leading marks in final approach to St Helier Harbour are a RW patch at the northern inshore end of the Albert Pier, and the other a W patch at the angle of the pier. The transit leaves the Dog's Nest to starboard and the Platte beacon (Photo No. 7) to port.

20.14. When the harbour entrance opens out abeam, alter course between the pierheads and receive instructions at the control tower.

Traffic signals are exhibited from the Control Station on the head of south pier (starboard hand) which is equipped with RT. At night a green light permits entry into harbour and a red permission to leave. Entry and exit is prohibited when both lights are exhibited.

A visiting yacht will be hailed as she enters the harbour and directed to a berth alongside one of the quays in deep water. The pontoons for yachts at No. 5 berth are no longer available, as this position has been converted to a Roll-on/Roll-off terminal. A press notice has been issued warning visiting yachtsmen that owing to lack of deep water berths they must expect to suffer inconveniences at the very least. This is serious because St Helier is the only port of refuge secure in all weathers, but it is added that the harbour authorities will do their best to help visitors seeking refuge in bad weather. No doubt every effort will be made to alleviate the berthing problem, possibly by laying moorings outside the harbour but in the long term the construction of a marina of some kind appears to be the only solution for an island of the importance of Jersey. In the meantime greater use must be made of the open anchorage at St Catherine's, Gorey and St Aubin. St Helier is a busy commercial port with very limited room for berthing in deep water, especially during the potato season and the tomato season. Consequently yachts, if allowed to remain for any length of time, may have to berth in the upper part of the harbour, beyond a concrete sill (dries 3m7 marked by danger notice and red lights at night) on the bottom, or in the old harbour. Both positions dry out, but large yachts can remain afloat in the main pool if permission is granted by the Harbour Master*.

Berthing alongside a quay wall is not difficult with a long-keeled yacht, and the yacht settles quickly, once she takes the ground, as the tide falls very rapidly. Good fenders are, of course, essential.

* Note: two pontoons for a dozen (often more) yachts have been added between the old pierheads.

Jersey

Facilities are excellent. Water at quayside, two yacht yards and engineers. Petrol and oil, hotels, amusement, and the town is an exceptionally good shopping centre. Charts at South Pier Shipyard. The St Helier Yacht Club is most hospitable and local advice may be obtained there. Good air connections. Passenger service to St Peter Port and Weymouth. Hydrofoil, weather permitting, to St Malo. Buses to all parts.

St Aubin. This harbour is situated 2 miles west of St Helier across St Aubin's Bay, and is the headquarters of the Royal Channel Islands Yacht Club. The harbour dries out 6m4 and should only be entered with sufficient rise of tide. When there is less than a 9m5 tide care should be taken to keep to the north side of the entrance, and to avoid running aground on the central mud bank, but dredging and other improvements have been made. At low water the causeway between the Fort and the shore dries 5m5. There are shipwrights at St Aubin and shops. The harbour is very full of boats and moorings and there are also many boats on moorings to the north of the Fort where they dry out. A deep draft yacht will have to take soundings to find a suitable depth, according to the state of the tide, in which to anchor east of Platt Rock pole beacon. The anchorage is good, being open only on its south side but it is a long distance from the harbour. It has just been announced that the R Channel Islands YC are putting down 3 safe visitors moorings with one ton concrete sinkers in Belcroute Bay just W of St Aubins Fort. This is within the drying area shown on the chart but the minimum depth is stated to be 1m4 MLWS. Note that the stream runs south along the shore from half flood to low water St Helier.

20.15. St Aubin Fort which dries out at LAT.

20.16. St Aubin Harbour. Keep close to northern pier. A 9m5 tide gives 2m7 of water at the iron ladder inside the northern arm. It is often crowded.

Gorey. This is a charming little town, or large village, on the east side of Jersey, nestling under Mont Orgueil, on which stands the castle dominating the harbour and its approaches. There are hotels, restaurants and several shops. Gorey Yacht Service Ltd. provides diesel, petrol and water from the end of the pier, as well as shipwright and engineering services, winter yacht care, chandlery, clothing etc. There is a yacht club on the pier and Gorey is the only harbour, other than St Helier, where Customs can be cleared. Some yachtsmen prefer it

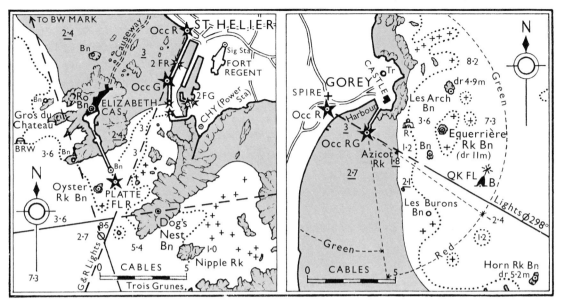

St Helier and Gorey: (Based on British Admiralty Chart No. 3367 with the permission of the Controller of HM Stationery Office and of the Hydrographer of the Navy.)

to the larger port. There are vedettes in summer to Carteret and a service to Portbail will probably be added.

When approaching Gorey keep a distance of 1 cable outside all local beacons until the leading marks are identified. These are Gorey Pier lighthouse on with the rear lighthouse (with rectangular white surround with vertical orange edges) at 298°. The black conical buoy (*Qk Fl*, established in summer months, 7 cables off the pierhead is left close to starboard.

At low water entry to the harbour is impossible, and the flat Azicot Rock (dries 1m8) which is almost on the leading marks 2 cables from Gorey pierhead, may be avoided by a detour to the north, where temporary anchorage may be found while waiting rise of tide.

From the NE a short cut can be made by day, passing close SE of Les Arch Beacon and, with sufficient rise of tide, making straight for the pierhead, remembering to give the rocks under the NE side of the pierhead a berth of ½ cable.

By night. Approach in the green sector of Gorey Pier Light (*RG Occ 5 sec 10 M*) in transit at 298° with the rear shore light (*Occ R 5 sec 8 M*).

Harbour and Anchorage. As Gorey Harbour dries out the only position where a deep keeled yacht can remain is at the landing stage, shown in photograph No. 19. There is about 1m8 at half tide or when 0m6 shows at the fuel station steps marker. The Port Authorities prefer yachts from foreign countries to report here for Customs, and in any case this is necessary to obtain instructions from the Harbour Master if wishing to remain there or elsewhere in the harbour, which is often very crowded. Other possibilities for visiting boats are: (a) 8 sets of moorings inside harbour which dry at half tide or earlier, (b) swinging moorings off the end of the harbour which dry at low water, (c) a deep water mooring outside the harbour and another owned by Gorey Yacht Service by arrangement. Although the harbour may be crowded, it is stated that in bad weather refuge can usually be found

Jersey

20.17. Mont Orgeul Castle just north of Gorey Pier affords a conspicuous landmark. There is an anchorage in offshore winds and neap tides near the white mooring buoys.

20.18. The light structure at the end of Gorey pier is the front leading mark. The rear mark is an oblong white light structure with vertical red borders between the two white houses on the left.

somewhere within it and yachts equipped with legs should move well up the harbour to find the best shelter.

The outside anchorages are suitable only in offshore winds and reasonably settled weather. As the sands dry out 2 cables off the pier at LAT the state of the tide and the draft of the boat are the principal considerations, and soundings should always be taken. At MLWS there is 1m3 and at MLWN 4m1 above the LAT chart datum, which makes a great difference. At neaps a shallow draft yacht can anchor near or even just inside the pierhead, but clear of the fairway and the rock ledge marked by E Quadrant RW beacon. East of the pier

20.19. The yacht is berthed alongside the part of the quay reserved for yachts, where the Harbour Master gives directions. The whole harbour dries out at LW and all the craft on moorings have legs to remain upright.

there are several moorings for shallow draft local craft and usually room to anchor just north of them, clear of the rocks when LW is 2m0 above LAT datum. A small jetty or drain runs out from the steps, which facilitates dinghy work. At spring tides yachts of say 1m8 will have to anchor about 2 cables off the pierhead just north of the leading line but no more west than S mag of the red States buoy.

St Catherine's Bay. Situated rather over 1 mile north of the prominent Mont Orgueil Castle and $\frac{1}{2}$ mile south of La Coupe, and made conspicuous by its long breakwater on the north side, St Catherine is easy to find and enter by day or night. It is protected from the north by the breakwater and from the west and SW by the land. The southern part of the bay contains many rocks, extending beyond and to northward of the Fara beacon which is south (mag) of the breakwater head. To clear these dangers when approaching from the south, keep the lighthouse at the end of the breakwater on with the guard tower on La Coupe Point, which is conspicuous on a transit of 315° true (NW by N mag). From north of east there are no outlying dangers, other than the overfalls in rough weather on two shoals $1\frac{1}{2}$ cables from the breakwater head. The tide is very fast in the offing and there is an eddy along the breakwater.

When close to the breakwater follow it up on the south side, keeping within a cable of it and anchoring off about the middle of its length. The holding ground on mud or fine sand is good. There is a rock a cable south of the inner end of the breakwater. The breakwater lighthouse (*Fl $1\frac{1}{2}$ sec 8 M*) enables the anchorage to be used at night, and it is often a most

143

Jersey

convenient one. There is a sailing club and café but no other facilities other than buses to Gorey and St Helier.

Rozel Bay lies on the NE coast of Jersey, under a mile west of La Coupe, and is sheltered from SSE through S to W. There is a small drying jetty on the west side against which a yacht can lay alongside. Approach from the north is made with the end of the jetty bearing 250°, leaving drying rocks NE of it to starboard. Anchor in 2 metres off the jetty. With sufficient rise of tide enter the harbour close to the end of the jetty leaving to port a rock, dries 5m5, marked by iron beacon with RW globe top. The entrance is only 18m0 wide. Rozel is a picturesque fishing village with hotel, restaurants and café.

Bouley Bay. This wide bay on the NE side is a popular anchorage, which is easy to enter and is sheltered on west and south. There is a shoal Les Troupeurs (1m8 over) in approach on the NE and the Oyster Rocks (dry 4m3) 2½ cables NE of Etaquerel Fort, but the west half of the bay is clean beyond 150 metres of the shore. There is a jetty near the corner of the bay in the SW side and anchorage off it.

Bonne Nuit Bay. This pretty bay is situated near the centre of the north side of Jersey 1½ miles east of Sorel Point and close east of Fremont Point, ¼ mile off which there is the Demie Rock, marked by a conical BW cheq buoy. There is a stone jetty, which dries out, fringed by drying rocks at low water, in the SW corner of the bay and anchorage off it. Approach in a SW direction leaving to port the Cheval Rock (dries 10m7) and rocks ½ cable north of it. At night there are two leading lights *FG* at 223°.

21 Les Ecrehou and Plateau des Minquiers

Streams. The NNW stream begins +5 h 05 m Dover (−2 h 25 m St Helier), and S stream −0 h 40 m Dover (+4 h 15 m St Helier).

(Use Admiralty Chart No. 62a but note that drying heights in this Chapter are increased to conform with LAT datum).

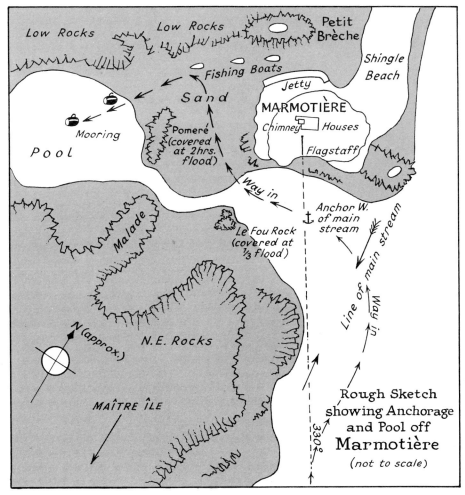

Rough Sketch showing Anchorage and Pool off Marmotière (not to scale)

Les Ecrehou: For approach to Les Ecrehou it is essential to use the large-scale Admiralty Chart No. 62. This sketch is intended only to illustrate the anchorages described and the slight alteration of course necessary to avoid rocks NE of Maître Ile, which at low water touch the transit of the flagstaff and chimney.

Les Ecrehou and Plateau des Minquiers

Although Les Ecrehou and Minquiers are difficult, and regarded as dangerous to navigate without local knowledge, this book would be incomplete without mention of them.

The Ecrehou group of islets and rocks lies 5 miles off the NE coast of Jersey, and once formed part of the continent with Jersey. Maître Ile, some 600 metres long, is the largest, and in medieval times had a Priory where monks lived, sung masses for the souls of the dead, and tended a beacon for mariners. The ruins are still to be seen.

The only inhabited island is Marmotière just to the north of Maître Ile, which is a mere fistful of rock capped by a tiny cluster of stone-walled cottages. They are crammed close together, and look like a Grimm's Fairy Story village, with grey and red roofs, bright against the summer sky, and below them the craggy islet, completely devoid of vegetation, standing in the fast-running tide. It is difficult to imagine how the original inhabitants lived in such an inhospitable place, but the buildings are used now by a few lucky Jersey yachtsmen who lease them for use in the summer. The third island is Blanche Ile, which is connected with Marmotière by a long curving ridge of shingle covered at high tides and smoothed by the fast-running currents. The rest of Les Ecrehou is composed of islets, countless rocks, seaweed and sands, all in a compact group a bare $2\frac{1}{2}$ miles long. Sea birds make their nesting places in the higher rocks, and lobsters, prawns and shrimps multiply in the channels between them. Les Ecrehou are well worth seeing, and there is a temporary anchorage in deep water south of Marmotière. Yachts fitted with legs can feel their way into shallower and more protected water and dry out at low tide.

Navigation in the approach and up to Marmotière is intricate, and it is advisable to obtain the help of a yachtsman or a pilot from Gorey, when visiting Les Ecrehou for the first occasion. On no account attempt it at high water or at Spring tides. The tide is so strong that a yacht with a good breeze may be passing over the bottom at 10 knots, in restricted waters peppered with rocks. Furthermore, when bringing up, it may be difficult for the anchor to get a hold when the tide is pouring through the reefs at its maximum rate. The following notes by Mr D. P. Richardson, a Jersey yachtsman, which appeared in *The Yachtsman*, describe the approach very clearly:

The approach is from the south-west leaving the Maître Ile with its survey beacon surmounted by a barrel to port. Coming from Gorey or the south, arrange to arrive at half ebb. Southward and westward of the Ecrehou the tide will be running very strongly to the north so that a course must be set as if to pass to the southward of the Ecrevière Bank, SE of which there is black bell buoy *Fl 5 sec Ra Refl.* Eastward of the Maître Ile is a fine rock known as the Bigorne (4m9 high) which cannot be mistaken. It appears as a giant's inverted eye-tooth or a bull's horn. North-eastward of the Bigorne are two massive rocks, the Grande Galère (4m0 high) and the Sablonière (1m8 high). The former is a long red granite rock (white with bird lime) which gives the impression, especially when well uncovered at low tide, of being an old Roman Galley, as its name implies. The Sablonière would appear as if part of the Grand Galère if the tide is low. This is because the Pierre des Femmes, which lies to the north-east and near the Sablonière, merges into it from certain angles, but at high water the Pierre des Femmes covers.

But a check bearing on the Bigorne will immediately show the navigator whether he has the Bigorne as he should have, mid-way between the Grand Galère and the Sablonière. The true bearing for this is 022°. Proceed towards the Bigorne on this bearing remembering that the tide will be pushing your ship to the north-east very hard.

Do not get south of the line of Bigorne mid-way between the Grand Galère and

21.1. Bigorne in the centre is the key rock in the approach to the Ecrehou with Grand Galère to left and Sablonière to right.

21.2. This photograph near LW shows how different is the picture when the rocks dry out and the groups merge with each other, but Bigorne remains clear in the centre for the first line of the approach.

21.3. The temporary anchorage at Marmotière. The picture is taken at LW with a number of week-end yachts from Jersey rafted on two moorings. At HW Marmotière is only a fistful of rocks capped by a cluster of stone walled cottages. The front leading mark is a white flagstaff (over a white patch on the rock below it) in line with the left hand chimney at 330°, but when passing the rocks off Maître Ile (shown on left of picture) it is best to open the chimney to east of the flagstaff. The entrance to the pool is on the left side of the picture and the Sound with its fierce tidal streams is to the right of the big right hand rock at Marmotière.

Les Ecrehou and Plateau des Minquiers

Sablonière, as this will bring you very near the 'Noire' and its neighbouring heads. The yacht may pass to the north of this line until the Bigorne touches the north side of the Sablonière.

When a cable and half short of the Bigorne the leading marks to run up the Sount to the Marmotière will have come on, and their line must not be passed. These are the Flagstaff on a white-washed rock which is very prominent on the Marmotière Island, and a low black square chimney on a house to the north of this in transit. It is the most left-hand or western chimney on the cluster of dwellings at Marmotière. It is necessary to approach on this transit of 330° exactly to clear two rocks (drying 6m7 and 4m0 respectively) to SE of Maître Ile which must be left to port and the Sardrière (dries 8m5 and showing by quarter ebb) about 2 cables east of the north end of Maître Ile, which is left to starboard.

Note 1973. Alterations to the gable of the house on which the leading mark chimney stands, may involve the removal of the chimney, but possibly it will be replaced by a dummy.

Continuing up towards the Marmotière, take care to keep the marks dead on as you clear the Maître Ile north end or open the chimney well to the eastward. (This is to avoid the rocks shown uncovered in the photograph from Maître Ile.) Anchor within a stone's throw of the pebble beach below the south side of the Marmotière and its flag-staff. (This is referred to as the "temporary anchorage" in the notes below). During the low tide your ship will lie safely to an anchor in the pool and you can land on the slipway. Until you have gained local knowledge and there is a mooring available, it would not be advisable to remain in the anchorage during the high water, or at night. The tide will turn to run down the Sound to the south an hour before low water and will allow you to make a quick get-away. But be warned, don't go into the Ecrehous with a falling barometer and the south-west looking black, for a strong blow will test any ship's gear, and the hearts of the bravest will have many bad moments when clearing the Noire Rocks and the south-western approaches. A sailing boat in a headwind without the help of an auxiliary will probably not make it and will have to return to shelter in the Ecrehou, as many have done before.

Anchorages. There are two anchorages, and to avoid confusion these may be referred to as the 'Temporary Anchorage' and the 'Pool'. The temporary anchorage is the obvious one just south of Marmotière, which is shown in photograph 1. It lies in the bight between Marmotière and Maître Ile and nearer the former. The yacht should enter between the two islands to get out of the strength of the stream, which pours approximately parallel with the eastern rocky shores of Maître Ile and Marmotière. At high water the edge of the main stream is close to the anchorage, but when the rocks dry out at low water it is farther eastward. The visitor should pilot his yacht far enough into the anchorage to get out of the worst of the tide, but take soundings as the water rapidly shoals, especially on spring tides, which is not the best time to pay a first visit. There are two moorings belonging to Jersey owners.

The Pool or 'Mare' is ½ cable WSW of Marmotière. A yacht drawing 2 metres will always remain afloat in this Pool, even at MLWS, but at low water on big springs there is barely an average depth of 1m5 in the middle of the Pool. There are three yacht moorings in this Pool, and that of *St Yves* RCYC, the middle of the three, can be used by a visiting yacht by invitation of the owner, but the chain requires to be brought right aboard. The holding ground nearby is good and, except at high water springs, it is well sheltered. The Pool is connected with the outer temporary anchorage by a narrow channel, a kind of gutter in the sand, which never dries out; but this should not be attempted until it has been examined at low water.

In order to attain the Pool a stranger should pass from the south side of Marmotière round its west side to the line of fishing boats generally moored off the jetty slipway. From this point turn SW towards the two buoys generally to be seen 140 metres to the SW. Do not attempt this until the Roche Pomeré has just covered or wait until half flood. Better still, anchor the yacht in the temporary anchorage out of the main stream of the Sound, SW of the Marmotière until you have been able to explore and examine the passage and the dangers to be avoided—namely the Roche Pomeré—which will become clear at low water.

Plateau des Minquiers (Minkies)

(Admiralty Chart No. 2100)

This group of rocks is situated some 9 miles south of Jersey, and covers an area greater than Jersey itself. Unlike Les Ecrehou and Les Iles Chausey (Chapter 29) there are only about a dozen very high rocks on the whole plateau which never cover, and the only one worthy of the name of island is Maîtresse Ile, a narrow slice of rock about 300 metres long and 9m7 high. On this island there are about twenty single-room stone cottages built in the eighteenth century for men from Jersey to quarry rock. More recently they have been used by fishermen and some are now leased, as at the Ecrehou, to Jersey yachtsmen. The area around Maîtresse Ile is alive with low-water fishermen on the big March and September tides, who look for Ormers (shell fish), and by bird watchers in the spring and early summer. An Anglo-French helicopter air/sea rescue landing platform is established.

At low water the whole Plateau des Minquiers is a maze of rocks and sands with shallow passages between them, and countless below-water rocks. The only island worth visiting is Maîtresse Ile. The anchorage here is to the SE of the island. At low water springs it almost dries out. Above half tide it can become most uncomfortable and at high water springs it is very exposed and boatwork at the slip is often dangerous. In parts the bottom is mud and soft sand so that a boat must be allowed to heel over at LW and no attempt to ship legs should be made. Local advice (if any is available) is needed here. However, it has not been heard that any boat has foundered in the anchorage and a visit is worth while, even if it has to be a short one.

The easiest deep water anchorage is ½ mile WNW of the Coq Beacon, which can be reached with the aid of Chart No. 2100. It is very exposed but in calm weather at neap tides the 1-mile passage to Maîtresse Ile slipway might be made by a reliable motor dinghy, though the streams are very strong.

The Minquiers are undoubtedly dangerous owing to the combination of rocks and tidal streams said to attain 8 knots in places. For a first visit a pilot is desirable and the Harbour Master at St Helier may be able to give advice on this matter.

The following notes are based on an article in *Motor Boat and Yachting* by Mr John Marriner and are reproduced here by permission.

The best way to approach Maîtresse Ile is from St Helier direct. It is perhaps wisest first of all to make the beacon tower SSE of St Helier, known as the Demie de Pas, and to use this as point of departure, making good a course of roughly 180° magnetic, allowing for the estimated speed of the vessel and the rate of tidal flow and whether the tide is east-going on the flood or west-going on the ebb.

The correct approach from the north to Maîtresse Ile involves first making the black conical buoy with Ra Refl, known as Demies du Vascelin, whence course should be altered to make good 165°. This course takes a vessel south to the Jetée des Fontaines de Bas RW concrete beacon which is left about 3 cables to port, and very close indeed to the long sandbank shown on chart No. 2100 and which one leaves to starboard. A tide rip caused by the west-going eddy which forms here generally indicates its edge, so it is not usually a great danger. The red and white buoy shown on some charts has been removed and is not likely to be replaced. The whole of this approach passage can be easily checked, at least in fine weather, by bringing the two beacons on the Rocher du Sud Bas (SSW of Maîtresse Ile) into line and keeping them so until the pole beacon on the rock known as the Demies is immediately on the port beam. Then alter course into the anchorage. A useful indication of the amount of water over the sandbank (over which one is now forced to pass on this approach) is that, when the Demies rock is itself awash, there is at least a fathom of water over the higher part of this bank, and probably more over the lowest part near the rock itself. At this point, the chart loses some of its value as the dangers are too close to each other to be accurately reproduced: they can best be memorized by stating that there are two 'heads', one of which dries 5m8 and the other 2m7 (allowing for the new chart datum), immediately to port on entering the anchorages, where there is a mooring buoy not marked on any chart to date. Note that in the part of the Minquiers described there is often a westerly running eddy.

If wishing to leave the Maîtresse Ile anchorage and go over to a French port, which is perfectly proper if one has cleared outwards in St Helier, a course of 165° can be steered with the two Rocher du Sud Bas beacons in line. The southerly of these two beacons is to be painted white and the northerly (now bent) black at the first opportunity, to make them stand out more clearly. Due care must be taken, when rounding the Rocher du Sud Bas beacons, to avoid the several dangers shown on chart 2100. The SE Minquiers Buoy, formerly known as 'Les Sauvages', is sighted shortly and course may then be set for St Malo or other local port.

PART 4
DIELETTE TO ST MALO

Introduction

Chart Datum: The chart datums in this part IV of the book correspond to the datums of the individual French Charts on which they or the Admiralty Charts are based. For most practical purposes the datums correspond approximately to those given in Admiralty Tide Tables Vol I. **Local Magnetic Variation:** The *Channel Pilot* states that abnormal magnetic variation, due to local magnetic anomalies, may be experienced within an area bounded by lines joining Cap de Flamanville, the island of Sark and Cap de Carteret.

The harbours of Goury, Diélette, Carteret and Portbail are included in the following part of this book, instead of Part II with those of the Cherbourg Peninsula, as they are visited more conveniently on the way to or from the Channel Islands, which have just been described.

The west coast of the Cherbourg Peninsula and the French coast to the south of it as far as Granville is inhospitable, as it is open to the prevailing winds, and from Cap Carteret southwards it is fringed by reefs of rocks which dry out high, and reach far seaward. Goury, which is $\frac{1}{2}$ mile SE of Cap de la Hague, is approached through the Race of Alderney, and is a tiny drying harbour. Diélette, which is just north of Cap Flamanville, is also a drying harbour, but provides an anchorage which is sometimes very useful in offshore winds when waiting for a tide through Alderney Race. Carteret is a pleasant village with a harbour which is well worth visiting during a spell of fine easterly weather, though a visiting yacht must dry out alongside a quay or use legs. Portbail, included in this book for the first time, likewise dries out but is liked by Jersey yachtsmen.

There are no harbours on the 35-mile stretch of French coast between Carteret and Granville, other than Regneville and a few small inlets which are difficult to approach over the outlying ledges, and dry 8 metres or more. Granville itself, though it faces west and dries out, is a first rate harbour once inside, and a yacht can lie in the wet dock in complete security, with a pleasant French town conveniently at hand.

Immediately west of Granville lie the Iles Chausey, which should certainly be visited. They are of similar formation to the Ecrehou, the Minquiers and the other plateaux which lie off the Jersey coast, but they offer a good anchorage which is easy of access. Here is seen at its best the combination of islets, rocks and sands subjected to nearly the greatest range of tide in Europe.

The principal harbours in the SE corner of the Gulf of St Malo are St Malo itself with a wet dock, a new yacht harbour and the roadstead off Dinard on the opposite side of the river. Dinard, St Malo and the River Rance provide a cruising ground of their own, offering many anchorages.

To reach the SE corner of the Gulf of St Malo is a matter of chart work (Chart No. 2669) and careful tidal calculations both for directions, rates and heights. The passages are not difficult in clear weather, especially near neap tides but can be horrid when it is thick. Several options are open.

From St Peter Port or St Helier the simplest passage lies west of the well-marked Minquiers to St Malo or to Grande Ile, Iles Chausey, but from St Helier the quickest lies east of the

Introduction

Minquiers through the Entrée de la Déroute to Grande Ile or the Déroute de Terre to Granville.

From the north and Carteret the direct course is to follow the French coast southward in the Déroute de Terre. This passage can be very rough in strong westerly winds as it crosses shoals and uneven bottom close to a lee shore. Carteret cannot be left except near high water when the tide will be foul. The stream off Cap de Carteret will be strong but once south of Les Ecrehou it becomes much weaker. The line to follow on chart 2669 is given as Hautville Sandhills shut in with Cap Carteret at 349°, but it is easier to keep Cap Carteret lighthouse itself on this stern bearing. The shallowest part lies when crossing the Banc Félés in 1m2 LAT, which gives 2m5 at MLWS and plenty of water at most states of the tide. The line leads to Basse Jourdan whistle buoy between the Boeufs and Le Sénéquet lighthouse, where the stream turns SW about HW Dover (+ 5 h St Helier) and south just over an hour later.

Continuing south after passing Le Sénéquet the bottom becomes very irregular and there are shoals 0m3 LAT and rocks. But the dangers are marked by buoys, except for one wreck, and with the aid of the chart and sufficient rise of tide there should not be any great difficulty in reaching Granville or off the east and south of Iles Chausey to Grande Ile.

From Gorey the passages round the Boeufs have been referred to on page 138 and can be continued to Granville or Iles Chausey as described above or through the Entrée de la Déroute to St Malo.

A great help for navigation on the French coast are the numerous beacon towers and buoys, and the excellent lights, even for harbours of minor importance. If there is any ground for criticism it is that there are almost too many lights.

In other respects problems of navigation in the SE corner of the Gulf of St Malo are much the same as for the Channel Islands, but strangely enough although the range of the tide is higher than in the Channel Islands, and in fact reaches its maximum in the Baie du Mont St Michel, the rates of the streams are generally less.

22 Goury

High Water: −4 h 20 m Dover (−1 h 05 m Cherbourg).
Heights above Datum: MHWS 8m1. MLWS 1m2. MHWN 6m5. MLWN 3m2.
Depths: Harbour dries up to 4m8. Anchorage outside 3m7 to 1m3.

This very small drying harbour snuggles among rocks on the west side of the Cherbourg Peninsula, little over ½ mile SE of Cap de la Hague lighthouse. The approach appears singularly uninviting when a yacht is being swept in a 7-knot stream past La Foraine beacon tower in the Race of Alderney. The sailing instructions, given by Mr J. M. Robson of Sark, in the last edition of this book, provided an excellent introduction to the harbour which the author followed in 1972, adding photographs, a few additional notes covering the change in the leading marks and carrying the area covered by the chart further southward to include the Gréniquet Plateau. The accompanying chart is based on the large scale French Chart No. 5631, 'Abords de Goury', which also covers Omonville. Alternatively use the smaller scale No. 5636, covering whole coast from Nez de Jobourg almost to Cherbourg.

In the approach allowance must be made for the fierce streams in the offing and a leading wind or auxiliary power is needed. It should only be attempted for the first time in good weather conditions and at the right state of the tide near neaps, consulting the *Pocket Tidal Stream Atlas*. The streams weaken inshore and the difficulties are over when the rock Diotret and the leading marks have been identified with certainty.

The best time for the approach is stated to be on the last of the south-going stream through Alderney Race to arrive south of La Foraine Beacon Tower at 5 hours after HW Dover, which is about half flood locally. Alternatively, on the last of the north-going stream arriving 1½ to 1 hour before HW Dover, which is about half ebb locally. See also Alderney Race Tidal Streams, page 91.

Approach and Entrance. Make good a position about half mile to SSE of La Foraine beacon tower, BW2 cones, points together. Owing to the strength of the athwartship stream it is necessary to keep La Foraine on the stern bearing of NNW as near as possible. When the right distance of ½ mile has been made good the large rock Gréniquet (1m8 high, and sometimes white at top) will bear about 110° distant ½ mile on the port bow, and other nearer rocks in the groups (see charts) may be uncovered. By then the leading marks (daylight only) will be identified as they will be less than a mile away and course can be altered to port on their transit shown on the large scale French chart as 066°.

The front leading mark is a narrow circular stone beacon with a black cone point upward on a rock called Hervieu, (dries 5m2) and the rear is an iron pole (also with a black cone point upward) on Jet d'Aval which dries 6m3. This line after passing very close to Bau Charlin shoal (1m6 LAT), leaves:

(a) Grios, dangerous twin rocks drying 2m9 100 metres to port, and

Goury

22.1. Approaching Goury, showing the leading beacons (details see below) and the rock Diotret on the right. This is an important rock in the approach and must be identified, but at HW on a big spring tide only 1m2 remains above water. When on the leading marks it is left not more than 70 metres on the starboard hand. On the left of the picture can be seen the hexagonal life-boat house and the white patch at the end of the inner breakwater.

22.2. Facing east from the anchorage showing the outer stone beacon on Hervieu rock and the inner iron pole beacon. The beacon to the left and to the right of the octagonal lifeboat house is the port hand red Jet d'Amont beacon, which is not a leading mark, and in the centre is the white patch on the end of the harbour breakwater.

22.3. Looking NNW from the anchorage showing Cap de la Hague (Gros du Raz) lighthouse and rocks drying out near LW.

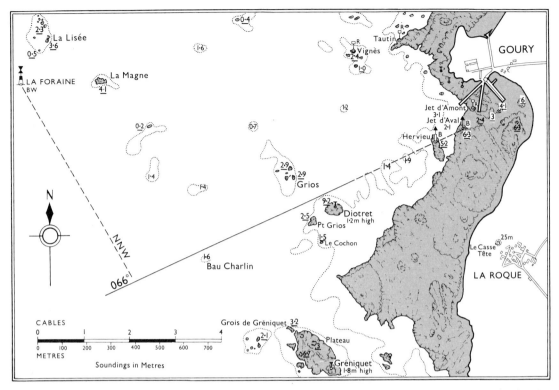

Goury: Dotted contours indicate 3 metre lines. T indicates a rock which never covers. (Based on French chart No. 5631 by permission of the Service Hydrographique de la Marine.)

(b) Diotret, a rock drying 9m2 (the summit of which is always above water) 70 metres to starboard, or less.

Carry on until front beacon is about 50 m off, then steer as to leave both beacons 25 m to starboard, and a perch, Jet d'Amont, red cylinder, 30 m to port, and thus close around the end of the quay into the harbour. This harbour dries up to 4m8 level shingle and sand. It is used by the lifeboat and local small fishing boats only. Berth alongside in NW corner. Very good shelter in almost all winds, but Instructions Nautiques states that there can be a heavy surge.

If entry is not possible anchor outside in 3 metres, sand and rocks, ½ cable north of Hervieu. The anchorage is sheltered in winds from NE to SSE. It has been said that Alderney Race affords some degree of protection from the west to which it is completely exposed, but in winds from this direction it can only be regarded as a temporary anchorage in fine settled weather and in the absence of swell.

Facilities. Excellent restaurant within 100 m but no other facilities. The unique lifeboat house is hexagonal and the lifeboat is housed on a turntable ready to be launched at one of the two slips, according to tide. A village, Auderville lies ¾ miles to east.

23 Diélette

High Water: −4 h 35 m Dover (+0 h 12 m St Helier).
Heights above Datum: MHWS 9m7. MLWS 1m3. MHWN 7m4. MLWN 3m6.
Stream sets off the anchorage to the SW about −2 h 30 m Dover and to the NE +4 h Dover.
Depths: Harbour dries out, and the entrance dries about 2m1 off the end of the outer breakwater.

Diélette is a small artificial harbour situated some 11 miles south of Cap de la Hague. It is not a particularly good harbour, but the temporary anchorage is useful in offshore winds when waiting a fair tide through Alderney Race or along the coast. Yachts can only use the anchorage or harbour in offshore winds.

The Approach. From the southward the approach is easy enough. Cape Flamanville is a prominent headland with a signal station, and it is only necessary to follow the coast keeping a mile offshore to avoid off-lying rocks. A mile or so north of the Cape a conspicuous white tower and dolphin will be seen and also an overhead transporter. This dolphin is left to starboard, and then, a mile beyond, the harbour will be seen. There is a shoal with 0m5 to 1m5 water west of the southern breakwater, which need only be considered near low water or if conditions are rough. Streams in vicinity of the Dolphin are strong.

From the northward, after passing through Alderney Race, the three shoals, Basses St Gilles, Les Huquets Jobourg and Huquets de Vauville must be avoided. This may be done by keeping outside them, with the pitch of Pointe du Rozel (south of Flamanville) well open of Cape Flamanville or by going inside between the shoals and the coast, which is possible with a good chart as the passage is over a mile wide. In the outside passage allow for strong tides setting rather athwart on the shoals, and for the inside passage remember that the tide turns early. The shore south of Vauville to within a mile of Diélette is clear, with a shelving sandy shore, but for a mile north of Diélette there are rocky ledges extending 4 cables seaward. In settled weather there is anchorage SW of Vauville with an offshore wind.

The Entrance. The harbour entrance dries 2m1, so that it can only be approached with sufficient rise of tide. The entrance is with the lighthouse on the outer pier (*Occ WR G 4 sec vis W 8, RG 5 M, sectors W 072°–138°, R 138°–206°, G 206°–072°*) in line with a fixed light (*FR visible 11 M intensified 122°–129°*) in the window of a white house ashore, at 125°. Approaching with the end of the inner pier just open of the outer one is quite accurate enough.

The water shoals about 100 metres off the pierhead. On close approach (at suitable tide only) alter course to pass about 25 to 50 metres off the outer pier. In the harbour the stream runs SE towards the old jetty when the stream outside is NE, and westward along the old inner jetty.

The Harbour. A yacht can berth alongside the inner wall of the outer pier near the end where the bottom dries out about 2m1. A yacht equipped with legs can anchor and put a stern line out to the quay. There are steps near end which are used by local boats, and best berth appears beyond steps at first or second ladder. There is a steel obstruction under the wall beyond the third ladder. Some 100 metres inside the end of the breakwater the harbour dries out 4 to 5 m. The section between the outer and inner breakwater is called the Nou-

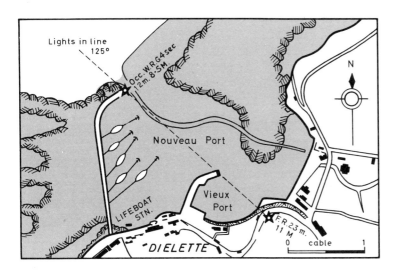

Sketch map of Diélette.

veau Port, and the section inside the inner breakwater is the Vieux Port, which dries even higher, leaving only one berth alongside the outer end of its breakwater. The harbour can only be used in settled weather and an offshore wind. There is surge under many conditions, and in westerly winds even the inner harbour may be untenable.

There is room to anchor temporarily in the new or the old harbour, but poor holding ground on the bottom of thin sand on rock. There is no sign of the former chain from the end of the outer jetty to the arm of the inner and another across the mouth of the Vieux Harbour, but there is a steel hawser from near the outer pier end which runs in a S direction, so buoy the anchor.

23.1. Diélette Harbour. Approach with the inner breakwater just open, or at night with the leading lights in transit (lighthouse on jetty, and light in white house with gable) until close to the entrance.

Anchorage. Outside. With offshore winds and in the absence of swell the anchorage outside, just E of the line of the leading lights, seems quite good, although the holding ground is stated to be bad, as it may be if there is swell or sea. There is about a fathom of water at a distance of rather less than a cable off the pier, and plenty of water farther out. At neap tides it is possible to anchor closer to the pierhead if soundings are taken, and the steps barely dry out.

Facilities. The village is small, but on a main road with a bus stop opposite Hôtel de la Falaise. There are three hotels (Hôtel du Commerce gave a meal at 10 p.m.), small shops and two garages. Lifeboat station. The Harbour Master/Customs Officer/Mayor speaks English. Baker is up the hill on west side of village, but bread can be obtained at the épicerie. At HW one can go by dinghy and land close to the east garage for petrol.

24 Carteret

High Water: −4 h 36 m Dover (+0 h 6 m St Helier).
Heights above Datum: Admiralty Tide Tables, Vol I. MHWS 10m9. MLWS 1m3. MHWN 8m2.
MLWN 3m9.
The stream near Cap de Carteret begins NW at −5 h 47 m Dover (−1 h St Helier) and to SE at HW
Dover (+4 h 47 m St Helier), both streams attaining 3.8 knots.
Depths: The sands forming the bar vary from time to time in position and height, in some years drying
7m0. Of recent years there has been more water over the bar but a high sandbank has developed off the
west jetty.

The small fishing port of Carteret is an attractive place and a popular summer holiday resort
for those who need no organized amusements. Entry and departure are made only near HW
and by day, so that a visit to the Port usually entails a stay of either an hour or two or at least
24 hours. In westerly or SW winds the approach is generally rough, as the yacht is approaching a shallow lee shore, but in winds from N to E the harbour is sheltered.

Approaches and Entrance. The dark headland, over 76 m high, on which is the Cap
de Carteret Lighthouse (*Gp Fl (2 + 1) 15 sec*) usually shows up well in the line of sandy
beach and dunes along this coast.

To the east of the headland lies a number of buildings, those sheltering behind the headland being the town of Carteret. On the coast to the ESE about a mile from Carteret Harbour
lies the seaside resort of Barneville Plage, where a large red-roofed building on the shore gives
a good line of approach from the west until the Carteret stone jetty can be seen, with a white
light structure (*Fixed R, illuminated −2 h to +2 h HW*) at its end. When the tide has risen
high enough, steer east to leave the jetty end about a cable to port and pick up the leading
marks for the harbour.

Outside Carteret it is slack water about 1 hour before local HW and arrival at HW
−½ hour is the best time for approach. At spring tides in the absence of strong onshore winds
entry over the bar presents no difficulties, but at neaps only light draft craft can cross it
even at the top of the tide, and there is no water to reach the Petit Port (dries 8m8) beyond
the second slipway. On the flood immediately before and particularly after HW the inshore
stream sets strongly westerly across the entrance.

There is an eastern mole ½ cable east of the West Jetty. It submerges at HW and is marked
at its south end by a pole beacon (see photograph 2). The transit for entry which gives the
best water over the sandbank (but this varies in position and depth) is this *Eastern* mole-end
beacon in line with the Life Boat shed, a long building with a large door at 007°, in front of
which is a tall telegraph pylon at the top of the second slipway. On this transit there should
be about 1m8 over the bar when ATT Vol. 1 gives a height of 8 metres. In 1972 a depth of
1m8 was found 2 hours before HW on an ordinary spring tide. When the stones at the foot
of the eastern mole-end beacon, referred to above, are seen to be awash, the tide has risen
to 8m8 above datum. In 1972 a depth of 1m8 was found on the bar 2 hours before HW on
an ordinary spring tide, but it is safer to wait for more water.

An alternative transit is the eastern mole-end beacon in line with a large cream-coloured
house with green woodwork and a Mansard roof. This is easier to identify and avoids the
westerly running eddy, but it used to cross the bar in rather less water than on the other
transit.

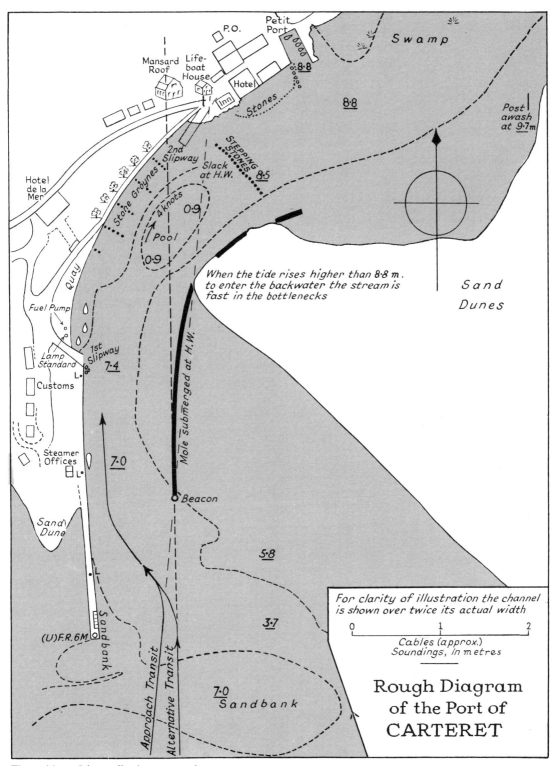

Rough Diagram
of the Port of
CARTERET

For clarity of illustration the channel
is shown over twice its actual width

0   1   2

Cables (approx.)
Soundings, in metres

The positions of the sandbanks vary year by year.

Carteret

24.1. Cap de Carteret from the NW.

24.2. The west jetty and light structure which should not be approached closely. Towards the right is seen the starboard hand beacon marking the end of the nearly submerged mole and behind it the lifeboat house and the house with a mansard roof just to the left.

When entering on either transit, the course should be altered as given in the diagram, where the channel is shown over twice its actual width. A high sandbank which bulges into the channel is growing off and along the end of the jetty, but soon after it comes abeam alter course towards the steamer offices. When the eastern mole-end beacon comes abeam to starboard the best water lies within 10 metres of the West Jetty side and there are high drying sands extending off the west side of the submerged eastern mole.

The Harbour. A berth alongside the West Jetty can be reached under sail in fair weather when the tide is slack but, if arriving early or late on the tide, the stream is strong and then entry is easier under engine. Yachts berth and dry out alongside the jetty and quay. A good position is just beyond the first slipway and petrol pump but not beyond the ladders where the quay is sloping. As the position is in constant use nowadays the usual berths lie betweeh the Steamer Offices (where the vedettes berth) and the first slipway but not too close to the slipway where there is a small dangerous ledge. Quayside ladders have also been added south of the Steamer Offices. The harbour is increasingly being used by fishing vessels and yachts so it may be necessary to moor temporarily alongside another vessel and obtain local advice. The jetty is rough so plenty of fat fenders are required and the bottom is uneven with numerous stones etc. The streams run very fast near HW on ebb and flood so bow and stern and breast ropes require careful attention until the yacht has taken the bottom.

160

Craft equipped with legs can anchor some 30 to 40 metres out from the first slipway, but except at Neaps the streams are very strong and a yacht may drag unless she has good ground tackle. It is best to secure the anchors fore and aft on foot as soon as the channel has dried out.

The Petit Port. This provides a secure but high-drying harbour which can only be used by shoal draft yachts as until the height of the tide is 10m5 a vessel drawing 1m5 should not attempt to pass the second slipway (see photo 3) either to reach or to leave it.

The Petit Port should be entered cautiously at right-angle to the stream to avoid a stone groyne built on the SW corner. If the tide is still flooding it may be wise to turn and stem the tide before edging into the port. If this is much in demand by fishing craft it is as well to take a berth outside them or if equipped with legs to ship them and moor end on to the east side of the Petit Port, using a small anchor and a couple of bow lines.

Anchorage. In calm weather, it is possible to anchor in shallow water just over $\frac{1}{2}$ mile south of Carteret Harbour Light. Fishing boats sometimes anchor here while the smaller dories fish inshore for bait, but strangers should take soundings and anchor well outside the fringe of rocks which dry out over a long distance from the shore and the stream is strong.

Ashore. The day can well start by collecting the milk from the grocer, and bread and croissants from the baker. About 0700 there is a bus to Cherbourg and other places of interest. Hotels in Carteret produce the usual attractive French meals and can usually find accommodation for those who would like a spell ashore. Vedette to Jersey.

24.3. View of Carteret Harbour from the first slipway facing upstream. Yachts can berth alongside the quay beyond the petrol pumps but not beyond the ladders where the quay is sloped. These berths are crowded nowadays and it is better to bring up at the quay south or north but not opposite the steamer offices.

Carteret

24.4. Inshore end of the western jetty, showing vessels dried out alongside. *H. A. Stevenson.*

On the NE side of Petit Port lies old Carteret, where the buildings, some dating back to the seventeenth century, have their foundations only a few feet above sea level.

Petrol is supplied at the garage. Water from tap near the Custom's House or near the fuelling place or at the well near the Petit Port if berthed there. There is a Yacht Club, hotels and shops. Bus to Cherbourg.

Departure. It is not advisable to leave if it is blowing hard from the SW, because of the difficulties met with on a lee shore and because the falling tide will close the harbour and prevent return if the weather worsens. The navigator must leave at HW or just before. As the tide makes northward it becomes necessary to stem the tide if making for the south or for Jersey. If bound south leave early to gain distance before the tide runs hard to the north. The Author has never been at Carteret in strong or gale force SW or S winds, and would not care to be caught there in such conditions in a yacht of draft too deep to permit entry to the Petit Port. With the threat of bad weather from this quarter, it would be best to leave before it arrives.

25 Portbail

High Water and Chart Datum approximately as at Carteret.

Portbail is an interesting drying harbour which is increasingly used by moderate and shallow draft yachts in suitable weather. The entrance is situated some $4\frac{1}{2}$ miles SE of Cap Carteret and is approached by a passage over low reefs to seaward and sandbanks closer inshore. Due to continual gravel dredging within the fringe of outer rocks the sand and gravel banks bordering the entrance channel have been appreciably reduced with resultant greater depths of water than those indicated on charts. It is inadvisable to attempt entry (even with only 1m2 draft) more than, say, $1\frac{1}{2}$ hours either side of HW. At springs 2 hours after HW the tide pours out and the jetty area dries out completely before $\frac{1}{2}$ ebb. Vessels alongside are left high and dry.

Approach and Entrance

There is no official large scale chart of Portbail, but the French Chart No. 827 shows the harbour approaches and covers the coast north to Diélette and No. 826 also includes the harbour and the coastline south of it. Entry can be made with either chart aided by the following notes, for which the Author is indebted to Mr V. R. Richardson, as also for the photographs, as he has not as yet visited the harbour himself.

The entrance is not readily identified from seaward. However, a large, high, slightly funnel-topped, white water tower, standing close to the coast line westward of the small town and northward of the entrance channel, is conspicuous and serves well as a first location landmark for approach. Approach from a SW direction and when the water tower is identified bring it on to a bearing of approximately 025° and continue on it until a very small red fairway buoy (Fl R) (possibly to be replaced by a larger one) is identified. Steer for the buoy until it is 3 or 4 cables distant when course may be altered to bring the church at Portbail on to a bearing of 042°. Then steer on this bearing for the church, allowing if necessary for a tide on the beam. The small town and church are some distance back from the shoreline and, due to the height of the land and sand dunes nearer the shore, the church tower is only visible over a narrow arc when seen from seaward. The church is shown in the photograph and must not be confused with another church east of it. The fairway buoy will be left over a cable to port and the line crosses a 0m9 shoal and drying rocks with a head drying 5m3 a cable to starboard. By then the next buoys will be seen, the first being red to be left to port and the next black left to starboard. Both have been moved further north than shown on the charts and mark the shallow bar area, the water being deeper to seaward and in the channel shoreward up to the small harbour jetty. Both dry out at LW. The line then leaves a ruler-straight stone training wall about 10 metres to port which when covered is marked by four balise poles. On arrival off the third balise continue for a distance equal to $\frac{2}{3}$ of that between the third and fourth balises and parallel with their line. Then alter course to starboard for the jetty end. Except at dead neap tides the training wall covers for its entire length over the HW period.

Yachts may lie alongside the far (SE) face of the jetty and take the ground on a firm,

Portbail

25.1. The end of the training wall at low water springs, and the four beacon poles marking it when covered. The approach is made with the church bearing 042°, leaving the training wall about 10 metres to port. *V. R. Richardson.*

25.2. The jetty with sloping slipway for half its length, and the yacht *St. Yves* berthed alongside the higher end. Note the RW beacon at the jetty end. *V. R. Richardson.*

even mud bottom which extends about 35 metres from the jetty. Local yachts dry out on legs at their moorings in 3 lines parallel to the jetty. On the extreme end of the jetty is a beacon pole painted in alternating red and white bands and surmounted by a red can top mark. A very small black, spherical buoy is moored approximately 20 metres off the jetty end and east of it. Pass between this buoy and the jetty in coming alongside.

The jetty as to half its length from the end is a slipway sloping upward towards the shore end. This slipway submerges over the top of the higher tides periods for nearly half the approximately 100 metre long jetty, so when mooring against the jetty select a position away from the end. There are eight ladders and adequate, small mooring bollards. It may be necessary on occasions to secure alongside vessels (double and even triple banked) moored to the jetty.

There is a red light showing from the church tower at the entrance to the town and there was formerly a forward light hoisted on a gantry close to the shoreward end of the jetty, which may be used again by 1974. These give an entrance transit on 042°, but strangers are not likely to enter at night.

Facilities

It is desirable to obtain local advice on mooring. The yacht club has a bar and members are most helpful to visitors. From the jetty to the little town there is a motor road on a raised causeway about $\frac{3}{4}$ mile long.

There is a water tap at the shoreward end of the jetty and it may be possible to borrow a hose pipe. There are several very adequate restaurants in the town as well as shops, PO, bureau de change and a garage (at the upper end of the town, $1\frac{1}{2}$ miles from the jetty) where fuel can be obtained and which is able to deal with some marine engine work.

26 Granville

High Water: −5 h 02 m Dover (−0 h 15 m St Helier).
Heights above Datum: MHWS 13m1. MLWS 1m4. MHWN 10m0. MLWN 4m5.
Streams 1½ miles off Pointe du Roc are rotary anti-clockwise. Just after local high water (−5 h 02 m
Dover) the stream is NE, then it backs through N to W which it reaches about −1 h 30 m Dover, S at
about +3 h Dover, E at about +5¼ h Dover. The rate is a little over or under 1 knot. For tides offshore
refer to tidal atlas.
Depths: The outer harbour dries out 5m9 to 6m7 and the approaches dry out from 0m6 to 2m1 as far
west as Le Loup tower, and just beyond. The lock gates to the wet basin open about 1 hour either side
of HW.

Although the harbour is a commercial one, Granville is a very pleasant place to visit. The
yacht is secure in the wet dock with all the facilities of a considerable and attractive town at
hand. The shops are particularly good and there are plenty of hotels and inexpensive
restaurants, since Granville is as much a holiday resort as a commercial town. There is an
active yacht club, where local advice may be obtained. The Customs are quick and obliging,
though they usually require passports to be stamped at the police station if formal entry to
France has not already been made.

The Approach and Entrance. The approach to Granville is rough in strong winds
between west and NW, and is exposed to the south though the seas will not be so high from
this quarter. The entrance is sheltered from the north and east. In good weather or in offshore winds Granville is easy of access, granted sufficient rise of tide.

Approaching from the northward the Iles Chausey will be left to the west, together with
their rocks and beacons and a RW buoy. There is also a green wreck buoy to be left to starboard, as also an unmarked wreck just over a mile to the south. To the east an extensive area
off the mainland coast dries out, and in the approach to Pointe du Roc there are rocky
patches with 1 metre or less. These shoals are rarely of any concern to the navigator as
Granville harbour can only be entered near HW, so that the approach will not normally be
made at low tide.

The principal feature in the approach on which bearings will be taken is the Pointe du
Roc, a prominent headland with a white lighthouse and a signal station—see photograph.
Le Videcoq buoy, BW marking a rock which dries 0m8, lies 3½ miles off Pointe du Roc.
There is another prominent headland, the Pointe de Champeaux, 5 miles south of Pointe
du Roc, but this has no lighthouse and will not be seen from so great a distance.

The Pointe du Roc is fringed by reefs extending nearly ¼ mile. There is La Fourchie beacon
on the NW of the reef, but there are detached rocks seaward of it. Despite the great range
of tide, the streams are not unduly fast and, as shown at the head of this chapter, 1½ miles
off Pointe du Roc they are rotary and anti-clockwise, attaining a rate of a little over a knot,
though they are faster inshore.

When Pointe du Roc comes abeam the harbour breakwater will be sighted. There are
high rocks immediately under the headland on its south side, and reefs extend 3 cables in
this direction which dry out from 2 to 2m5. Accordingly, except near HW, do not alter
course until nearly ½ mile S of the headland when the leading marks are identified. These
are the clock on the spire of St Nicholas church at 78° true, just open of the Pointe de Roche
Gautier. The Pointe de Roche Gautier is a cliffy headland easily identified, but St Nicholas

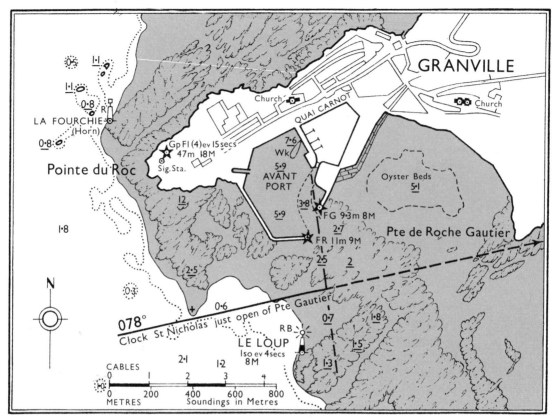

Granville: Dotted contour indicates the 1 metre line. (Based on French chart No. 5897 by permission of the Service Hydrographique de la Marine.)

is by no means conspicuous and stands among trees above a village.

However, near HW there is plenty of water, and it is only necessary to steer midway between the end of the harbour breakwater and Le Loup beacon (see photograph) ¼ mile south of it. This beacon has a tide gauge on it. Note also that there is 4m5 more water at low water neaps.

The entrance of the harbour faces SE, and when the entrance opens up, and the end of the inner pier just opens up with the extreme end of the eastern breakwater, course may be altered to enter the harbour (see photographs). Note that this course takes the yacht well clear of the end of the southern breakwater but close to the end of the eastern breakwater head into the Avant Port.

The tidal streams off the harbour and along the south of Pointe du Roc are stronger than outside. The flood runs at up to 2 knots from half tide to ½ hour before local high water into the entrance and along the eastern jetty. At this state of the flood there is a sharp counter-current close to the head of the eastern jetty, which, at high water and after, increases in width in the entrance and runs fast northward along the western jetty and toward Pointe du Roc.

26.1. Pointe du Roc from NW.

26.2. Pointe du Roc, as seen when approaching the harbour.

26.3. Le Loup Tower at low water. Pointe de Roche Gautier to left, St Nicholas church clock-tower in background. The tower just open of the Pointe are the leading marks, until the harbour entrance opens up. At high water just steer midway between the breakwater and Le Loup.

26.4. Entrance to Granville at low water.

The approach from westward is easier. The yacht will sail south of Iles Chausey in water free from dangers except for the isolated rock Le Videcoq mentioned 3 miles E of Pointe du Roc, and a 1 metre shoal NE of it. She will cross a shoal with 1 metre least water and approach Le Loup beacon and Pointe Gautier following the directions given above. It need only be noted that the Banc de Tombelaine with depths from −0m1 to 0m3 lies a mile W by S mag of Le Loup, which is south of the course. Avoid making the passage below half tide in rough weather because of seas over banks.

By Night. Pointe du Roc lighthouse (*Gp Fl (4) ev 15 sec*) is visible 18 miles and Le Videcoq

Granville

26.5. The Avant Port and the Lock entrance. This photograph was taken one year when the wet basin was emptied. It shows the configuration of the bottom towards low water (but the tide will fall much lower).

buoy 3½ miles west carries a light *Gp Fl (2)*. Having passed between these lights, the fixed red light at the end of the western harbour jetty will be seen and to the south of it the light on Le Loup beacon (*iso ev 4 sec visible 8 miles*). Steer east (mag) midway between the two until the *fixed green* light on the eastern jetty head opens up, then alter course for the eastern jetty, giving a berth to the end of the western jetty.

The Harbour. The outer harbour (Avant Port) is large, but it dries from 5m9 near the entrance to 7m6 at the north quay. It is dredged to dry about 3m8 from the entrance to the locks, which are situated about a cable inside the eastern breakwater. There is a tide gauge on the W jetty-head.

The lock gates are open about 1½ before to 1 hour after high water (the exact time depending on tidal conditions) and signals are exhibited, see page 11.

Notice should be given to the Harbour Master if departure at night will be required, and occasionally the locks are kept open for repairs and the inner basin dries out.

Except for a temporary stay at high water, yachts berth in the wet dock. On the north side is the Quai Carnot, the most convenient quay, alongside which coasters and fishing boats lie, but yachts berth at pontoons near the yacht club on the west side. Directions are usually given as to the pontoon at which to lie alongside. The east and south quays, which suffer from coal dust, are used principally by commercial vessels.

Anchorage. In offshore winds the best position to anchor outside the harbour is 1½ to 2 cables west of Le Loup beacon in 1m5 to 2m0 LAT. There is a reef of rocks extending about ¼ cable SSW of Le Loup. This anchorage is exposed and in quite strong tides ½-mile from the harbour. However, at neaps a yacht can proceed nearer to the entrance.

Facilities. First rate and hospitable yacht club. Water at club or from tap at street side at NE corner of Avant Port. Customs office is on the Quai Carnot. Repairs to yachts can be arranged. Banks, hotels, restaurants and excellent shops of all kinds. Casino and places of entertainment. Station and vedette service to Iles Chausey.

168

27 Mont Saint Michel

Tidal Heights at MHWS stated to be nearly 1 metre higher than at Cancale, see page 175.

High Water: −0 h 10 m St Helier.

Depths: The bay dries out for some 6 miles seawards. Within the Cousesnon Channel, just west of Mont St Michel, a depth at high water of 2m9 was found on a 10m5 tide St Helier.

Mont St Michel, looking in the distance like an anchored battleship, can hardly fail to provoke the interest of the passing yachtsman cruising in the SE corner of the Gulf of St Malo. It is one of the great historical monuments of France. The islet, part abbey, once part fortress and part state prison, with houses clothing the lower slopes on its southern, and trees on its steeper northern sides, though now joined to the mainland by a wide causeway, is one which should fittingly be approached from the sea. Its aspect, from that quarter more especially, is peculiarly majestic and beautiful.

Many yachtsmen have cast wistful eyes in the direction of the 'Mount', for on the chart it does not look difficult of access on a high spring tide. Nevertheless, it is said that the tide runs at the speed of galloping horses. There were quicksands, and if by chance the yacht ran aground she might never lift again, since the suction on the keel might hold her in deadly embrace. There are also fish stakes in various unspecified parts of the bay.

This apparently is true, for although the locations of the quicksands are not stated, many people from Jersey as well as elsewhere, within not so distant times, have been engulfed and lost in them. The famous Bayeux Tapestry is on record as showing that William the Conqueror personally pulled some poor unfortunate out of one over 900 years ago. All this, of course was before the time of the modern causeway.

The following notes were provided by a Jersey yachtsman who visited Mont St Michel in his yacht in 1955 and was probably the first British yachtsman to do so. The information he has kindly given will satisfy the curiosity of those who have wondered whether Mont St Michel is approachable in a yacht.

The yacht was a 5-tonner of 1 metre draft and equipped with legs. The instructions given are therefore for similar yachts which can safely take the bottom at low water. From the depths noted it will be seen that there is enough water for a yacht of 1m8 draft to reach Mont St Michel, but it is difficult to find anywhere to remain afloat or lie alongside at low water.

The Approach

Mont St Michel is best approached from Granville, and it should not be approached in a vessel from west of N by W, at least for the last 1½ miles. Obviously, a passage to Mont St Michel should be made before the maximum spring tides, as if it were attempted at the top of springs or with tides falling off, the yacht might get neaped if by mischance she ran aground. For the approach use French chart No. 824.

Arrival should be timed say between ½ hour and an hour before high water. The shallow part of the Baie de Mont St Michel lies between S and SW of Pointe de Champeaux. Here the tide runs at an awe-inspiring rate. The sea water soon becomes the colour of café-au-lait and perfectly opaque. At low water there appear to be no rocks, stones, pebbles or even

169

gravel in the approach except near Tombelaine* islet and in the immediate vicinity of the Mont and the main causeway. The bottom on the recommended line of approach appears to consist of firm, clean, lightly rippled sand, except to the west and to north of the river's western training wall where it is very soft and glutinous. These types of bottom are remarkably different, though so close together, and a yacht could easily touch bottom where it is soft without knowing it.

Approach the Mount from slightly east of north, leaving the islet of Tombelaine say $\frac{3}{4}$ mile to the eastward. The rock appears to be fairly steep-to.

The leading marks used were a very small detached chapel (St Aubert) just above the HW mark at the NW corner of the Mount in transit with the conical roof-top capping the central turret of the large, round *western* tower (Tour Gabriel) whose base is on the beach and is lapped by the sea at high water.

To the west of this transit is the Cousesnon river estuary channel, which is the entrance to the small river of that name. (This river is the boundary between the ancient provinces of Normandy and Brittany. This places Mont St Michel just in Normandy, though at one time the river debouched to the eastward.) The entrance channel lies between two training walls of rough, dumped stone. The western one is apparently higher than the adjacent mud to the west of it and is visible for its whole length to seaward. At its extreme seaward end there used to be a beacon according to the chart, but now there remains only a vestige of a stump. The eastern training wall has become silted over and at its seaward end it is barely if at all visible. The mud bank rises steeply above it to the beach car park at the foot of the causeway embankment.

As the yacht approaches the Mount from the northward the town of Avranches is visible to the south-eastward on the skyline. A tall church tower with short steeple (or pitched roof) is the most obvious feature, silhouetted against the sky with the lower mass of the cathedral close to its western side.

Course should be altered from the chapel and Gabriel tower transit, when the church and cathedral of Avranches appear open eastward of the Mount, at a horizontal distance equal to not less than 6 times their apparent height above the shore line directly beneath them. Course will then be in a slight arc to the entrance of the Cousesnon estuary channel, which is about 50 metres west of the Mount and is about 30 metres wide. There are no landmarks which can be used as leading marks and it is therefore a matter of judging distance off, to enter between the training walls, which vary in height from a minimum at their seaward end to about 1m2 above the river bed opposite the Gabriel Tower. These walls are, of course, submerged at HW. If in doubt when entering, it is best to steer straight to the anchorage and to err on the side of being too close rather than too far off the Mount. It is safe to approach Chapelle St Aubert fairly closely, within not less than 18 m. There are no rocks as much as 21 m out from the high water mark.

The object of these directions is that a yacht may avoid the great mud banks which extend seawards for a long distance westward of a line running roughly in a N by W direction from the end of the western training wall. These banks (which may be up to 1m8 higher than the level of minimum estuary outflow water) are fairly steep-to along their eastern limits but

*It is of some small historic interest perhaps that there exist still on Tombelaine one archway and the lower parts of some walls erected by the English in the troublous times of the French wars. Using Tombelaine as their advance base the English were continually keeping an eye on Mont St Michel and from time to time attempting across the sands at low tide to surprise the French garrison and take the Mount.

are avoided on leading line Chapelle St Aubert—Tour Gabriel. To eastward of this line the French buoyage authorities have now laid a number of conical black buoys to be left to the westward, best water. Although the bottom is fairly flat their line should be followed closely to avoid the new silt bank of very considerable area which has been created of recent years between Tombelaine islet and the Mount. With Tombelaine approximately ¾-mile to the eastward the first of these buoys should be readily visible southward, but in 1967 the most southerly one was reported to be on top of the mudbank west of the west training wall.

According to a French yachtsman correspondent, resident of the areas, the rivers Couesnon, Selune and See have created much additional silting of recent years. At low water the estuary run-off waters fan-out over the nearly flat sands, after leaving the constriction of the training walls, from a depth of about 0m5.

Anchorages

A vessel may take the ground in the centre of the channel some 50 metres west of the centre of Tour Gabriel. However, though there is adequate latitude in a north and south direction for anchoring in the estuary channel (roughly along the position line of the Abbey in transit the western tower) there is little latitude laterally or east and west along such line as the channel is narrow. Soundings should be taken (over both sides) to check that the position is satisfactory. The bottom between training walls is flat, even and firm under about 5 cm of loose silt sand. At low water of any tide there appears to be about 0m5 of very fast running river outflow water. It is very desirable to lie on the ebb to two anchors laid some metres upstream (southward) over the stern after HW and to time of grounding. Later these anchors should be transferred at leisure over the bow well before the ensuing flood tide reaches the vessel. Movements of the latter, with the arrival of the tidal bore, are liable to be violent. It would be difficult to lay out anchors from a dinghy on account of the high rate of water flow. The operation can be done wading. This is a most desirable precaution in view of the bore which arrives about 1½ hours before HW, and at a speed said to attain about 10 knots, rushing southward up the estuary to fill 2 kilometres of canalized river.

An alternative and easier anchorage, particularly for the less shallow draft vessel, is ½ cable northward of La Chapelle St Aubert on firm, flat sand. Similar type precautions as above to ground the vessel, headed bow northward in readiness to receive the flooding tide bore, are very strongly recommended. This would require anchors fore and aft to control position at grounding. This anchorage affords much greater latitude and obviates the change of course towards the channel entrance between submerged training walls but is appreciably further to walk ashore after drying out. Also, the ebb leaves a runnel of water to cross which, though it dries out in due course, does not drop to comfortable paddling depth for some while.

These instructions are only applicable to yachts with legs, or which can take the ground. As far as is known there is nowhere for a deep-keeled yacht to berth, since the banks of the canalized river, some 200 metres and farther inland, slope downwards to the water at an angle of about 45 deg., and there are no quays. If the passage were attempted in a deep-keeled yacht, the visit to Mont St Michel would have to be very brief indeed, to allow a safe margin of time for exit in waters where the tide falls as much as 14 metres in 6 hours.

Notes 1968. Mont Saint Michel is still rarely visited by yachts but two Bobcats made the passage successfully in 1966 and other shallow draft yachts have been there. For yachts with fixed keels and deeper draft it provides one of the most interesting but risky expeditions on

Mont Saint Michel

27.1. Tombelaine, which should be left about ¾ mile to the eastward. Mont St Michel in the distance. *Combier Macon.*

27.2. Aspect of the Mount when on the leading line of the small detached chapel (St Aubert) on with the Central turret of the western tower (Tour Gabriel). *Combier Macon.*

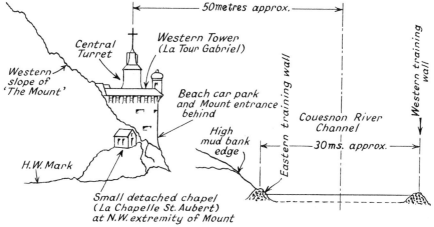

General approach to Mont St Michel

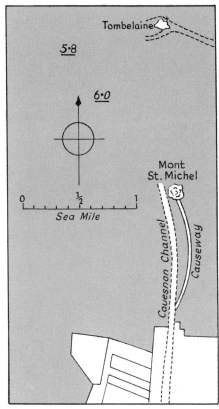

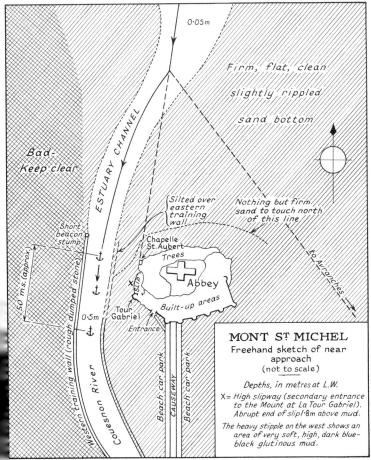

Tombelaine

5·8

6·0

0   ½   1
Sea Mile

Mont
St. Michel

Couesnon Channel

Causeway

0·05m

Firm, flat, clean

slightly rippled

sand bottom

ESTUARY CHANNEL

*Bad-
Keep clear*

*Silted over
eastern
training
wall*

*Nothing but firm
sand to touch north
of this line*

Short
beacon
stump

Chapelle
St. Aubert

Trees

to Avranches

Abbey

Built-up areas

50 ms. (approx)

Western training wall (rough dumped stone)

Couesnon River

0·5m

Tour
Gabriel

Entrance

Beach car park

CAUSEWAY

Beach car park

MONT St MICHEL
Freehand sketch of near
approach
(not to scale)

Depths, in metres at L.W.

*X = High slipway (secondary entrance
to the Mount at La Tour Gabriel).
Abrupt end of slip 1·8m above mud.*

*The heavy stipple on the west shows an
area of very soft, high, dark blue-
black glutinous mud.*

Mont Saint Michel

the Brittany coast. Captain C. W. McMullen in *Alexa* of 1m5 draft (see *Royal Cruising Club Journal* 1966) sailed to the anchorage south of Tour Gabriel. From his experience and those of others attention is drawn to:

(1) The weather must be set fair as otherwise there might be difficulty in returning out of the bay. (2) The possibility of grounding on the way with the tide sweeping the boat at about 3½ knots or riding on the back of the bore over the flats. (3) Legs may dig deep into the sand, which the stream tends to scour away, and the yacht must be made to list towards the side on which the sand is highest.

The Mount was reached by Mr C. Dunn in his Stella yacht *Merrily* (draft 1m2) on 21st August 1967, HW St Helier 10m0. The two training walls are now marked by flimsy withies. The tidal bore proved to be at the speed of 'galloping horses'—apparently over 10 knots.

A better anchorage, clear of the tidal bore, was found *east* of the eastern training wall some 200 metres south of the Mount, i.e., in the stippled area of the sketch between the east training wall and the causeway, with 2m4 at low water on that day. This 'pool' (which may only be temporary), close to moored fishing boats, can only be reached by crossing the training wall (a nasty place to ground on) over a low part 10 metres wide on the line of a small conical roofed turret at the west end of a minor fortification wall about one-third height up the Mount in transit the triangular 'hipped' end of the Gendarmerie building's roof at the Mount. (As seen from southward and in the estuary, Tour Gabriel is seen on the extreme left and the large, high Gendarmerie building to its right side. A tricolour invariably flies at the building which may assist in identification). The depth over the wall is thought to be between 1m2 and 1m8 on a 10m3 tide at St Helier.

Information both on the approach and anchorage at the Mount is incomplete as it is so rarely visited by yachts and no reports have been received since 1968. It is thus safer to visit it first by land to obtain the latest information and to make a survey at low water. Advice and pilotage may be obtained from Monsieur Constant Beaufils, Mairie de Mont St Michel, tel. Mont St Michel No. 6.

28 Cancale and Rothéneuf

High Water: −5 h 02 m Dover (−0 h 15 m St Helier).
Heights above Datum: MHWS 13m5. MLWS 2m0. MHWN 10m4. MLWN 4m8.
Stream sets off Herpin Lighthouse to NW −5 h 15 m Dover and to SE +1 h 15 m Dover, and to S and N off Cancale N −6 h Dover, S +1 h Dover.
Depths: The harbour dries 5m8 at head of jetty.

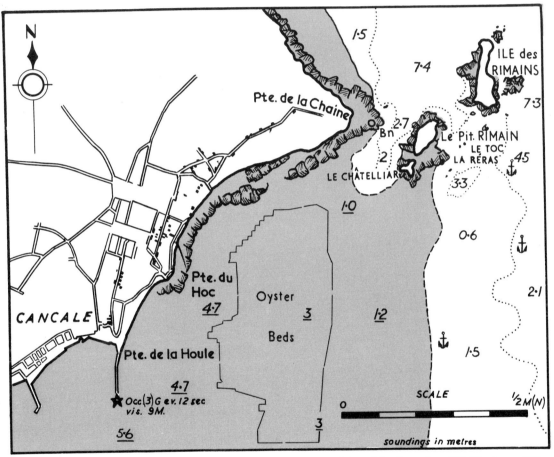

Cancale: (Based on English Channel Handbook Misc. 679, with the permission of the Controller of HM Stationery Office and of the Hydrographer of the Navy.)

The small fishing harbour of Cancale is situated on the west side of the Bay of St Michel, 3 miles south of Pointe du Grouin. The town consists of the seaside resort of Cancale with the fishing quarter of La Houle to its south. As the harbour dries out, and the deep anchorage is exposed and a long way offshore, it is not often visited by yachtsmen.

175

Cancale and Rothéneuf

The Approach. The feature of the approach to Cancale is the line of rocks and ledges off the Pointe du Grouin, 3 miles N of Cancale, which project NE to Pierre d'Herpin lighthouse (*Gp Occ (2) 6 sec 13 M. Siren Mo (N) 60 sec*) and beyond to La Fille buoy (whistle). There are channels between these dangers which require either local knowledge or very great care to navigate. Immediately E of Pte du Grouin lies the Channel de la Vieille Rivière, between the

28.1. Cancale (La Houle) Harbour near high water with fishing vessels alongside its east jetty.

Pointe and Ile des Landes, which offers a short cut when approaching from the westward. It is very narrow, and the tide rushes through it like a torrent. However, the author has found it possible to beat through under sail near slack tide. The best water is somewhat on the Ile des Landes side, and the wind is baffled between the land. Large scale French Chart No. 5644 is necessary. With sufficient rise of tide it is possible to continue inshore passing between Pointe de la Chaine (off which there are rocks marked by a beacon) and Le Petit Rimain island.

For a stranger it is best to round La Fille buoy, giving it a good berth, and to leave all these dangers to the west. Plenty of allowance must be made for the tides. These are very strong in the vicinity—a good 5 knots or more at Springs—and set across the ledges. Course may then be set for the Ile des Rimains, the outer of three islets off Pointe de la Chaine, the prominent headland a mile to the north of Cancale. The island has an old fort standing on it and should be left ½ mile to the west. Course shortly afterwards should be altered outside the oyster beds and then towards the harbour which will then be seen. The water will shoal rapidly and the bottom dries out at low water springs south of the inner islands named Le Petit Rimain and Le Chatellier. There is a rock awash at extreme low water situated about a cable SSE of Le Chatellier.

Anchorages and Harbour. The nearest anchorage to Cancale is south of Ile des Rimains and it is necessary to take soundings to find the best position. At neaps a yacht can anchor nearer the harbour, but seaward of the fish stakes referred to below. The tide attains a rate

176

of 3 knots in the anchorage, and the anchorage is only moderately sheltered even in offshore wind, and over a mile from the harbour. Alternative anchorages are found NE of Pointe de la Chaine, or off Port Picain south of Pointe Chatry, or off the Anse de Port Mer north of Pointe Chatry. These anchorages are protected from the west only. The tidal stream is strong except at neaps, when after taking soundings a yacht can work into the shallow water just within the line of the headlands where the stream is weaker.

If intending to enter Cancale (La Houle) harbour from off Ile des Rimains, look out for the fish stakes, stretching from the oyster beds south of Pointe de la Chaine across the approaches to the harbour, which can only be crossed near high water.

The harbour, which dries out 5m8 to 7m6, consists of a western jetty and an eastern jetty and is open to the south. Yachts can berth on the western side of either jetty. The eastern jetty is convenient, but is in frequent use by fishing vessels when there is enough water. There is a light at the end of the eastern jetty (*Gp Occ (G) (3) ev 12 sec*). Minor repairs can be effected at La Houle. Water and fuel are available. There are plenty of shops, hotels and restaurants.

Rothéneuf
(For chart datum see St Malo)

Rothéneuf, which is situated $3\frac{1}{2}$ miles E of St Malo, is a spacious natural harbour which dries out entirely and has a very narrow entrance, which is approached from La Bigne Channel, for which Admiralty Chart No. 2700 is essential. On La Varde Pte, the headland

28.2. Facing seaward across the entrance from Rothéneuf. When entering near high water the beacon in centre is left to starboard.

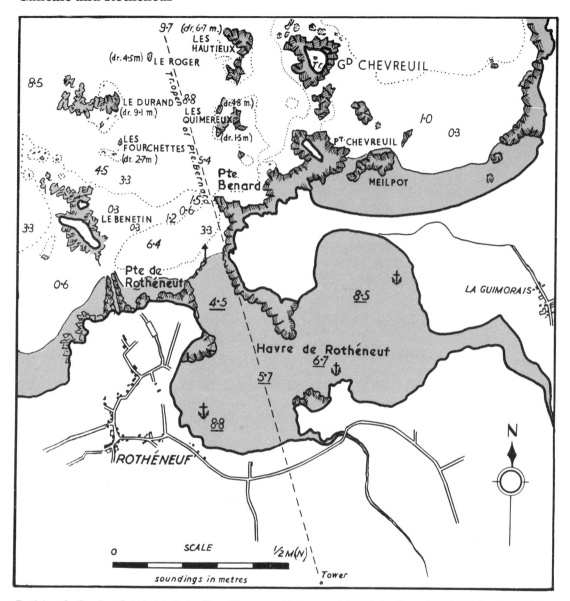

9·7 (dr. 6·7 m.)
LES HAUTIEUX

(dr. 4·5m) Ø LE ROGER

8·5

LE DURAND 8·8
(dr. 9·1 m.) LES QUIMEREUX
(dr. 4·8 m.)

Ø LES FOURCHETTES
(dr. 2·7 m)

4·5
3·3

0·3 5·4
LE BENETIN 1·2 0·6
0·3

3·3 6·4

Pte de Rothéneuf

0·6

Pte. Benard

GD CHEVREUIL

1·0 0·3

PT CHEVREUIL

MEILPOT

5·5
3·3

LA GUIMORAIS

4·5

8·5

Havre de Rothéneuf
6·7

5·7

8·8

ROTHÉNEUF

N

SCALE
0   ½M(N)

soundings in metres   Tower

Rothéneuf: (Based on British Admiralty Chart No. 2700 with the permission of the Controller of HM Stationery Office and of the Hydrographer of the Navy.)

a mile to the W of Rothéneuf, there is a rifle range and, although La Bigne Channel is a recognized fairway, firing continues when red flags are exhibited and spent bullets ricochet close to a yacht, but the range does not interfere with the approach from seaward. The approach to Rothéneuf lies between Le Roger rock (dries 4m6) on the W side and the reefs of Les Hautieux on the E side, which dry in places 7m8 and 8m0. The width of the channel here is only about 2 cables. The leading line is stated to be the tower of a windmill held just open of the headland (Pte Bernard) on the E side of the entrance. The author found his own way in twice, sailing in *Cohoe III*. Near HW all rocks were covered except for breakers on Le Durand (dries 9m1) which lies SW of Le Roger, and by which he navigated, as no windmill could be seen. There is a strong athwartship tide, attaining 3 to 4 knots at springs and the approach when the rocks are covered may be regarded as difficult, if not dangerous, for strangers.

On close approach to the entrance of Rothéneuf, what appeared to be the leading mark was found. There is a round tower close over a yellow house with a small group of trees to the left and a few higher trees behind it. Below it, near the shore, is a white house with a slate roof. This mark is not guaranteed, but when leaving in *Cohoe III* near LW it appeared correct, though leading close to Le Roger. The bearing with the W edge of the headland on with the tower marked on the chart is 163° true. It is much easier to approach near LW, when the rocks would uncover and Le Durand, Le Roger and Les Hautieux can be identified, and allow for cross tide. Note also that the approach leads close to Les Quimereux and, in particular, the reef extending NW of Bernard Pte, with the outer rock, dries 5m7, only 20 metres east of the transit line, so keep the tower well open of Pte Bernard here. The harbour itself can only be entered with sufficient rise of tide, but there is anchorage in 2m0 to 4m0 to the northward of the beacon in the entrance. Little stream and no swell with an ENE wind was found here, but the anchorage is safe only in settled weather and an offshore wind. Presumably, streams would be strong off the narrow entrance of the wide expanse of harbour in the first hours of a spring flood or ebb.

There is a reef of rocks on the SW side of the entrance between the headlands, culminating in a high rock on which the beacon stands. This is left to starboard when entering. The bottom in the entrance between the beacon and rocks at the foot of the E cliff appears to be sand. The whole harbour (once notorious for its pirates) dries out except for a rivulet with steep sandy shores and, although excellent for yachts equipped with legs, multi-hullers and the like, the harbour cannot be used by deep-keeled yachts except at HW. The village and yacht club are in the SW corner, and appear to provide a happy little seaside resort. There are shops, hotels, restaurants and a bus service. The anchorage just north of the beacon is worth a visit under suitable conditions.

29 Iles Chausey

High Water: −5 h 01 m Dover (−0 h 14 m St Helier).
Heights above Datum: MHWS 12m6. MLWS 1m5. MHWN 9m7. MLWN 4m4.
Depths: The southern entrance of the Sound nearly dries out at LAT but at MLWS there is nearly 1m5. The northern passage dries 4m6 west of La Saunière.
Streams: See Admiralty *Pocket Tidal Atlas* for streams in the area between the Minquiers, Chausey and St Malo.

Les Iles Chausey form a group of islets and rocks, measuring some 6 miles from east to west, and 2½ miles from north to south. The plateau is compact, with few detached rocks outside the encircling line of islets and submerged reefs. Several navigable channels lead into or through the group, but the principal one is the Sound de Chausey, which is entered on the NW at the Grande Entrée, crosses a wide area of drying sands, and then deepens into a clearly defined channel along the NE of Grande Ile, where it provides the anchorage, and finally emerges into open water SE of the lighthouse.

At high water the Iles Chausey are seen as a group of islets and rocks rising from the sea, but owing to the immense range of tide, at low water land becomes the predominating feature—a vast area of islets, weed-covered rocks and sands, penetrated by narrow channels of water. The scene changes hour by hour as the tide rises or falls, and with its strange rock formations contrasting with the gentle colouring of the sands it is often very beautiful.

Grande Ile is the largest and the only populated island. Although less than a mile long, it is deeply indented and has a long sea-shore, with four sandy bays between five pronounced headlands, two of which are miniature peninsulas. It is composed of rock thinly covered by soil, on which have been built the lighthouse and the old fort near by, a large château belonging to the Renault family, a small church, the house of Marin Marie, the marine artist and sailor, a farm, two hotels, shops and a few other buildings and cottages. The permanent population numbers little more than forty, who live principally by fishing; but in the summer months there are streams of visitors who arrive by the motor boats from Granville.

Foreign yachts are not allowed to visit Chausey without having first made official entry into France at Granville or some other port.

The anchorage at Chausey is one of those which used to be regarded as difficult of access by strangers, but this reputation is unjustified and today it is so well beaconed that it is easy from the southward. Then again, although Chausey is subject to almost the greatest range of tide in Europe, the actual streams are not excessively strong, attaining rates of little more than are found in the Hamble River.

The Approach and Entrance. On the occasion of a first visit to Chausey, the approach is best made from the southward, as the leading marks for the northern entrance are not so easily picked up and much of the channel dries out.

The southern entrance to the Chausey Sound lies SE of Pointe de la Tour, the SE promontory of Grande Ile on which the lighthouse stands (*Fl 5 sec visible 17 miles*).

Rocks extend seaward from Pointe de la Tour for a distance of just over a cable, but are now marked by three RW beacons (with cones, bases together), but there is a rock awash at LAT about 50 metres SSW of the outer beacon.

Approach to the entrance is made from SSE, leaving the three RW beacons on the rocks

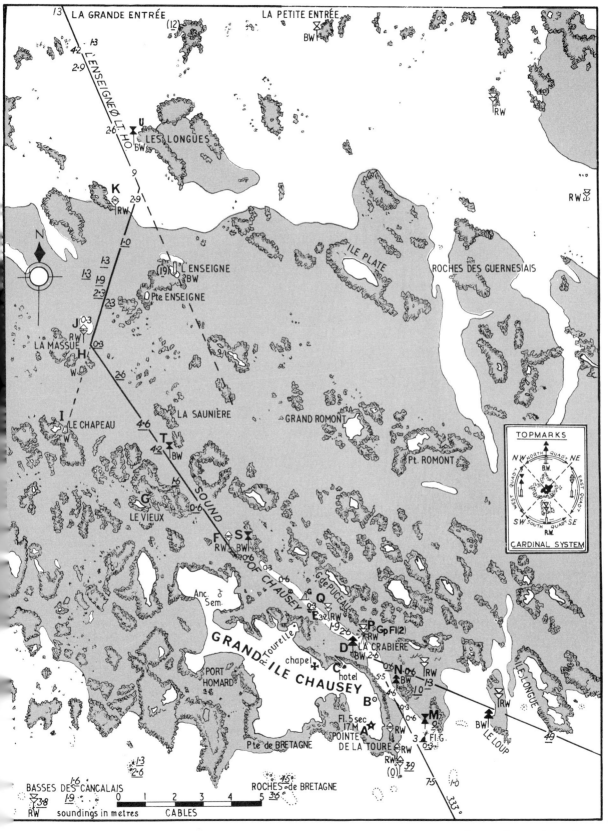

Sound De Chausey: Drying areas at LAT shaded, not drying white. (Based on French chart No. 829, by permission of the Service Hydrographique de la Marine.)

Iles Chausey

29.1. Approaching Grande Ile from the SE. The entrance is marked by three RW beacons on the west side, of which two are shown.

to port and black buoy (*Fl G ev 2 sec*) to starboard. The transit is the RW beacon marked P on chart, with two cones points down (which now has a tripod base and a light *Gp Fl (2) 6 sec* and the L'Enseigne BW beacon tower 19 m high on an islet nearly 2 miles away at 333°. Near LW L'Enseigne is hidden behind Grande Puceau islet but the passage is so well marked that no transit is needed. On the starboard side after passing the buoy there are two BW beacons, marked M (2 cones points together) on chart and N (2 cones points up).

At LAT the transit crosses the edge of the sand to port which dries out and the channel is narrow and shallow, but at MLWS there is nearly 1m5 or 2m5 after an hour's flood and at neaps there is plenty of water.

When the yacht has passed the second starboard-hand beacon, the channel is deep and there are moorings for the vedettes. The anchorage will soon be seen to the northwest round the corner of the island, but the yacht has first to pass between a pair of beacons shown as D (marking the east side of the big La Crabière rock) and the tripod light beacon P (marking a rock on the north side). She then enters the Sound where the fairway runs approximately NW. On the starboard side there are rocks, the most southerly of which is marked by beacon Q. On the port side will be seen a landing slip and a small bay. Many boats and shallow draft yachts are moored there and dry out at low water, so they afford a useful indication of shallow water. Fishing vessels and a few yachts may be moored in mid-stream. The beacons are placed on the tops of rocks and should never be approached closely. There is over 1m9 at LAT as far as beacon Q but beyond that the channel soon shoals to 0m6 least water, and there is a rock which dries 0m3 on the west side of the channel about ½ cable NW of Q.

There is also an approach, with sufficient of tide, to the Sound off Grande Ile from the ESE with La Crabière (beacon D) in transit with Rocher Tourelle and the Semaphore at 292°. Borrow to the south temporarily to clear the rock (dries 4m9) south of Ile Longue. This transit crosses a shoal awash at LAT between a BW beacon (two cones points up) left to port and a RW beacon (two cones points down) to starboard and another a broad stretch of sands which dries 2m3 at LAT but carries about 2m0 at LW neaps. See photographs:

29.2. On the east side of the entrance channel there is the conical black light buoy, the beacons on the two rocks (M) and (N) and the tripod light beacon (P) just to the left of the vedettes on moorings.

29.3. Here, the channel turns to NW between the light beacon (P) starboard and La Crabière rock (Beacon (D)) port. Most of the mooring buoys lie between the starboard hand beacons (Q and S). The picture is taken near LW.

29.4. Sailing through the Sound from the southward, the next beacons are a pair at the northward end of Grande Ile. (F) is left to port and (S) to starboard. The course is then towards the island La Massue (H), leaving the beacon (T) to starboard. The transit after passing F is a stern bearing of beacon F in line with the lighthouse.

29.5. After passing the next beacon (T) the yacht crosses the shallowest part of the sound which dries 4m6. The best water is found on the direct line of (T) to the beacon (J) just north of La Massue.

Just before reaching (J) the chimney beacon on La Massue (see photograph No. 6) will come in line with a similar beacon on an islet named Le Chapeau, which is hidden in the above photograph by the island (G).

The transit of the two chimney beacons leads north of the slug-like island of L'Enseigne with beacon, and east of beacon (K) shown on the chart. Allow here for an athwartship tide.

Iles Chausey

When L'Enseigne comes in line with Grand Ile lighthouse, come onto this stern transit of 156° leaving to starboard beacon (U) marking Les Longues reefs and leaving very close to port the rocks on the west side of the Grande Entrée. To give these rocks a wider berth keep the lighthouse just touching to the east of L'Enseigne.

29.6. The chimney beacon on La Massue. A yacht will leave this island to port, then, altering course on the transit of the chimney beacon and a similar one on Le Chapeau, she will sail towards L'Enseigne shown below, leaving it to starboard.

29.7. L'Enseigne and associated reefs taken at half tide.

29.8. The Grande Entrée taken from north. The lighthouse is just open east of the L'Enseigne and to the left is the beacon (U) marking Les Longues.

29.9. Grande Ile as viewed from the Sound after passing La Crabière (beacon D). The yachts are either shoal draft or equipped with legs as the whole area south of the channel dries out. The picture shows the Hotel du Fort and the Blondel Hotel on the hill and the landing place below. To the right is the chapel.

Northern part of the Sound. The northern part of the Sound dries out for a considerable part of its length, the shallowest part being west of La Saunière where it dries its maximum of some 4m6 at LAT. Thus it is navigable shortly after half flood until say ¼ ebb, when at Springs the water may be falling at a rate of as much as 1 metre in 30 minutes. The channel affords a useful short cut, and is not difficult when followed through on the first occasion from the south. The illustrations Nos. 6 to 8 and accompanying descriptions provide the simplest method of indicating the course.

By night. The general approach to Grand Ile is easy as the lighthouse light on the SE of the island *Fl 5 sec* has a range of 17 miles. On near approach bring the light on beacon P *Gp Fl (2) 6 sec* on at 333° true and steer for it on this bearing leaving the light *Fl G* on the buoy close to starboard. Sufficient night visibility to identify the beacons at a short distance (say ½ cable) is required and it is probably best to anchor short of the beacon P (see Anchorages) as for strangers it can be difficult to continue up the Sound (with no further lights) and find a vacant mooring or anchorage at night unless there is good moonlight.

Other passages. There are many deep inlets among the islands, and another important channel named the Chenal des Roquettes à l'Homme. This is entered in the north at La Petite Entrée, and runs roughly SE and south, entering open water on the south through the Passe de la Conchée. This and the other inlets are beyond the scope of this book, but are mentioned as they provide interesting sailing with the aid of the large-scale French Chart No. 829, which is essential for their navigation.

Moorings and Anchorages

Owing to the great range of tide at Iles Chausey the state of the tide is the first thing to consider, and it is necessary to take soundings whether picking up a mooring or anchoring. At LW neaps there is 4m4 more water than shown on the chart at LAT. Thus there will be plenty of water at the moorings and much more room for anchoring in parts where the depth is inadequate near springs. The streams will be moderate at neaps and the Sound better sheltered.

At spring tides the deep water channel is narrow and ends at beacon Q. The NW current, which runs for about 9 hours out of the 12 from about + 2 h Dover, attains about 3 knots. The anchorage will be uncomfortable in fresh or strong NW or SE winds if contrary to the streams, and very rough in gales from these directions. Yachts sometimes drag their moorings or anchors and it may be too rough to get ashore in a dinghy. The Sound is only fully protected under the lee of Grande Ile during gales between south and west, but the islets and rocks afford some protection from the NE (and the wind is across rather than contrary to the streams) and to a lesser extent from east.

There are a few deep water moorings in mid-channel between beacons P and Q which are used by fishing and other local vessels and yachts. Anchorage may be possible just NE of them and SW of the lobster boxes, but there is little room at springs and there is rocky bottom and weed in places if too near the lobster boxes. Use a trip line with the anchor.

Many yacht moorings have been laid in the reach NW of beacon Q, those in mid-channel having 0m6 and those at the sides drying LAT. Some are marked *privé* and others belong to the Granville Yacht Club or to its individual members. Nearly all are occupied at the peak of the holiday season and at fine week-ends, but at other times some may be vacant. Enquiries should be made before picking up one. Do not judge a mooring by the size or colour of its buoy as the holding power varies, the majority being for small yachts. Except near spring tides it is possible with the aid of soundings to find room to anchor just clear of moorings in this reach. Rough landing at R Tourelle headland or at half tide or above at the slipway C.

During westerly winds anchorage may be found near the entrance, west and NW of beacon N, but the water is deep and the streams are strong. This is the easiest anchorage if arriving at night. The moorings nearby belong to the vedettes, but no objection is made to their use after the last has left for Granville provided the mooring is cast off *before* the first vedette arrives the following morning. Being in the fairway an anchor light is necessary. Landing west of beacon N or with rise of tide at the slipway.

Anchorage south and SE of Grande Ile is prohibited on account of telegraph cables.

Facilities. The Hotel du Fort has a good restaurant. The former smaller restaurant nearby has been converted into an hotel–restaurant with splendid views over the Sound. There is a shop, PO and telephone at the back. There is another small shop near the landing slip. Milk and vegetables may be obtained at the farm near Rocher Tourelle. Water appears to be rather a scarce commodity in the summer season but the restaurants may oblige customers. Vedettes maintain frequent communication with Granville on the mainland, except in bad weather.

30 Dinard and St Malo

High Water: −5 h 15 m Dover (−0 h 28 m St Helier).
Heights above Datum: MHWS 12m0. MLWS 1m3. MHWN 9m3. MLWN 4m0.
Stream sets off the Cézembre to the eastward +2 h 20 m Dover and to the westward −4 h 25 m Dover.
Depths in Channel: Ample at any state of the tide.
Yacht Club: Yacht Club de Dinard. Yacht Club de St Malo.

Dinard and St Malo are situated at the entrance of the River Rance on the west and east side respectively. Dinard is one of the best known holiday resorts in France, and has many hotels, restaurants, shops, a casino, good bathing beaches but rather an exposed anchorage for yachts. The yacht club, which is very hospitable to British yachtsmen, overlooks the anchorage. St Malo is an important commercial port, but the town is an historic one, founded in the sixth century, and is famous in maritime history. Perhaps because of its antiquity some yachtsmen prefer St Malo to the modern Dinard. Yachts lock into the wet docks where entry and departure can only be made at near high water. The docks include a sheltered marina close to the town. There is a yacht club. Another marina is under construction at Anse des Bas-Sablons, which is referred to on page 195.

The Approach

Yachts bound for Dinard from England or from the Channel Isles will usually sail west of the Minquiers. There are buoys off outer rocks on the western and southern sides, never more than 3 miles apart.

If the yacht has passed close to the SW Minquiers whistle buoy the course to Dinard outer fairway buoy (distance 15 miles) will be about SSE. In either case the land on the starboard hand likely first to be identified is Cap Fréhel, 9 miles west of the entrance. Cap Fréhel has an octagonal lighthouse (*Gp Fl 2 ev 10 sec visible 23 miles siren (2) 60 sec*) and coastguard station on its promontory, and is usually seen from a considerable distance. Six miles ENE of Cap Fréhel is the Basse des Sauvages, a 4-fathom shoal with overfalls in bad weather.

When Cap Fréhel comes abeam the landmark to look for is Ile Cézembre, which is situated on the east side of the entrance, and will then be about 5 miles away. From a distance there are other islets and cliff formations which could be confused with it, but the photograph will help identification. A lighthouse (Grand Jardin) will be seen ½ mile SW of Cézembre and a lower one (Les Courtis) to the W of Cézembre, and the spires of St Malo in the background.

The course will bring the yacht close NE of a bell buoy (BW), and another BW buoy (*Gp Fl 4*) to the SW of it on Le Vieux Banc. Both are left to starboard, and the *Fairway whistle buoy* (*Occ*) (see photograph) will then come into sight. It is situated 2 miles approximately NW of the Grand Jardin lighthouse and may be regarded as the first mark in the entrance.

If the yacht is approaching from the eastward, having come through the Entrée de la Déroute between the Minquiers and Chausey, or the channel east of Chausey, a course should be set for the Fairway buoy, and a good offing should be given to the coast east of the Cézembre. Alternatively, use Grande Conchée Channel—see page 194.

Entrances

Petite Porte Channel. Wide ledges extend $\frac{1}{2}$ mile on the SW of Ile Cézembre, and Le Grand Jardin lighthouse (*Gp Fl (2) Red 10 sec 13 M*) is erected on the SW side of this reef, westward of which lies the entrance.

Leave the Fairway buoy about $\frac{1}{2}$ cable to starboard and steer on the lighthouse at 130° when the distant lighthouse of La Balue (*FG, 21 miles*) on a hill beyond St Malo will come into transit. Except at slack water, allowance must be made for the stream, setting up to nearly 4 knots at Springs athwart the course.

On the east side of this approach is La Grande Hupée (which, except in rough water, may usually be ignored since there is 1m3 of water over it even at the lowest tide) and Le Brunel, which dries 3m8 but is easily found as there is a BW bell buoy a cable NW of it.

On the W side of the approach, 6 cables NW of Grand Jardin lighthouse, lies the reef Les Courtis (dries 10m0), now marked by a black tower (*Gp Fl (3) 12 sec 13 m 8 M*). A cable WSW of Les Courtis is a double reef (dries 6m3 and 11 metres) which is marked on the S side by a red beacon tower.

The Jardin/Balue transit leads about $1\frac{3}{4}$ cables E of Les Courtis lighthouse, which is thus left to starboard, together with a shoal with 1m9 least water situated about a cable NE of the lighthouse.

Continue on the transit of Le Grand Jardin and La Balue lighthouses until Les Courtis lighthouse bears 275° (W by N magnetic). Then steer S for a cable or more until on the new transit which is Les Bas Sablons lighthouse (*FG, 13 miles*) (situated on the land just eastward of the La Cité promontory on the E side of the river entrance, S of St Malo mole), on with La Balue lighthouse (*FG, 20 miles*).

Steer on this new transit at 129° leaving to port Le Grand Jardin lighthouse, off which rocks bulge nearly 50 metres SW into the fairway to the red beacon marking them on the S side of the lighthouse. Next leave to starboard a black buoy (*Iso G*), 2 cables to the S, on a bank with 1m1 over it at LAT. The channel thus lies between the red beacon and the black buoy, and it is merely necessary to keep between the two.

Once past these marks the sea moderates and the rest is easy, allowing near HW for an athwartship stream. The lighthouses, including a smaller one on the end of St Malo mole, lead up the channel leaving to starboard the Buron Tower (*Iso ev 4 sec*) and to port three red buoys and a RW one. When within $\frac{1}{2}$ mile of St Malo mole there is a middle ground, Plateau de la Rance, marked by a RW buoy at its northern end and a RW light buoy (*FR*) on its S end. The transit leaves the north buoy to starboard and when 2 cables past it alter course towards the middle of La Cité on the headland until the entrance locks of St Malo open up. Note that sands to port dry out at LAT over a cable west of the mole head.

If bound for Dinard or the Rance River leave the transit earlier in order to pass on the west side of Plateau de la Rance, keeping well west of both buoys. South of the lightbuoy, in the fairway $3\frac{1}{2}$ cables eastward of Pointe de Dinard, is the Rat de la Mercière, but except in rough weather this may be ignored as it has a least depth of 2m1 over it.

By night. Approach and entry to St Malo is almost easier by night than by day, as the lights are excellent. Off the NW Minquiers there is a buoy (*Gp Fl (2) Bell*), a whistle buoy (*Gp Fl (4)*) SW, and a buoy (*Gp Fl (2) R*) and Les Sauvages buoy (*Gp Fl (3) Bell*) on the

30.1. Cape Frehel, 9 miles west of the entrance, is a prominent landmark in the approach. At night its powerful lighthouse, is sometimes sighted off the Minquiers.

30.2. Whistle Fairway buoy in approach, Ile Cézembre in background and Grand Jardin Lighthouse to right. The distance between the Island and the lighthouse is less than it appears in the picture.

30.3. Cézembre on the port hand, lighthouse ahead.

30.4. Grand Jardin Lighthouse and beacon to be left to port, and black buoy and Le Buron tower to starboard. The lighthouse is erected on extensive reefs which bulge towards the fairway on the NW and SW of the lighthouse.

30.5. Le Buron light tower is left to starboard. There is a red buoy on the opposite side of the fairway.

30.6. Entrance channel to St Malo locks. A yacht should not turn to port until the lock gates are well open at the end of the mole.

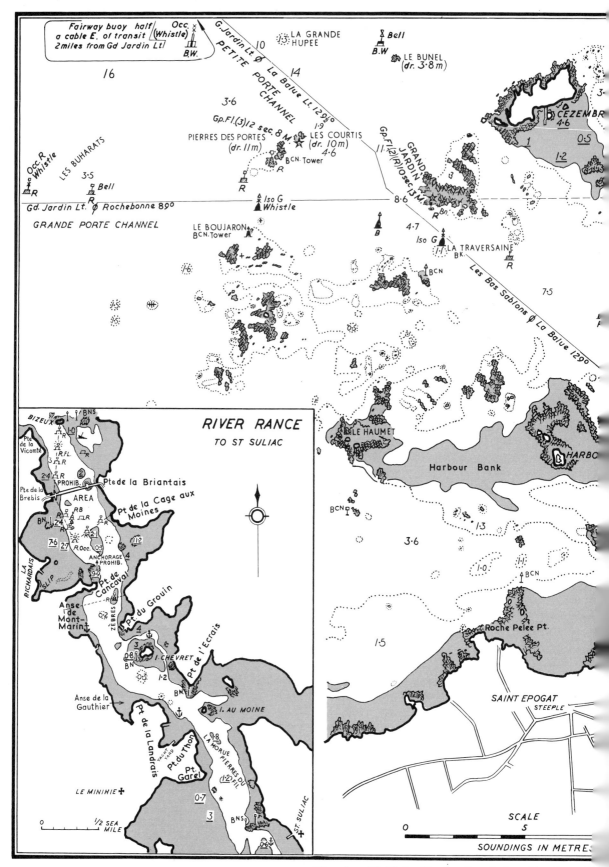

Fairway buoy half a cable E. of transit 2 miles from Gd Jardin Lt¹

Occ.× (Whistle) B.W.

16

G. Jardin Lt ∅ La Balue Lt 129½°

10

PETITE PORTE CHANNEL

14

·13 LA GRANDE HUPÉE

Bell B.W.

LE BUNEL (dr. 3·8 m)

CEZEMBR 4·6

3·6

Gp.Fl.(3)12 sec. 8 M. PIERRES DES PORTES (dr. 11m)

·1·9 LES COURTIS (dr. 10m)

R BCN. Tower 4·6

R

1

0·5

1·2

3·

Occ. R Whistle R

LES BUHARATS

3·5

Bell R

Gp.Fl.(2)(R)10 sec.13 M. GRAND JARDIN 11

R BN

R

8·6

Gd. Jardin Lt. ∅ Rochebonne 89°

GRANDE PORTE CHANNEL

Iso G Whistle

LE BOUJARON BCN. Tower

B

Les Bas Sablons ∅ La Balue 129°

4·7

Iso G ·1·1 LA TRAVERSAINE BK. R

BCN

7·5

1·6

·1·5

·1·5

ILE HAUMET

Harbour Bank

HARBO B

BCN

1·3

3·6

1·0

1·1

BCN

1·5

Roche Pelée Pt.

SAINT EPOGAT STEEPLE

RIVER RANCE
TO ST SULIAC

BIZEUX BNS 1·0 R Pte de la Vicomté R.FL. 3·1 R 2·4 R PROHIB. Pte de la Brebis AREA BN 2·4 R RB 7·6 2·7 R.Occ. 0·3 ANCHORAGE PROHIB. 4 LA RICHARDAIS SLIP Pt de Cancaval ZÈBRES Anse de Mont-Marin 4 3 0·8 BN I. CHEVRET Anse de la Gauthier Pt de la Landrais Pt. Garel LE MINIHIE Pte de la Briantais Pt de la Cage aux Moines ·12 Pt du Grouin Pt de l'Ecrais 1·2 BN I. AU MOINE 0·8 LA MORUE PIERRES DU 1·2 Fl. 0·7 3 BNS 0·6 ST. SULIAC

0   ½ SEA MILE

SCALE

0   5

SOUNDINGS IN METRES

Dinard and St Malo: (Based on French charts No. 5645 and

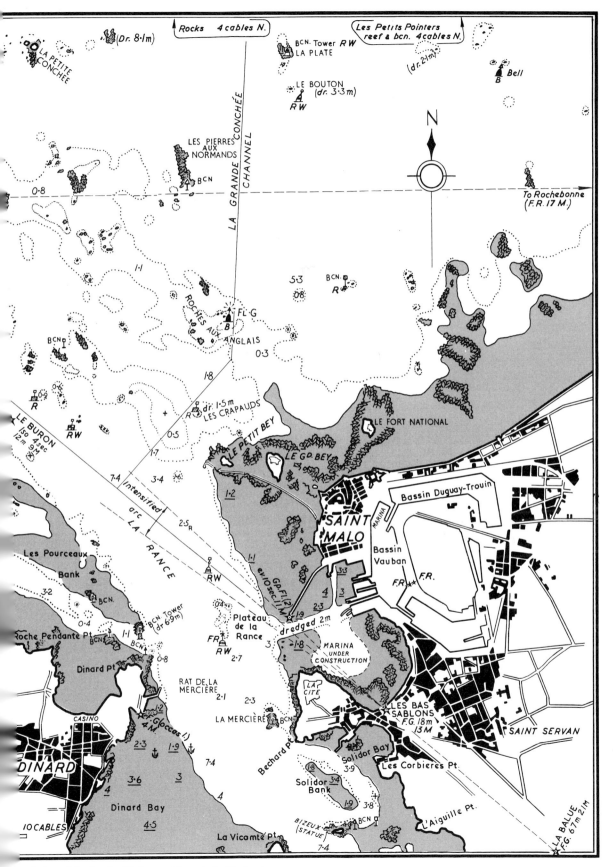

Rocks 4 cables N.

Les Petits Pointers reef & bcn. 4 cables N.

(Dr. 8·1m)

LA PETITE CONCHÉE

BCN. Tower *R W* LA PLATE

B Bell

(dr. 2·1m)

LE BOUTON (dr. 3·3 m)

R W

N

LES PIERRES AUX NORMANDS

LES GRANDE CONCHÉE CHANNEL

BCN

0·8

To Rochebonne (F.R. 17 M.)

1·1

5·3

BCN.

0·8

R

FL.G

ROCHES AUX ANGLAIS

B

0·3

BCN

1·8

R dr 1·5 m LES CRAPAUDS

R

0·5

LE FORT NATIONAL

LE PETIT BEY

LE BURON Iso 4sec 12 m 9 M

R

R W

1·7

0·6

LE GD. BEY

Bassin Duguay-Trouin

7·4 intensified

3·4 ·6

1·2

SAINT MALO

arc

2·5 *R*

LA RANCE

1·1

Les Pourceaux

Bank

R W

Bassin Vauban

F.R.

F.R.

3·2

0·4

BCN.

Gp.Fl.(2) ev10sec.11M

3·3

4

3

0·4

BCN. Tower (dr 6·9m)

Plateau de la Rance

dredged 2m

2·3

1·9

Roche Pendante Pt

BCN

1·1

BCN

0·8

F.R.

3

1·8

MARINA UNDER CONSTRUCTION

Dinard Pt

R W

2·7

RAT DE LA MERCIÈRE

2·1

2·3

LA CITE

CASINO

LA MERCIÈRE

BCN

LES BAS SABLONS F.G. 18m 13 M

SAINT SERVAN

G/loccos I) 4 M

2·3

1·9

7·4

Bechard Pt

Solidor Bay

3·9

Les Corbieres Pt

DINARD

3·6

3

4

Solidor Bank

3·4

1·8

1·9

3·8

l'Aiguille Pt.

10 CABLES

4

Dinard Bay

4·5

La Vicomte Pt

BIZEUX (STATUE)

BCN

7·4

LA BALUE F.G. 67m 2 I M

Dinard and St Malo

S side. The dominating lights in the vicinity are Cape Fréhel (*Gp Fl (2) 10 sec 23 miles, siren (2) 60 sec*) which is exceptionally powerful, having a range of 23 miles, and Chausey (*Fl 5 sec 17 miles*). Do not confuse Fréhel light with NW Minquiers light, both being double flash.

La Balue lighthouse is *fixed green, 21 miles*, and Grand Jardin lighthouse is *Gp Fl (2) ev 10 sec red 13 miles*. Approaching on this transit Le Vieux lightbuoy (*Gp Fl (4)*) and the unlit buoy will be left to starboard, as also the fairway buoy (*occ 4 sec*); and Les Courtis (*Fl (3) 12 sec 8 miles*).

On a dark night when approaching Grand Jardin lighthouse it may be difficult to judge when to leave the transit of Le Grand Jardin and La Balue lighthouses at 130°, but this may be done when Les Courtis and Le Grand Jardin lighthouses are equidistant and Les Courtis bears 275° (W by N magnetic). Then steer south onto the transit of Les Bas Sablons and La Balue, both *fixed green* at 129°. With these in line Grand Jardin lighthouse will be left to port (give it a good berth to clear rocks and unlighted beacon) and a lightbuoy *green isophase* will be left to starboard. This transit leads up the Channel, leaving Le Buron (*Iso ev 6 sec*) to starboard. On close approach the transit leads east of the Plateau de la Rance and over the tip of the shoal water off St Malo mole, which dries 0m9 at LAT. In this vicinity the following lights assist navigators for St Malo; the lighthouse on the end of the mole (*Gp Fl (2) ev 10 sec 11 miles*) and the lightbuoy *F red* at the south of the Plateau de la Rance.

If bound for Dinard roads then, after passing Le Buron and continuing on the transit of the green lights for ½ mile, alter course for the Plateau de la Rance lightbuoy (*FR*), to leave it about a cable on the port hand, and then steer for the anchorage, SE of a *FG occasional* light on the S side of the Pointe de Dinard. There are many shore lights at Dinard and usually the lights of a big hotel on La Vicomté Point which assist in estimating position.

30.7. The entrance to the locks. To the left are yachts at moorings on the north side of the entrance awaiting signals to enter the lock. Centre is the control office. The Blue Peter indicates that the locks are opened at both ends. The red flag prohibiting entry has just been replaced by the green flag which allows entry but not departure.

Grande Porte Channel. Although not so well known to yachtsmen, entry to Dinard by the Grande Porte Channel is if anything easier than by the Petite Porte, and it is certainly quicker when approaching from the westward.

This entry is true west of the Grand Jardin lighthouse. The approach is made at Les Burharats whistle buoy, which is red and exhibits a *red occulting light*. This buoy should be left on the port hand, and the leading marks line up about $\frac{1}{2}$ cable south of it. They consist of the Grand Jardin lighthouse in transit with Rochebonne lighthouse (on the land 4 miles beyond) at 089° or, more simply, just keep Grand Jardin lighthouse true east. Approaching on this course two red buoys will be left to port, the second being SW of the beacon tower on the reefs SW of Les Courtis. Here on the opposite side of the channel is a black whistle buoy (*Iso G*), the one which may be used when using the Petite Porte Entrance to determine where to alter course. Continue steering towards Grand Jardin lighthouse until on the transit of Les Bas Sablons Lt. and La Balue Lt., both *green*, which leads as before between the beacon and the buoy south of Grand Jardin.

By night. Follow the red leading lights, Grand Jardin (*Gp Fl R (2)*) and Rochebonne (*fixed Red*) until the *green fixed* leading lights of Les Bas Sablons and La Balue come into line. Then follow them.

Other Channels. There are several other entries to the east of Cézembre. These are shallow in parts and unlighted and require a large-scale chart, Admiralty No. 2700. With the help of this chart they present no particular difficulties in clear weather, though acquaintance is best made by using them as exits rather than attempting entry by them, when the groups of rocks and beacons may be confusing.

However, the North Eastern or Grande Conchée Channel, recommended by Lieut.-Colonel H. A. Stevenson, is so much used by Jerseymen and so straightforward that it should be included, particularly as there is talk of it being marked and lighted.

La Grande Conchée Channel. For $\frac{3}{4}$ mile E of Cézembre there are groups of rocks in which La Petite Conchée (11m0 high) and a rock NW of it are most conspicuous in the centre, although there are reefs farther E drying 11m0 and 8m1 respectively.

La Grande Conchée lies even farther E, a mile E of Cézembre. It is only 4m0 high and is steep-to, but what makes it conspicuous and different from the other rocks is the fortress erected upon it.

The Grande Conchée channel lies eastward of Grande Conchée, and note that there is a group of rocks named Les Haies de la Conchée, over $\frac{1}{4}$ mile to the NNW of Grande Conchée, one of which is 5m0 high.

The recognized leading marks for the channel are Le Petit Bey Fort (the outer islet $\frac{1}{2}$ mile NW of St Malo) open east of La Roche Reservoir at 183°. However, the bearing on Petit Bey Fort is sufficient for approach leaving Les Rousses shoal (2m8 at LAT, 4m0 MLWS) to port and Les Haies de la Conchée to starboard.

Steer to pass between La Grande Conchée (leave it about 3 cables to starboard) and La Plate RW Beacon tower about 2 cables to port. The line leaves Les Pierres Normands black beacon and Les Roches aux Anglais black buoy to starboard. When the black buoy is a cable astern alter course to starboard towards SW to leave Les Crapauds red buoy to port and thence into the main channel to St Malo.

The only difficulties in the Grande Conchée Channel are the E or W going streams which have to be allowed for in the approach, and the shallows, 0m7 to the E and SE of Les Roches aux Anglais and about the same depth W of Les Crapauds. That is, the channel has at least

30.8. La Grande Conchée fort from
the SE.

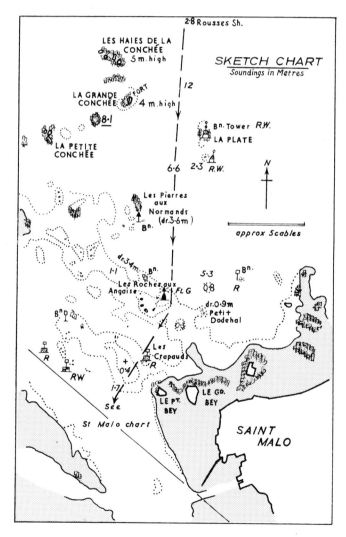

Sketch of La Grande Conchée Channel

depth of about 2m0 at MLWS, and is easily navigable at most states of the tide. This applies to all the east channels, as the minimum depths are found near Les Roches aux Anglais and Les Crapauds.

30.9. The yacht marina at the end of the bassin Vauban. It provides long pontoons with water laid on. The hospitable Yacht Club de St Malo is the low building on the left.

St Malo Docks. The locks are open at intervals between $1\frac{1}{2}$ hours each side of high water, and the approach channel is dredged 2m0 and is entered SW of St Malo mole. It should not be entered until after crossing the line of the lightbuoy south of Plateau de la Rance and the end of the mole. The end of the mole should be given a wide berth, and the area both north and SW of the dredged channel dries out. Anchorage in the dredged channel or in the approach as far west as Plateau de la Rance is prohibited. There is temporary anchorage east of Plateau de la Rance, keeping east of the busy fairway, or in Dinard Roads.

British yachtsmen speak well of St Malo, as the town, with its thick masonry, and heavy fortifications, has a character of its own. Facilities at St Malo are excellent. Yachts can berth in the first basin (Bassin Vauban) or beyond in the Bassin Duquay-Trouin, but the best position is alongside one of the pontoons at the north end of the first basin near the St Malo Yacht Club. The club harbour master usually directs a visitor to a berth or alongside another yacht. As in a marina, the visitor just steps ashore at a pontoon. Yacht repairers, ships' chandlers, water and petrol are handy at the quay and there are many hotels (Hotel l'Univers seems most popular), restaurants and shops. The Libraire Maritime, 5 Rue Broussais, centre of town, stocks French charts. Vedettes to Dinard, St Servan and the River Rance to Dinan. Main line station (at St Servan) and bus services. Air service from Dinard.

Regulating Signals. These are displayed on the N side of the lock's entrance. Red flag by day, or red light by night, prohibits entrance. Green flag by day or green light by night prohibits departure. Red flag over green, or red light over green light prohibits both entrance and departure. (Code flag P indicates both lock and gates open; at such times there may be considerable current in the lock). Wait for entry signal. While waiting, mooring buoys will be found on the port hand. They dry at LW. There are also special signals for the cross-Channel and large vessels.

New Yacht Harbour. A new Port de Plaisance is being constructed at the Anse des Bas-Sablons, between La Cité and the locks. A considerable area has already been dredged to 0m4 LAT giving about 1m8 at MLWS, 4m4 MLWN. There are 5 buoys in the area marked 'Plaisance attente' to be used by those waiting for the lock. To reach these leave the

30.10. Facing west across the Anse de Dinard. At neap tides with the aid of soundings it may be possible to find anchorage near the vedette moorings.

30.11. The approach from northward to the lock on the River Rance. The last of the yachts leaving from the river has left the lock and the cone point downwards has been hoisted to permit the vedette and other craft to enter from seaward.

undredged spit off La Cité to starboard and proceed nearly to the lock before swinging round to starboard, approaching the buoys from the east. A half-tide wall and jetty are to be constructed to complete the proposed marina with all facilities and with depths ranging up to 2m5.

Dinard and Dinard Roads

This roadstead is sheltered from south through west to NW but, as the whole area almost dries out at spring tides between from Pointe Dinard to La Vicomté Pointe to the SE, a yacht has to moor far out in the strong streams. At neaps a yacht can anchor close in to the SE of the moorings of the vedettes, by taking soundings to find the appropriate depth, but it is still quite a long row in the dinghy to the town. The rise and fall of tide is immense, so dinghies are left on the endless lines just south of the yacht club, or pulled up the ramp in the bay to the northward. The yacht club welcomes visiting yachtsmen, and water in small quantities can be obtained there. To fill large tanks, however, it is necessary to make arrangements, and at high water go alongside the quay to the south. There are many hotels, banks, restaurants, shops and a casino. Frequent vedettes to St Malo. Airport and station.

The River Rance

This river is only referred to here in general terms as it is included in detail in my book *North Brittany Pilot*. Since completion of the dam and lock between Pointe de la Brebis on the west and Pointe de la Briantais on the east the levels in the river above the dam and the rate of the streams are very much as they were before it was built (which were fierce at springs), but the times are different. The procedure on arrival at St Malo is to ask at the Port Master's office or yacht club or at the locks on the dam for a copy of the programme giving the levels above chart datum in the river. Often it does not fall below 4 metres above chart datum and there may be periods of 4 to 5 hours while the water is above 8·5 metres. The chart on page 190 shows the river as far as St Suliac, but it is better to buy the large scale French Chart No. 4233, so that additional anchorages may be found when the level of water permits.

There is a prohibited zone to north and south of the dam. Yachts must keep to the west

30.12. Tacking up the River Rance and approaching the Pont St Hubert and over head high tension cables.

Dinard and St Malo

side of the river between Pointe de la Vicomté and the lock leaving red buoys to port and two black beacons to starboard. The lock usually opens at the exact hours between 4 hours before to 4 hours after high water by day. *Signals*: cone point *down* permits entry from *downstream*, prohibits it from upstream. A *sphere* permits entry from *upstream*, prohibits it from downstream. *Both signals* together prohibit entry from *either direction*.

After passing through the lock leave the further red buoys to port and two more black beacons to starboard. Then proceed by chart which shows depths at LAT to which the level at which the water is held may be added. There is 2m3 in the channel as far as Le Chaudron red beacon west of St Suliac, but in the absence of a large scale chart it is better to regard it as drying 1m8 LAT. There are anchorages on the west side at the southern end of Anse de Montmarin, Anse de Gauthier and off the bay SE of Pte de Langrognais (where there are many moorings, a yacht yard and a good restaurant) and on the east side N of Ile Chevret and 2 cables off St Suliac. The currents are very strong at times, as maximum variation of level may be 1 metre in 10 minutes or 1m40 in 10 minutes in exceptional circumstances. At neaps or when the level of water is held up it is possible to anchor closer in out of the strength of the stream, and as stated other anchorages can be found with the aid of a big scale chart.

Conversion Tables

Ft	Metres		Metres	Ft
1	0·3		1	3·3
2	0·6		2	6·6
3	0·9		3	9·8
4	1·2		4	13·1
5	1·5		5	16·4
(1 fathom) 6	1·8		6	19·7
7	2·1		7	23·0
8	2·4		8	26·2
9	2·7		9	29·5
10	3·0		10	32·8
20	6·1		20	65·6
30	9·1		30	98·4
40	12·2		40	131·2
50	15·2		50	164·0
60	18·3		60	196·9
70	21·3		70	229·7
80	24·4		80	262·5
90	27·4		90	295·3
100	30·5		100	328·1

Cable: British 0·1 nautical mile (185 metres), French 200 metres.
Miles: Nautical 1·9 kilometres, Statute 1·6 kilometres.

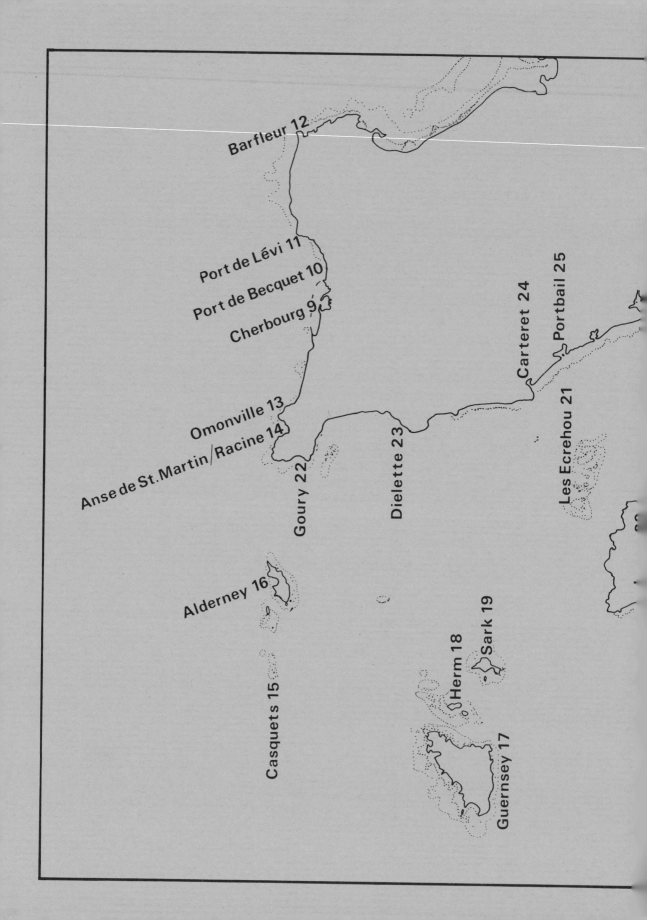

Barfleur 12

Port de Lévi 11
Port de Becquet 10
Cherbourg 9

Omonville 13
Anse de St.Martin/Racine 14

Goury 22

Dielette 23

Carteret 24

Portbail 25

Les Ecrehou 21

Alderney 16

Casquets 15

Herm 18

Sark 19

Guernsey 17